AMERICAN REBOOT

AN IDEALIST'S GUIDE TO GETTING BIG THINGS DONE

WILL HURD

SIMON & SCHUSTER

NEW YORK   LONDON   TORONTO   SYDNEY   NEW DELHI

Simon & Schuster
1230 Avenue of the Americas
New York, NY 10020

First Simon & Schuster hardcover edition February 2022

SIMON & SCHUSTER and colophon are registered trademarks
of Simon & Schuster, Inc.

For information about special discounts for bulk purchases,
please contact Simon & Schuster Special Sales at 1-866-506-1949
or business@simonandschuster.com.

The Simon & Schuster Speakers Bureau can bring authors
to your live event. For more information or to book an event,
contact the Simon & Schuster Speakers Bureau at 1-866-248-3049
or visit our website at www.simonspeakers.com.

Interior design by Kathryn A. Kenney-Peterson

Manufactured in the United States of America

10   9   8   7   6   5   4   3   2   1

Library of Congress Control Number: 2021951377

ISBN 978-1-9821-6070-8
ISBN 978-1-9821-6081-4 (ebook)

To Mary Alice and Bob
for always believing in me
and teaching me to be honest
and do the right thing.

CONTENTS

PART IV: ENEMIES SHOULD FEAR US, FRIENDS SHOULD LOVE US

PART V: TAKE ADVANTAGE OF TECHNOLOGY BEFORE IT TAKES ADVANTAGE OF US

AMERICAN REBOOT

INTRODUCTION

GET OFF THE X

Imagine you are behind the steering wheel of a car parked in a narrow alley of a foreign city, with a mob of people shaking and banging on your vehicle as you bake inside from the oppressive heat and humidity. Angry faces peer in the windows. The situation is spiraling out of control.

That was what I faced in a South Asian city as I neared the completion of the first year of my inaugural overseas assignment in the National Clandestine Service, the division of the CIA responsible for recruiting spies and stealing secrets oftentimes while having to live and work undercover. I was there to conduct an operation to meet my "asset," a person risking their life and the lives of their family to give secrets to the U.S. government. To determine whether I was being followed, I was performing a surveillance detection route, or SDR. I had inspected parts of my route the day before and had found an alley that would force surveillance—if I had it—to follow me closely, making them easier to spot.

This alley happened to be in a neighborhood that "polite society" considered dangerous. It was home to the lower strata of society who had been laboring in a social order that had been dividing citizens of this country into rigid hierarchical groups for more than three thousand years.

My problem was that I had committed a rookie mistake. I had cased the alley in the morning when it was empty of people. But when I maneuvered my two-door Toyota Tercel into the alley that afternoon, I found myself on the busiest street I had ever seen. Hundreds of people were walking in all directions. Pack animals clogged the street, and vendors were hawking their wares.

I was inching my car along when a woman walked in front of my vehicle. I mashed on my brakes, but my tire came to a stop on the back of her flip-flop, dragging her foot across the road. Her big toe busted wide open. Suddenly blood was everywhere.

The woman looked at me, and realizing I was a foreigner, she screamed. The scene changed instantly. I braced myself inside the car, as the roar of the angry mob pushing and pulling at the vehicle became deafening.

The CIA had taught me about situations like this. The first thing you are supposed to do is get off the X. The X is where something is going down—an ambush, a riot, or general chaos erupting or about to erupt. Staying on the X is the last place you want to be. But my little Tercel wouldn't get me through this mass of people. I had a firearm, but it wasn't going to help me out of this situation. So I got out of the car.

When I unfolded my six-foot-three-inch frame, I shocked the crowd. They didn't expect me to get out, and I was much larger than most of the congregation. Since I only knew a little of the local language, I yelled, "Does anyone speak English?"

A teenager pushed through the enraged crowd, parting it with his arms like he was doing the breaststroke. He proclaimed triumphantly, "I speak the English."

I asked, "Where is the closest hospital?"

He consulted with the crowd, then turned back to me, pointing to the east and said, "Four blocks that way."

I handed some money to the woman, and helped her into a rickshaw—a three-wheeled passenger cart used primarily in Asia—and I told the driver to take her to the hospital, *immediately*.

Then something entirely unexpected happen. The mob calmed. People started clapping and patting me on my back. Some guy opened my car door and helped stuff me back inside. I drove away to my meeting, and when

I looked in the rear-view mirror the crowd was waving and smiling behind me.

I've had years to reflect on why an incensed mob went from rage to happiness within minutes. I have concluded that the mob appreciated a show of
warmheartedness from someone they did not expect to show kindness. They
had seen me, a foreigner, as a representation of an apparatus of oppression
perpetuated on them by members of the upper classes of society. Their rage
was checked when they saw an act of compassion—me getting out of the car,
trying to do something about the situation I had put the woman in.

On its surface, what I experienced in that crowded alley seems to have
little in common with the United States today. But the incident is reflective of
where we are as a nation and how we must move past divisions and hostility
preventing us from solving our problems.

In the U.S., both political parties are crammed into separate little cars,
stuck in the same place, with millions of Americans shaking and banging
on them. Anger and resentment are threatening to upend the cars. Unfortunately, most of the elected officials in the cars are oblivious to the chaos
around them. Others are turning away and choosing to ignore it, and some
are screaming, trying to further incite drama.

This unattended chaos will prevent the United States from doing for the
next 245 years what it has done for the last 245 years—improve the quality of
life for all Americans, while uplifting humanity. It's time for elected officials
to get off the X. They need to step outside their bubbles and listen to what is
happening to *all* Americans, not just the ones in their own political party. If
this were to happen, I think we would see the same reaction from the American electorate that I experienced the day my car was almost flipped over, and
political contempt could be transformed into something positive.

Getting off the X will be like a "Ctrl+Alt+Delete" for our country. I
started my career in technology, working in a college computer lab, and I
learned a simple lesson. When you are troubleshooting a computer problem and you can't figure out why the computer is acting weirdly, the best

thing you can do is reboot. This is what our country needs now, an American Reboot.

I'm not talking about starting from the beginning. An American Reboot doesn't mean re-forming our more perfect Union in a radically different way. And it doesn't involve tearing up our Constitution and starting over. Instead, it's an opportunity to refresh our operating system so that it's operating on our core values that have sustained us as a nation for close to 250 years.

Just like a computer slows down when its memory is filled up with garbage from running bad programs for too long, it's getting harder to get big things done in our country because the gears of our democracy have been mucked up by political nonsense. If we are going to meet the generational-defining challenges of the twenty-first century, our country needs to be at peak performance.

I've seen some of the challenges of the twenty-first century up close and personal. I grew up the youngest of three children in a loving, interracial South Texas family. I helped my community through a horrific tragedy in college. I served in dangerous places as a member of the CIA, living in places where the concentration of power in the hands of a few eroded principles like rule of law, freedom of the press, and separation of powers. I helped build a cyber-security company and saw firsthand how the sophistication of our adversaries has evolved. I served three terms in Congress, winning multiple campaigns in one of the country's toughest districts while interacting with people from all walks of life. Today, I help entrepreneurs working on the cutting edge of science and technology, to ensure their efforts help transform society for the better.

Through these experiences, I have seen five generational-defining challenges facing our country. The Republican Party is failing to be competitive with the largest growing groups of voters. There is a lack of leadership in Washington, DC. People are anxious about their future because of an inability to handle unexpected expenses and growing income inequality. U.S. economic and military dominance is no longer guaranteed. And the technological explosion we are going to see in the next thirty years will make the advancements over the last thirty years look trivial.

The cost of ignoring these challenges—of not getting off the X—is that the world we leave to our children or grandchildren will be worse than the one we inherited. To meet these seismic problems facing our country, we need an American Reboot that gets our country back on an operating system that can adapt to a chaotic and uncertain future but is based on the shared values that have solved the challenges of the past.

An American Reboot of moving beyond political contempt—fueled by only focusing on, listening to, and interacting with people who think and act the same—will allow us to update our operating system with what I like to call *pragmatic idealism*: achieving what is actually achievable while improving life for the greatest number of people possible.

To realize a vision of uplifting humanity for another 250 years, we are going to need a Republican Party that looks like America. The GOP will need to align its actions with its values. We will need to show up to places we have never been, and listen. The party can't have in it assholes, racists, misogynists, and homophobes. For our party to more accurately reflect a broader America, we will need to appeal to the middle, not the edges.

This vision of continuing to help humanity is unattainable without leaders who inspire rather than fearmonger. Leaders will need to be honest and do the right thing. They need to ensure their audio and video match. They need to stop pandering and build trust. Most important, we need leaders who focus on what unites us, not what divides us.

Continuing this experiment we call America requires a domestic policy based on the idea that prosperity should be a product of empowering people not the government. While everyone hasn't excelled under democracy and capitalism, you don't throw the baby out with the bathwater. Rather, you increase access to healthcare while decreasing its cost; provide our seniors quality care and compassion while treating our kids like they are our future. We need to build a workforce for tomorrow, not yesterday, encourage a global "brain gain" through immigration, and prevent planet Earth from teaching us a terrible lesson.

Success in the rest of the twenty-first century requires a foreign policy where our enemies fear us and our friends love us. This starts with understanding the source of American power, being tough with tough guys and being nice with nice guys, while preparing for the wars of the future, not the ones of the past.

Uplifting humanity requires us to take advantage of technology before it takes advantage of us. We need to recognize that we are in a New Cold War with the Chinese government. This begins with an understanding of what "Made in China" really means. This New Cold War necessitates America achieving technical fitness for cyber war and winning the struggle for global leadership in advanced technology.

We all know we can do better. It's time to get out of our cars, get off the X, and hit Ctrl+Alt+Delete to start the American Reboot. Pragmatic idealism—a concept rooted in the timeless American ideals of bipartisanship, inclusivity, and democratic values—can get our country back to where most Americans are, and inspire Americans to take back their country from the fringes that dominate our politics.

Understanding how pragmatic idealism can help us address these generational-defining challenges of our time is what *American Reboot* is all about.

PART I

THE GOP NEEDS TO LOOK LIKE AMERICA

CHAPTER 1

ALIGN OUR ACTIONS
WITH OUR VALUES

With help from a paper map and directions from cowboys on horseback, I found *El Rancho Escupe Sangre No Raja* down a long dirt road. It was 2009 and I was in the middle of my first campaign for the 23rd Congressional District of Texas. I'd been invited to a *tardeada a la Mexicana* in the Democratic stronghold of Eagle Pass, Texas, located on the U.S.-Mexico border.

Quick Spanish lesson: *tardeada* is an afternoon party. The translation for the party's location is a little trickier. *El rancho* means "ranch." *Escupe sangre* means "spit blood," and *no raja* is Mexican slang for "don't give up" or "don't quit."

So, this party was at the "Don't Quit, Spit Blood Ranch" in the biggest city of Maverick County, a place that was largely Latino and hadn't held a Republican primary consistently until 2010. When it did, only fifty-nine people voted. The professional Republican political consultant types had warned me against spending time in Maverick County. They said it was futile for a Republican candidate to earn votes there.

But I thought it was an opportunity. And since my name was the one on the ballot, I got the final say.

I learned in the CIA that when you can, always have backup, so I asked a good friend of mine, Mel, to go with me to the *tardeada*. She is smart, always up for adventure, and had helped me with Spanish translation services when I was in the private sector. Most candidates would have been joined by a campaign staffer who had campaign experience, but those kinds of folks didn't think I had a chance in hell. So I had to rely on my friends.

Even though I had taken Spanish in middle school and high school, studied in Mexico City while in college, and had grown up in San Antonio, my *español* still wasn't great. I used to say I knew "dance floor Spanish"—enough Spanish to get by on the dance floor—but when I got elected, my staff said this comment wasn't congressional. So the apology I gave for not speaking better Spanish was *"Entiendo mucho pero hablo muy despacio como un niño en la escuela primaria."* It means "I understand a lot of Spanish, but I speak slowly like a kid in elementary school." This was even better than my dance floor wisecrack because it always got a laugh. I don't know why, but I guess people find the image of a six-foot-three, 230-pound guy in elementary school funny.

Mel and I crammed my Toyota 4Runner into a spot alongside hundreds of other cars in a makeshift dirt parking lot. I wore a white guayabera—a casual Mexican shirt—and Mel, whose family is from Mexico, looked like a movie star.

The party's nerve center was a cream-colored, one-story cinder block building where the food was being prepared and distributed. A large, greenish awning jutting off one of the structure's sides provided shade, under which a band was playing popular Tejano tunes. The smell of slow-roasting pork was making us hungry. We could see dozens of couples dancing and eating. This was a popping party. But when we got closer, hundreds of heads turned and fixated their gaze on us. It got real quiet. It was like an old Western. Three members of the band, who happened to be local elected officials, literally stopped playing.

I thought everyone was staring at Mel. Then she whispered in my ear, "Are all these people staring at you because you are a Republican?"

Okay, so they weren't staring at Mel.

I had been trained for this situation. It was like being at a diplomatic reception when I was in the CIA looking to "bump" a target of interest. A "bump" means using a piece of information about a target to strike up a seemingly benign conversation with them. A "target of interest" is anyone who might have access to information we seek. A bump is the first step in the long process of recruiting a spy. I had pulled off bumps in restaurants, ski lifts, airplanes—even a terrorist training camp.

Usually when you perform a bump, you have a target in mind. This was the first time I was doing a bump without a specific target. At the same time, everyone in the crowd was an appropriate target for the kind of bump I needed to perform.

No one at that *tardeada*—not me, not the people around the yard staring curiously at me—could anticipate what was coming in the years ahead. The people of Maverick County would be dragged through hell in 2020 when COVID slammed into them. It was one of the worst-hit communities in the country.

But all this was not yet in front of this hardworking community, which I would get to know so well during my three terms in Congress. For the moment, on this dusty, warm November day, there were curious eyes and the same baffled question hanging in the air, as Mel and I made our way to the bar: *Why are you here?*

We worked the room as well as we could. I was a novelty. Why was a Republican at a *tardeada* in Eagle Pass? Almost all the people at the event, including the hosts, were going to support the incumbent, Democrat Ciro Rodriguez.

I gave the same answer to everyone: "Why am I here? Because I like to drink beer and eat barbecue, too."

Everyone laughed and slapped me on the back. The conversation would then turn to everyday things—how oppressive the heat was, how bad the Dallas Cowboys were playing, and how fast time goes by when you realize your kids are becoming adults and about to graduate high school. Nothing political.

The next time I showed up in Eagle Pass, people would shake my hand. The next couple of times, a few people would walk by and whisper, "I'm a Republican."

After I got elected, I kept showing up, and people started telling me their problems: the Department of Veterans Affairs' slow response time to inquiries about a veteran's benefits; missing Social Security disability payments; and unnecessarily long lines at the border crossing between Eagle Pass and its sister city, Piedras Negras, due to insufficient staffing at the border checkpoints.

Then I would return and tell them how my staff and I had helped solve their problems by battling the bureaucracy in Washington, DC, getting answers to their questions, or, in some cases, passing laws to resolve the issue.

In all of my elections in Texas 23, I never won Maverick County. That's not the point. I never expected to. But by my third election, I increased my vote total by 50 percent in a Democratic, Latino county, and many people did what they never thought they would ever do—vote for a Republican.

Texas 23 sprawled along the south and west of the state, through two time zones, three geographic regions, and a political divide as wide as the nation's. Almost as large as Georgia, the district runs from the San Antonio suburbs, along 820 miles of U.S.-Mexican border, skims the New Mexico line, and reaches the outskirts of El Paso. The 23rd contains Big Bend National Park, towns like Eagle Pass, Fort Stockton, and Mentone—population 19.

Seventy percent of the population in Texas 23 is Latino, 24 percent is White, 3 percent is Black, and 2 percent is Asian American. The median household income is a little under $60,000 and almost 16 percent of the population is below the poverty line. Fifty-nine percent of the district is under forty years of age. Only about a quarter of the population has a bachelor's degree or higher, and half the district has someone in their household who speaks a language other than English. While 15 percent of the population is foreign-born, many people are descended from families that have lived in the area since Texas was a part of Mexico.

Most of the district is rural and dominated by gas, oil, and cattle, and trade with Mexico is the district's lifeblood. At the same time, a cybersecurity industry thrives in my hometown of San Antonio, the seventh-largest city in the U.S., and in El Paso, you have the largest and most valuable military installation in the nation and six international ports of entry.

For the last decade and a half, the 23rd voted consistently half Republican and half Democrat—for most of my adult life it was the only fifty-fifty district in Texas, and one of a few dozen remaining fifty-fifty districts in the country. Winning elections here is tough. I was the first person to hold the 23rd for successive cycles in a decade, including in 2016 when I was just one of three Republicans nationally to win a district carried by Hillary Clinton. Prior to my first victory, the seat had toggled back and forth between Democratic and Republican each election cycle since 2006.

For two of my three terms, I was one of two Black Republicans in the House of Representatives. In my last term, I was the only African American Republican in the House. But during my entire time in Congress, I represented a majority Latino district and took a conservative message on issues like healthcare, border security, and education to places that didn't often hear it.

My success in the 23rd is a bellwether for success across the rest of the country, and I was winning by righting the wrongs identified in the infamous Republican "autopsy" report written after Republican challenger Mitt Romney's defeat by President Barack Obama in 2012. Romney lost by almost four points even though he went into Election Day with most polls predicting he was in the lead over the incumbent president.

The "autopsy" conducted by senior Republican leaders, stalwarts, and activists explained that "The Republican Party needs to stop talking to itself. We have become expert in how to provide ideological reinforcement to like-minded people, but devastatingly, we have lost the ability to be persuasive with, or welcoming to, those who do not agree with us on every issue."

The GOP has tended to do the exact opposite, especially in presidential elections, and it has proven fatal. The Republican candidate has lost seven out of the last eight popular votes for president.

Almost a decade ago, the autopsy outlined what everyone knows—the U.S. is changing, and Republicans haven't caught up. A majority of the U.S. population will be non-white by the year 2050. Instead of pursuing a strategy of disenfranchising voters of color, like some Republican-controlled states have done because they believe people of color won't vote Republican, we as the inheritors of the party of Abraham Lincoln should be doing everything we can to ensure the GOP reflects the demographics of our broader society. If the Republican Party doesn't start looking like America, then there's not going to *be* a Republican Party in America.

In the four years of Donald Trump's presidency, Republicans lost the House, Senate, and the White House. Joe Biden won the presidency in 2020 in large part because President Trump ignored the advice in the 2012 Republican autopsy and failed to sufficiently appeal to the largest-growing groups of voters: people of color, female voters, and younger voters. Trump only received 26 percent of the non-white vote, only 36 percent of voters twenty-nine or younger, and 42 percent of all women voters.

The Republican Party can make inroads into these communities. I proved it during my time in Congress, and further evidence of our ability to be successful is the significant increase in Republican votes in Latino communities along the Texas-Mexico border in the 2020 election.

I've had a front-row seat to the Republican Party's inability to make inroads into critical voting communities, and my lessons from places like Eagle Pass give us a road map on how to reverse this trend. To be consistently successful at building a Republican Party that looks like America, we need to take four important steps.

First, we need to accept the fact that the 2020 election wasn't stolen. It was lost. Donald Trump lost because he failed to make the Republican Party look like America.

Second, the GOP must stop peddling conspiracy theories like those that led to the Capitol insurrection on January 6, 2021. This actual assault on our democracy was fomented by former president Donald Trump and is an example of the kinds of internal threats many of our military leaders have cautioned our political leaders to take as seriously as external threats. To prevent future manifestations of this threat from materializing, the Republican Party must drive out those who continue to push misinformation, disinformation, and subscribe to crackpot theories like QAnon—the crazy internet conspiracy that Donald Trump was trying to "take down" a shadowy cabal of Democratic pedophiles.

Third, the GOP needs to *broaden* family values from its historical views on religion, marriage, and family structure to everyday issues faced by families—whether that family consists of a man, a woman, and child; a woman and a child; or a man and a child. And yes, two moms or two dads.

When some Republicans talk about "family values," they mean being anti-abortion, pro-gun, and defining marriage as between a man and a woman. I believe the government shouldn't tell anyone who he or she can marry, and we should assume life begins at conception. While I am pro-life and pro–Second Amendment, and my record reflected that in Congress, I realize the debate around these two issues have devolved into a binary choice. You are either for or against. Neither side is going to change their position, and nobody is unaware of the Democratic or Republican positions on these topics.

The Republican Party can see increased electoral success if we become the champions of *new* family values. In addition to caring for our own health and that of our families, taking care of our kids and making sure they get a good education as well as protecting our parents, we need to be the party ensuring our country is open to those who can make it better, and our planet is habitable for future generations.

Finally, the Republican Party must realign our actions based on our principles—freedom enables opportunity, opportunity allows for growth, and growth leads to progress. These principles are not new; they were even written into the Republican platform in 1984. But despite this vision, the party has failed to be ideologically consistent in the pursuit of these noble ideals, instead pursuing a path of political expediency—saying or doing anything to win an election. We the people, individually as citizens but collectively as a nation, want to be inspired and we want pragmatic solutions that positively impact the greatest number of people. Results, not rhetoric.

Freedom means empowering people, not the government. A citizen should be able to make their own decision on how to take care of their own health rather than being told by the government how to do that. Opportunity means letting everyone move up the economic ladder through free and fair markets, not through market manipulation by a handful of people. Let a parent take control of ensuring their son or daughter gets the best education wherever they want. Growth and progress means being prepared to solve the generation-defining challenges like a New Cold War with the Chinese government on global leadership of advanced technology.

I'm the son of a Black father and White mother. I grew up in a neighborhood that wasn't my parents' first choice. It wasn't even their second or third. My folks met in Los Angeles and moved to San Antonio in 1971 a little over a year after getting married. When it was time to stop renting and buy their own house for their family of five, it took them almost a year to find a place. During the week, when my dad was traveling for his job, my mom would do the house hunting. At house after house, realtors would give encouraging signals to my mom, but when she returned with my dad fresh from the road, the real estate agent would lie and tell them the house had been sold. The realtor wasn't going to sell to an interracial couple.

It was neither en vogue nor widely accepted to be an interracial couple in the early 1970s in South Texas. My parents didn't let the hardships they faced define them or impact the values they taught my brother, sister, and me. Values like having the courage to do the things that haven't been done before, being truthful even if it leads to getting in trouble, and fighting for people who need help the most. These values gave their youngest son the tools and fortitude to serve in exotic places around the globe in the CIA, help build a cybersecurity company, and then get elected to Congress three times. Why?

Because, throughout my life, my parents, teachers, coaches, and mentors all worked hard to help me access opportunities, and they helped prepare me to take advantage of opportunities when they came my way. This allowed me to grow in ways neither my parents nor I expected and to progress through life in previously unimaginable ways.

Freedom, opportunity, growth, and progress—this is what the Republican Party should stand for. It's what has allowed people across this country to turn their American Dream into an American Reality.

The GOP has been widely known for standing for this before, when a guy like Jackie Robinson was a Republican. Yes, that Jackie Robinson. The first African American to break the color barrier in Major League Baseball was an ardent social justice warrior and vocal Republican, but he would unlikely be a Republican today.

The Republican Party has made mistakes over the years—being seen as embracing issues like white nationalism, xenophobia, misogyny, and callousness to people's suffering—culminating in a sitting Republican president losing reelection. If the GOP doesn't get back to being a party based on values and principles, then these losses will be the norm rather than the exception.

This is more than just a problem for Republicans. Democrats, Independents, and people who don't vote should care because two strong parties have enabled a competition of ideas that has been the hallmark of our success as a nation. We need two strong parties to participate in this competition of ideas. This is the only way we are going to be able to address the generation-defining challenges our country is facing at home and abroad. This is about leaving our country better off for our kids and their kids.

The GOP's inability to appeal to Americans of all walks of life enabled the Democratic Party to win the presidency in 2020. But the Democratic Party's own ineptitude prevented it from using this victory to influence races down the ballot. While the Democratic Party is experiencing its own vicious internal struggle for control of its soul, a strong GOP can be the only guaranteed foil to prevent the left-wing branch of the Democratic Party—those who are attempting to socialize the economy, constrict the free exchange of goods and services, and take power away from the governed and place it within the government—from deciding the future direction of our country for the next few decades.

To get back to winning, we must become a party that someone like Jackie Robinson and the millions of voters who voted for the first time in 2020 would be proud to join. The GOP can do it, and it starts by making the Republican Party look like America by aligning our actions as a party with our values of freedom, opportunity, growth, and progress.

It's going to be hard, but three terms in Congress, winning multiple campaigns in the toughest district in the country, successfully navigating a broken legislative process in Congress, and interacting with diverse constituents have taught me how. It starts with doing something simple that anybody can do.

CHAPTER 2

SHOW UP SO
YOU CAN LISTEN

"Why don't we round up all the Muslims and put them in internment camps?" That was the first question I was asked by a woman at a town hall in Fort Stockton, Texas, in late November 2014. I was fresh off my first victory in the state's 23rd Congressional District. Along with campaigning on my national security expertise, I'd committed to become the "gold standard" of constituent services while serving in Washington, DC. I promised to show up. I told the voters that if they elected me, I would visit every county before I was sworn into office so I could get my marching orders from my bosses—the seven hundred thousand or so people I would represent. I was fulfilling this promise.

My buddy Brian Jeffreys took personal leave from work to help me hit all twenty-nine counties of the 23rd. Jeffreys was one of those friends who had traveled with me after finding professional campaign staff proved difficult because most of them thought I couldn't win. In the 2014 election I did manage to have a professional campaign manager, Justin Hollis. He started volunteering on my first campaign the day he graduated from college. After that race, he went on to be involved in several campaigns across the country, gaining valuable experience that was put to good use in Texas 23.

While Justin participated in a few stops, it was mostly Jeffreys, me, and Pearl, my trusty gray Jeep Grand Cherokee. I would put more than 175,000 miles on Pearl in less than six years, and Jeffreys and I were responsible for three thousand of those miles on this one trip.

It takes ten and a half hours to drive from one corner of Texas 23 to the other at eighty miles per hour, which is the speed limit in most of the district. I learned the hard way that this wasn't the speed limit in all of the district.

Back in the winter of 2014, the Islamic terrorist group ISIS was in the front of people's minds. ISIS was filming beheadings and using social media to inspire lone-wolf acts of terrorism around the globe. The fear that terror spread caused national security to be a major issue for the 2014 election. Anti-Muslim sentiment was rising throughout the country, and the 23rd was no different.

Despite the backdrop of the national security threat, the woman's question was outlandish. Even the stone-faced ranchers and farmers with cowboy hats and mouths full of chewing tobacco showed signs of being uncomfortable with her inquiry. I took a few too many seconds to respond and started worrying that I was giving away that I thought her question was terrible, and I was afraid of upsetting her with my answer. Unfortunately, I screwed up my response, rambling on about ISIS and Syria.

On our drive to the next stop, I talked through with Jeffreys what my answer should have been. It should have started with a crystal-clear statement that violating someone's freedom by forcibly interning them was a terrible idea. Right there, barreling down the highway, I decided to challenge folks whenever they went too far. From then on, I didn't hesitate to admonish constituents for offensive comments and push back when they got facts wrong. One of my best friends, Lynlie Wallace, who knows more about Texas politics than just about anybody, used to be shocked at how I'd debate with people. But I've come to follow a very simple philosophy: agree when you agree and disagree when you disagree.

This outlook was hard for some to understand. Many in Washington and the media believe you must agree with your party 100 percent of the time and you must disagree with the other side 100 percent. That's just stupid. I was often criticized, even though I was being ideologically consistent, but I didn't care. I learned early on from my elementary PE teacher, Coach Clark, not to be easily influenced or affected by what other people say or think about me. I told everybody—the president, the leaders of my party, my colleagues, my constituents: "You're not always gonna agree with me, but you will know where I stand."

When Donald Trump came into office in 2016, I kept the same outlook. That didn't always fly with my congressional colleagues, especially as more of them came to ally themselves with Trump. There were tense moments. But throughout Trump's term, I advocated on behalf of my constituents and held on to my values, even when things got really screwy, which was pretty often over those four years.

I should have been prepared for the Fort Stockton woman's outlandish question. I got plenty of crazy questions on my first campaign when I took some wild forays outside of my hometown of San Antonio in 2009. After graduating from Texas A&M University in College Station, which is way outside the 23rd, I had spent almost a decade in the CIA, primarily overseas. Before I ran for office, I didn't know the parts of the district outside San Antonio that well, so I resorted to a tactic that had become a staple when I was in the CIA—area familiarization or "AreaFam."

In the espionage business, possessing a deep understanding of the city in which you were operating was critical to conducting a good Surveillance Detection Route (SDR), as well as finding a secure meeting sight or understanding the rhythms of a city. Do you know whether a street on a map allows you to drive a car through it or whether that street is one-way or two-way? Which shops, restaurants, and stores were always crowded inside and in which ones could you be inconspicuous? How do people dress in a particular neighborhood, what kind of cars do they drive, and what type of religious services do they attend? Some of this seems straightforward, but in a time before Google Maps and ubiquitous online guides, knowing the answers to these questions required you to find out the old-fashioned way: by hitting the streets.

So in late 2009, I jumped in my car and went on my inaugural campaign road trip to show up to places I was unfamiliar with in order to learn more.

I was joined by Barry Hammond, whose life I ruined by convincing him to quit his job in Houston and move to San Antonio to run my campaign.

Brad Heasley, one of my closest friends since I was thirteen years old, also joined. Barry is Black. Brad is White.

About a half hour drive west of San Antonio, in the town of Castroville, we had stopped at a coffee shop to grab a cup of joe. The owner, recognizing we weren't from around there, approached us and inquired why we were in town. Throughout the interaction, the proprietor looked puzzled. Then, at one point in the conversation, he matter-of-factly pointed at Brad and said: "I know what *you* are." He then pointed at Barry and said: "And I know what *you* are." Then he turned to me, whose skin is lighter than Barry's but darker than Brad's, and paused. "But what," he said, "are *you*?"

I didn't get pissed. He was just trying—in his blunt South Texas way—to figure me out. I'm pretty sure we convinced him to vote for me.

Throughout ten years of campaigning and serving the people of the 23rd, I crisscrossed the district hundreds of times. In my first term, I did about four hundred public events across the district, plus twenty-five town halls and countless private meetings—going to communities that literally had never seen a Republican politician show up before. I did this all the time—not just before an election. Showing up ninety days before the election is called pandering. Because I showed up when elections weren't on the top of people's minds, the people I was around told me their problems, they gave me their perspective, and they revealed their hopes and desires. I may have started the trips with the intention to have as many opportunities as possible to persuade my constituents to vote for me, but I realized early on that these trips presented opportunities for me to listen.

Just like getting out of that tiny Toyota Tercel in that crowded alley in that South Asian city, showing up and listening throughout the 23rd District of Texas showed empathy and enabled me to understand the emotional state of the folks I was representing. The resulting conversations inspired within me compassion to solve their problems or alleviate their suffering, as much as I could.

The visits were always fun, sometimes profound, occasionally weird, and every once in a while, riotous. People didn't always agree with what I said, but they always appreciated me showing up. In all my visits, I'd say the same thing: "How can I help?"

But showing up to all the places forced me to change a habit that I had forged during my time in the CIA to protect myself from Russian spies. The Russian equivalent of the CIA is the *Sluzhba Vneshney Razvedki*, which means Foreign Intelligence Service. They go by the acronym SVR and are notorious for trying to extort other people whom they suspect to be intelligence officers from other countries. They would manufacture scenarios where a suspected intelligence officer would be handed a packet of money in public while a hidden photographer took pictures. Because of these attempts at extortion, it was drilled into my head never to accept a packet from a stranger. But at every stop, while campaigning and in Congress, people I had never met were always trying to give me material about an issue they were dealing with. So I had to break my CIA habit and learn to accept unfamiliar material.

Jeffreys's and my trip in 2014 ended at a bar in San Elizario (San Eli to the locals) on the southeastern edge of El Paso County. In the 2014 election, I got 2.1 percent of the vote there. Although I ended up increasing my share of the vote by a factor of ten by my last election, I was never going to win El Paso. But I believe in showing up for people who will vote for me, people who won't vote for me, and people who won't vote at all, because I represent all of them.

We rolled into El Bandido Restaurant. The place was packed. Because of our poor showing in El Paso during the recent election, I thought we were in the wrong place. But these folks were genuinely excited to see me, and it was a hell of a party.

A group of Vietnam veterans came up to me and handed me some material. They had an astounding story about Private Marcelino Serna. He was an undocumented Mexican immigrant living in El Paso and had volunteered for the U.S. Army during World War I. He was shipped off to Europe to join the Allied Forces, but before battle, somebody discovered he was actually a Mexican citizen and gave him the option to withdraw.

Nope, he said. I'm staying with my buddies and fighting for the United States of America because I love this country. In one battle, he was injured and twelve of his compatriots were killed. He chased down the Germans and captured eight of them. Another time, he killed twenty-six enemy combatants and captured twenty-four more, refusing to allow them to be executed by his fellow soldiers.

Serna became the most decorated World War I veteran from Texas, honored with two Purple Hearts and the Distinguished Service Cross, the second-highest honor a soldier can receive. He became an American citizen, died in 1992, and is buried with full military honors at Fort Bliss National Cemetery near El Paso.

The vets wanted me to help get Serna the Medal of Honor, the nation's highest military honor. We looked into it, but it wasn't doable. Instead, one of the first bills I passed in Congress renamed the Tornillo Port of Entry outside El Paso as the Marcelino Serna Port of Entry.

At the renaming ceremony in April 2017, attended by six generations of the Serna family, they told me they hoped the honor would stand as a testament to the hardworking spirit of the people of the region and an example of how Latinos have long contributed to America's greatness. While Serna's accomplishments happened more than a century ago, his story reverberates now. When you show up, you learn what people really care about. If you just watch cable news and read your social media feed, it's easy to forget that all politics really is local.

On my trips through the deep-blue areas of the district, oftentimes people would come up to me and say: "Look, I'm a lifelong Democrat. I've never even seen a Republican. And I have no desire to vote for a Republican, but I'll vote for you. You listen to your community."

The 2014 trip, right before I took the oath of office to become a new member of Congress, was the inspiration for what became DC2DQ, my summer treks across all twenty-nine counties of the district in one week for town halls at Dairy Queens. Almost every county has a Dairy Queen, everybody knows where it is, and who doesn't love a cool treat on a hot day.

If you are going to show up, you can't be afraid of your constituents. The worst town hall I ever had was in Alpine, a small town in the 23rd north of Big Bend National Park in the Chihuahuan Desert. A natural gas pipeline was being proposed on the outskirts of the community, and people weren't happy about it. During a previous trip to Alpine, I screwed up and didn't know about the controversy. So I came back when I had more information.

Hundreds of people were gathered at Sul Ross State University. Everyone—and I mean everyone—was upset. People were coming up to the microphone at the front of the room and yelling at me. I was trying hard not to take it personally, but it wasn't fun.

As people were talking, I kept moving closer to their mic. One speaker shouted. I took a few steps closer. The next one went nuts. I stepped forward again. And so on. Pretty soon, I was close enough to shake the speaker's hand.

They calmed down. Then it became more "Hey, Will, thanks for coming here and listening to us. I know everybody's upset and angry, but we appreciate you being here and doing something." And we were able to have a productive session.

While it was uncomfortable, I learned that no one wants to scream right in your face. If they're in the back of the room, they'll scream at you from there. But they don't really want to yell at you when you're close and, ultimately, they just want to be heard.

While this hostile situation resolved in a productive way, it doesn't mean we weren't careful in these settings. I'd spent too long in the CIA not to be wary of crowds. In Texas, everyone carries guns and knives. That part didn't bother me. But people are unpredictable.

Like many government offices, we got death threats. After the shooting at the Capitol Hill baseball game practice in 2017, where Majority Whip Steve Scalise, U.S. Capitol Police officers David Bailey and Crystal Griner, congressional aide Zack Barth, and lobbyist Matt Mika were injured, we got even more careful. Scott Kafer—the toughest guy I know, who managed the security detail of the CIA director and who trained security forces for presidents, potentates, and kings—volunteered to show my team how to implement proper security protocols. I was never worried about my safety, but I did worry about my staff's.

Showing up so much meant you were building relationships in an environment of your choosing. You don't want the first time you show up somewhere to be during an emergency. That was clear to us when COVID-19 struck the 23rd. As a largely rural district outside the limelight, help was slow to arrive. In order to get desperately needed assistance, we drew on relationships developed over the years with community leaders as well as state and federal officials.

In a district of my size, driving means putting in long hours on the road. But distance driving is in my blood. My dad was a traveling salesman, and his territory was Texas, Louisiana, New Mexico, and sometimes portions of California. He was on the road five days a week, and when I was a kid, sometimes he took me with him. I remember one trip to Tyler, Texas. My dad and I did the drive—640 miles round-trip—in one day. I loved it.

You are probably thinking: Doesn't every politician do this? The answer is no. For years, Republicans have gotten locked into staying put and listening only to people who look and think like them. It's easy to represent a solidly Republican seat. It's easy to talk about conservative principles to a conservative audience; you get to preach to the choir. But if you are afraid of losing a primary, then you are a terrible politician because you haven't been taking a conservative message to new places, like explaining the negative repercussions of concentrating power in the hands of a few. Appealing to the fringes because they're the ones who always vote for you in the primary isn't a way to govern—or a way to gain new voters.

Many Republicans have neglected communities that are fighting for their inalienable rights. Communities that also believe in opportunities for all. Communities that think we don't care about them, although they actually believe in Republican principles and ideas.

In November 2020, Donald Trump failed because he did not demonstrate to a majority of the country that he cared about them, which prevented them from listening and understanding that our Republican principles—from eliminating achievement gaps through school choice to delivering real consequences to those who will do us harm—have been responsible for a lot of success and safety in this country. Some Republicans even tried to limit voting to help President Trump's reelection chances. That's insane—this notion that we can't be competitive if there are more voters. A benefit of showing up multiple times before an election is that you don't have to prevent people from showing up on Election Day. The more people exercising their right to have their voices heard, the better off we're going to be.

Republicans have an opportunity. The Democratic Party is tacking far left and cutting itself off from everyday America. Party leaders show a naivety on national security, an inability to accept a diversity of thought, and an unwillingness to embrace innovation when it comes to upskilling the worker of the future. The results of the 2020 election at the congressional and state level showed this is not what Americans want. So Republicans have a chance to bring their message of freedom, opportunity, growth, and progress to the entire country. We have an obligation to advocate for our ideals in *every* community. It is the only way we will endure and move our country forward.

The principles of empowering people, not the government, and helping people move up the economic ladder through free markets, not some flavor of socialism, produce better solutions for society. In a period when we need to solve generation-defining challenges, such as the fact that U.S. economic and military dominance is no longer guaranteed, the best ideas are necessary to succeed.

The Republican Party cherishes individual freedoms, like letting parents choose the best schools for their kids and deciding which doctors should be able to care for your family. The GOP believes in the power of opportunity. We believe income inequality is due to education inequality. We believe in effective government that should work on an individual's behalf, not telling that individual how he or she should live their life.

As I've learned in Texas 23, to make the GOP look like America is not complicated. Republicans need to show up to places where the party hasn't been before and listen. Listening shows you care, and we must *genuinely* care. Because if people don't think you care, they won't trust you. And if they don't trust you, then they're not gonna like you, even if you have better ideas than the other guy. That's pragmatic idealism in action.

Folks will support the GOP even more if we deliver results, not rhetoric, and stop doing and saying a few things that Republicans have, unfortunately, become known for.

CHAPTER 3

DON'T BE AN ASSHOLE, RACIST, MISOGYNIST, OR HOMOPHOBE

There was a good chance that going to the George Floyd march in Houston was a bad idea. When I first heard about the George Floyd video, I couldn't watch the entire clip. It literally made me sick to my stomach. It was made even worse because his murderer wore the blue uniform of the police, who are meant to protect and serve the public.

My decision to attend the June 2, 2020, march was easy for me, but most of my senior staff were either uncomfortable or downright opposed to it. They worried that an outcome of the trip would be headlines like "Republican Congressman Will Hurd Part of Protest that Killed People and Damaged Property."

It's true that some rioting and looting had occurred around the country at marches. None of that was justified. But I wanted to show my support to the family of George Floyd. When a large community deals with tragedy, it must grieve and heal together.

My older sister Liz, my friend Lynlie Wallace, and three staffers came along. As we marched, people chanted social justice slogans, but nobody was derogatory or mean. Tens of thousands of folks were there—the official count was north of sixty thousand. The interactions between the marchers and the police were pleasant and kind. The march was peaceful and a success.

At one point, Liz commented to me that she thought there were as many non-Black people marching as Black folks. It was invigorating to be with so many people from all walks of life committed to the same cause—to end the unnecessary deaths of Black folks in police custody. It felt as if a majority of Americans were finally understanding the realities of systemic racism in American society.

The country was having a long-overdue reckoning with issues like bigotry and hate across the board, including unjust police violence that has long marred this experiment called America. The public calls for social justice following George Floyd's murder were unique in their size and scope. I hadn't seen this type of universal outrage during my time in Congress, and I thought the outrage would create an environment to get something done legislatively on the issue of police violence.

But, getting legislation signed into law that would have improved the standard of policing across the country was made unnecessarily complex by far-left Democrats' demands to defund or even abolish the police. When such an extreme position gets into the public debate, it prevents nuance and thoughtfulness from ruling the day. People involved in the debate become scared to say anything other than voicing a full-throated rebuke of the extreme point of view for fear of any other position becoming viewed as acceptance of the extreme.

However, Republicans can't use the extremism of the far left as an excuse to stand on the sidelines on issues of social justice, especially since many Americans think the entire Republican Party is a bunch of bigots that condone racism, misogyny, and homophobia. Millions of Republicans, the overwhelming super majority, absolutely do not hold these beliefs. We believe, like those who created the party in the mid-1800s, in equal opportunity for everyone.

The Republican Party was officially created in 1856 from the efforts of anti-slavery proponents from the two major parties at the time, the Whigs and the Democrats. They formed a new party in opposition to the successful passage of the Kansas-Nebraska Act of 1854, which increased the territory within the United States where slavery would be permitted. Abraham Lincoln, who put this country on the long path toward equality, was the first GOP president. To this day, my dad—who lived through Jim Crow and has experienced brutal racism—is a lifelong Republican "because Lincoln freed us."

Republicans can't deny that people affiliated with our party, including former president Trump, have made intolerant, racist comments that give legitimacy to hateful ideologies like white supremacy. We also can't deny the legacy of the "Southern strategy," courting Southern white voters by stoking racial fears, begun by former Arizona senator Barry Goldwater in 1964 when he was the Republican nominee for president, and then perfected by President Richard Nixon in 1968 and 1972. In current times, being afraid to stand up to white nationalists for fear of losing a Republican primary is not a valid excuse to avoid rebuking racist rhetoric, behavior, and policy.

The way to achieve electoral success is to make sure the Republican Party looks like America by being a party based on the values with which we began—equal opportunity for everyone—and showing up in communities that have never seen us and listening to their concerns and offering attainable solutions.

After Floyd's murder, I was the first Republican official to issue a statement condemning his horrific killing, and I was one of the few Republicans who showed up at a protest of his murder. Reporters asked me if I was doing this because I was the only Black Republican in the House. That wasn't it at all. I was speaking out for my dad, my mom, my family, and my community. I wanted to show solidarity with Black America. I wanted to explain it was okay to be simultaneously outraged by a Black man being murdered in police custody, thankful that law enforcement puts themselves in harm's way to enable our First Amendment rights, and pissed off that criminals are treading on American values by looting and killing police officers. These emotions aren't mutually exclusive.

My father, Bob, now eighty-nine years old, grew up Marshall, Texas, just over the state line from Louisiana in East Texas. Within the state, East Texas was the region with the most recorded lynchings and the most members of the Ku Klux Klan. It embodied the Jim Crow South.

At a time when Black men in Marshall were basically limited to becoming a waiter or a bus boy, my dad managed to graduate from college. In the early 1950s, he was one of the first Black salesmen for the American Tobacco Company, responsible for selling Lucky Strikes to gas stations and small grocery stores. To make a successful sale, my dad had to get behind the counter of the store to see what cigarette merchandise was there and figure out what the attendant manning the store needed.

When he was on sales calls, he would pull up to an account in a company car, wearing a freshly pressed suit. Right before he walked through the door of the business, he looked up at the sky; he imagined the face of the guy he was about to talk to. He'd tell that guy, "Today is your lucky day."

He did this even though he knew, as soon as he walked in the store, the attendant would curse at him, call him the N-word, and demand that he leave because of the color of his skin. But my dad knew he could convince the guy to let him behind the counter. And by the end of the visit, the attendant would be shaking my dad's hand and asking when he would be back. My pops said the secret to his success was to have a PMA—a Positive Mental Attitude.

When we were growing up, we talked a lot in our family about maintaining a PMA. It's an attitude I keep even today. But I can't imagine the determination it took for my dad to walk into those gas stations and grocery stores day after day, week after week, year after year, confront the racism and hostility he experienced, and still maintain his PMA. Just like I can't imagine what it felt like for my mom to deal with those real estate agents who lied to her face every weekend while she kept losing out on a home for her family because of the skin color of the person with whom she wanted to spend the rest of her life.

Growing up in San Antonio, I experienced remnants of this bigotry. As a teenager, I'd go into stores and shopkeepers wouldn't want a young Black kid in their place of business so they'd call me the N-word and tell me to get out. Non-Black fathers of girls I dated tried to persuade their daughters not to date me because of my race. When I was doing recruiting for Texas A&M while a student there, I witnessed high school counselors discourage kids of color from applying to preeminent universities because they wouldn't "fit in."

I remember learning to drive at fifteen, and my dad giving me "The Talk"—not the one about the birds and the bees but the talk about what it means to be a Black man being pulled over by the police. He taught me that if I ever got pulled over by the police, I was to turn on the light in the car, roll down my window, and put my hands on the window seal so the police could see them. He instructed me not to make any movements unless I told the officer and received consent.

Today's Black parents still have to have The Talk with their kids. Some folks—exclusively White men—have told me they give their daughters similar advice. But I always point out that they were telling their daughters to do this so they would *stay calm* when interacting with the police. Black parents are trying to protect their children from getting *killed* by the police.

Here's the reality: communities of color, immigrants, the LGBTQ community, and the Asian American community (especially during COVID-19)—have been hit hard by hate crimes. While I was serving in Congress, hate-crime violence hit a sixteen-year high, according to the FBI. Mass shootings targeted the LGBTQ community at the Pulse nightclub in Orlando; Black parishioners at the Emanuel African Methodist Episcopal Church in Charleston, South Carolina; and Latinos at a Walmart in El Paso.

The entire country was sickened by acts like these, but Republicans were portrayed as being unsympathetic to these vulnerable groups suffering from these calamities. This portrayal will continue until Republican deeds match Republican rhetoric.

I shouldn't have been only one of a few Republicans who voted in May 2019 in favor of the Equality Act, a sweeping bill that would have banned discrimination on the basis of sexual orientation and gender identity under the Civil Rights Act of 1964 across important areas of life like housing, employment, and credit. Many of my colleagues opposed this. Why? Because they were worried about dudes playing women's sports, even though all major athletic conferences had already taken steps to address this situation. The other argument for opposing the Equality Act was that it didn't protect the freedom of religion. As a Christian, I've been to a bunch of different churches. I have lived in countries where the dominant religion was Islam or Hinduism, and I don't know of any faith that says it's okay to discriminate against anybody. They all teach to love one another.

I had many constituents upset with me over my LGBTQ antidiscrimination vote. That came with the territory, but my job was to do what my dad taught me—"be honest and do the right thing." Whenever I encountered an individual upset with this vote, I would think about my uncle Steve. Uncle Steve gave me my first computer. While he was alive, I never knew he wasn't my biological uncle. He was the longtime partner of my mom's actual uncle, Lester.

Uncle Steve, a Navy veteran, moved from California to San Antonio after Uncle Lester died. I was young when this happened and never really knew Uncle Lester, but Uncle Steve was a cool guy, and we were all close to him. In my house, there was a lot of loose language, mostly by my dad, but the one word we were absolutely never allowed to use was the f-word—the one that rhymes with bag (I can't even write the word because I'm worried my dad will read this and drive to my house and give me an open-handed slap to the mouth). I'm sure my dad's strict policy was because of my uncles Lester and Steve. They were the first ones to welcome my dad into my mom's family with open arms.

The vote on the Equality Act wasn't the only time I was one of the handful of Republicans standing up for the principle that started our party. Another time was in August 2017, when I was sitting in a chilly, darkened TV studio in San Antonio, waiting for the camera light to blink on so I could discuss the latest antics of North Korean Leader Kim Jong-Un with Wolf Blitzer on CNN's *The Situation Room*.

A few days prior, a white supremacist had driven into a peaceful group of marchers in Charlottesville, Virginia, protesting the far-right rally that had invaded their quiet city on that August weekend. The driver had killed a young woman.

As I was about to go on the air, President Trump had just said at a press conference that there were "very fine people on both sides."

I heard the remarks in my earpiece, and my reaction was instant revulsion. He had just called a bunch of white supremacist terrorists "very fine people."

"Congressman Hurd," Wolf asked as I went on the air. "You are a Republican member of the House of Representatives, but, more important, as an American, are you proud of the way the president of the United States handled this situation today?"

Instantly I thought of my dad's advice—"be honest and do the right thing."

"You know," I said into the camera, "if there's any kids watching the show—racism, bigotry, anti-Semitism, it's not okay. It's not okay. You can't support it in any fashion."

Speaking with increasing urgency, I talked about the bigotry my mom and dad had faced while trying to find a home for their family. I demanded that President Trump apologize.

"Racism, bigotry, anti-Semitism of any form is unacceptable," I told the CNN audience. "And the leader of the free world should be unambiguous about that."

And I added that, by the way, "if you're showing up to a Klan rally, you're probably a racist or a bigot."

The thing is, violent white supremacy meets the very definition of terrorism: it's politically motivated violence against noncombatants. President Trump should have known that. In 2020, his Department of Homeland Security warned that violent white supremacy was the "most persistent and lethal threat in the homeland," and that white supremacists were the most deadly among domestic terrorists in recent years.

White supremacists were responsible for what transpired in Charlottesville. They were responsible for the plot to kidnap the governor of Michigan in 2020. And a white supremacist was responsible for the August 2019 shooting spree at an El Paso Walmart that left twenty-three people dead and twenty-three more wounded—the deadliest attack on Latinos in modern American history.

I spoke at a memorial vigil for the El Paso victims and tried to make everyone's heart a little less heavy. I said, "El Paso, we are telling the rest of the world, that if you come into our community and try to scare us, we will not cower. If you try to come into our community and spread hate, we will respond with love."

That's not to say that Republican leaders never get it right. And it certainly doesn't mean that Democrats get it right more often. Republican House Minority Leader Kevin McCarthy rightfully kicked Rep. Steven King off his committee assignments in January 2019 after King questioned why white supremacy is considered offensive. But just a few months later, after Democratic Rep. Ilhan Omar made anti-Semitic comments, House Democratic leaders pushed through a watered-down resolution vaguely condemning "anti-Semitism, Islamophobia, racism, and other forms of bigotry" without actually naming her.

To be sure, plenty of Republicans condemned President Trump's repulsive *Access Hollywood* remarks ("grab 'em by the p***y") when they came to light in October 2016, and I was one of the handful of Texas Republican leaders to do so. I called Trump's remarks "utterly sickening and repulsive" and urged him to "step aside for a true conservative."

The long, hard process of removing the final vestiges of systemic racism, misogyny, and bigotry from our country to ensure our country actually reflects the revolutionary ideas in our founding documents starts with the words we use. It's okay to say the words black lives matter and agree with the concept while disagreeing with some of the tactics by the organization with the same name. You can be heterosexual and support the LGBTQ community. And, fellas, you should be comfortable with your wife, girlfriend, or sister making as much money as you or more.

The party that believes in freedom must fight for all citizens to have equal opportunity to access goods and services, economic resources, legal and political rights, and the decision-making that governs their lives. My parents didn't get to live in the neighborhoods with the best schools. Transgender kids in school don't drink water all day so that they don't have to go to a restroom. Women still get paid a little over 80 percent of what men make.

When a Republican is seen as a bigot, that affects all of us. If people don't like us, then they won't listen to our ideas. And we have better ideas. If we change our attitude, we change our behavior. When our behavior changes, so will our results. We can prepare the battlespace to win the competition of ideas by giving ourselves an opportunity to be heard. But if we play our cards right and get this chance, we can't throw it away by doing what we have been doing for the last twenty years.

CHAPTER 4

APPEAL TO THE MIDDLE,
NOT THE EDGES

The San Antonio Food Bank was a beehive of activity, and everyone looked haggard. This was the first time my district director, Stacy Arteaga, and I had been together since the 2020 COVID-19 pandemic began. After entering the building, we had our temperature taken by a woman who had the same look on her face as the Marine Security Guards I served with in the CIA when they were on watch all night. Food Bank CEO Eric Cooper and his director of government relations looked like they had been getting three hours of sleep a night.

COVID-19 slammed so hard into South Texas that people were running out of food. A few days before this meeting, Eric and his team had held a food distribution at an outdoor market where ten thousand cars waited hours in line for emergency food aid. A drone photo of the packed parking lot went viral.

"We can't feed this many" was Eric's first thought when he realized several thousand more people had showed up to the food distribution than had signed up. "Our country will see real desperation and chaos if people become afraid they can't feed their families."

Eric and his team explained how children on free and reduced-price lunch programs had lost access to meals because of school shutdowns. Seventy-five percent of kids who needed these programs weren't getting food. Parents were desperate.

Families weren't receiving access to emergency food aid included in the

Families First Coronavirus Response Act—one of three huge COVID relief packages a bipartisan Congress passed in the early weeks of the crisis.

It required the Secretary of Agriculture to approve a state agency plan for temporary emergency relief, and somewhere in the system, things had slowed down for Texas. We did some investigating and then some pushing and, shortly thereafter, Texas received approval from the U.S. Department of Agriculture to provide more than $1 billion in pandemic food benefits. It didn't solve all the crises we were dealing with during the pandemic, but a lot fewer kids went hungry.

Would the people we helped know my team and I were involved? Would they ever vote for a Republican? Would the people we helped vote at all? We didn't know and didn't care to ask. A representative doesn't represent just the people in his or her party. A representative is supposed to represent everyone. A problem was preventing parents from feeding their kids, so we helped solve it. Unfortunately, many elected officials fail to focus on solvable problems plaguing our communities because the problem lacks appeal among the loudest voices within their constituency.

The loudest voices are usually the most passionate. They dominate social media, and their perspectives get the most exposure on cable news. Even though the fringes on either side usually only make up a minority of general election voters, they push mainstream institutions into hyper-political positions that are out of touch with most of society, because they are oftentimes the largest block of voters in a primary. These people are on the extreme edges of both parties. An example within the GOP are those who believe the QAnon conspiracy theories that Hillary Clinton is part of a pedophile ring, and in the Democratic party, it's the people who advocate literally for abolishing the police. Sometimes these extremists on the edge get confused with "the Base"—the people who will only vote for a single party's candidates in general elections. While people on the edges would never vote for a candidate from the opposing party, they may not vote in a particular election if they don't believe the candidate is sufficiently "liberal" or "conservative."

Prior to Donald Trump's emergence as the Republican nominee for president in 2016, the GOP was an amalgamation of social conservatives, economic conservatives, and national security hawks. How you define these categories depends on the time period you are talking about. For some insights, we can turn to the pollster Tony Fabrizio, who has worked for a number of politicians for almost three decades. He has conducted three national polls since 1997 about the attitudes and views of the members of the Republican Party.

In the late '90s, a fiscal conservative could have been a deficit hawk who believed in reducing the federal deficit at all costs, including increasing taxes. Or a fiscal conservative could have meant a supply-sider—someone who believed the most important act the federal government could make was to cut taxes.

In the mid-2000s, social conservatives could have been moralists who were the successors of Ralph Reed/Pat Robertson Republicans (respectively the first executive director of the Christian Coalition and former Southern Baptist minister turned born-again Christian televangelist), who were primarily concerned about issues such as abortion and homosexuality. Or social conservatives could have been "Dennis Miller Republicans" (named after the *Saturday Night Live* alumnus turned political commentator/talk show host) who cared the most about illegal immigration and strongly opposed people gaming the system to get a "free lunch" and had mixed opinions on the issues of homosexuality or abortion.

In the current era, a national security hawk could mean a "border and order" Republican who cares about building a wall along our southern border and responds to law-and-order messaging or a neocon who favors a large military and believes the U.S. should be outward-facing on a global scale.

Further complicating the various segments that constitute the Republican Party is that after Donald Trump's election and defeat, an argument can be made that the Republican Party is made up of tribes based on their level of satisfaction with, and opinion of, the former president. However, the boundaries between these various ideological groups are not fixed. Within each of these segments exists those on the edge who believe it's either "my way or the highway."

A similar analysis could be performed on the Democratic Party, but the concept of the base and the edge are the same.

Understanding the edge matters because those on the edge get a disproportionate amount of attention from elected officials since they have historically been the largest individual block of voters who consistently vote in primaries. This focus contributes to a toxic political culture because so many races are decided by the winner of the primary from the party that is dominant in that district.

Going into the 2020 election cycle, only thirty-four House seats were considered split districts, meaning that in the previous presidential election, the candidate who won the congressional district was from a different party than the district's selection for president. Thirty-one Democrats represented districts that Donald Trump won in 2016 and only three Republicans represented districts won by Hillary Clinton. That is thirty-four out of 435 members of the House of Representatives—roughly 8 percent.

After the 2020 election, only sixteen split districts are still standing—seven Democrats hold districts that Donald Trump won and nine Republicans are serving in seats where the majority of those voters selected Joe Biden for president.

But go back twenty years: 86 seats were competitive. Twenty years before that, 143 seats were. This was back in the day when problems got solved through bipartisanship. Competitive seats create *problem solvers* because they force politicians to appeal to a cross-section of their district, not just those who show up in a partisan primary. Noncompetitive seats create *bomb throwers*.

In 2018, an average of 54,000 people voted in contested primaries, meaning a primary election for either a Republican or Democrat where there was more than one person a voter could select from on the ballot. This reality means a minimum of only 27,001 people decided who was going to represent their district. During my time in Congress, a member represented over

700,000 people, so in 92 percent of congressional districts, only 3 percent of the population decided who would get the opportunity to go to Washington, DC. In the 8 percent of competitive districts, roughly 265,000 people voted in the general election for their representative, meaning a minimum of 132,501 folks picked the winner. Would you rather have 27,001 or 132,501 deciding who goes to Congress?

Since 92 percent of districts are decided by the most partisan political blocs, then they are the only people who get spoken to, because professional political consultants advise candidates that if these voters don't vote for you, then you can't win. This fuels extremism.

That doesn't have to be the case. It's not like a majority of Americans are cool with our veterans returning home to lousy medical care or an immigration system that's still broken. When serious problems go unaddressed, people feel like they're not being heard or even ignored. The gridlock we experience in Washington is not because our problems are too complicated to solve, it's because there are too many people who appeal to the edges and won't work together.

Building coalitions, working with your political adversaries to find win-win solutions, has gotten a bad name. Some would even say it's old-fashioned. Folks who try this are scorned as "moderates."

I've hated labels my entire life. Don't tell me who I am, what I am, what I can do. And the word "moderate" annoys me. *Oxford Languages* says the adjective "moderate" means "average in amount, intensity, quality, or degree." While moderates generally do reflect the opinions of the supermajority of Americans, or the average American, moderates aren't average. The term is used as a pejorative synonym for squishy. It doesn't suggest boldness or ideological consistency. Most people using the term don't understand what really happens in politics. The moderates are the ones who behave the same way regardless of whether their party is in power or not. The moderates are critical to crafting and passing legislation that actually gets signed into law. The moderates are the ones who work the hardest.

Congressional representatives like me, who were in competitive seats, are the ones who actually have to campaign in our districts. We take a Republican message to communities where it's never been articulated. We are the ones taking ideas to people who don't agree with us.

Ideologues only have to talk to themselves, and it's easy to preach to that choir. But moderates have to change hearts and minds. We appeal to the middle—not the fringes—of the political spectrum.

And we are the ones who get shit done. Extremists do the most bitching and get the least accomplished.

Terrified parents trying to feed their families don't need ideologues. They need help—fast—from a Congress working together in a bipartisan fashion to pass bills to find solutions to the crises engulfing the country.

Our brothers and sisters in the military don't need idealogues. They need a federal government that can provide them with the tools, training, and facilities to enable them to defend our homeland.

One of the first bills I got signed into law originated from a stop at one of the forerunners to my DC2DQ trips. There, a civilian from Laughlin Air Force Base in Del Rio, west of San Antonio on the U.S.-Mexico border, raised his hand to tell me that the Laughlin airfield flooded after only one inch of rain and became unusable.

Laughlin produces more pilots than any facility in the country. So one inch of rain and they couldn't train pilots? That was crazy. Afterward, the guy showed me some aerial photos of what he was talking about. After a rainstorm, the area looked like a bathtub and the planes looked like toys floating in the water. No political leader had bothered to do anything about it for decades. It took us longer than we expected, but we were able to fix the problem.

Americans getting their digital information stolen on an almost daily basis also don't need ideologues. They need protection. When I got to Congress, I never thought I'd end up being the IT procurement expert. It's not exactly a sexy topic. But I was shocked to learn that the federal government spent $80 billion on buying IT goods and services—computers, software, and so on. And 80 percent of that money was spent on systems that any reasonable person would consider outdated.

How old? One example: The U.S. Department of Labor had a thirty-year-old system developed by people who were all dead. They had to resort to looking for old parts on eBay.

So I collaborated with Robin Kelly (D-Illinois) and Gerry Connolly (D-Virginia) on the Modernizing Government Technology (MGT) Act, signed into law by President Trump in December 2017. The MGT was designed to bring the government's IT systems into the twenty-first century by establishing an IT modernization fund at executive branch agencies so they could upgrade their technology systems. No more hunting through eBay for parts.

These are the types of solutions Americans *want*. On my trips through the 23rd, questions I got the most weren't about impeachment or Robert Mueller or whatever was obsessing Washington or the media at the time.

Instead, people asked: "Why won't DC get things done?" and "Why can't people work together?"

The reason little gets done in DC is largely because most candidates have to win elections by creating *contrast*, which fuels political and personal contempt. And if you win elections by throwing bombs and creating contrast, what do you do when it's time to legislate? Throw bombs and create contrast. But the contempt created from the bomb throwing and contrast making prevents us from solving the generation-defining challenges facing us as a country at home and abroad.

In his 2019 book *Love Your Enemies*, Arthur C. Brooks points out how political differences are ripping our country apart because of a culture of contempt—divisive politicians, along with screaming heads on TV, polarizing columnists, crazy social media posts, rants, and feuds. They stoke our own biases while affirming our worst assumptions about those who disagree with us. It makes political compromise—a dirty word in DC—and progress impossible.

A perfect example was Washington's failed attempt at police reform legislation after the horrific police killings of George Floyd, Breonna Taylor, Rayshard Brooks, and well over one hundred other African Americans in 2020.

When David Dorn, a seventy-seven-year-old, retired African American police captain, was killed by looters, and several other officers in St. Louis, New York, and Las Vegas were shot at during protests, the far right felt justified to view all peaceful protesters as looters and criminals. Around the same time, the far left began their outrageous demands to defund and even abolish the police. With such extreme positions gaining traction, two factions that were mutually exclusive began to develop in Congress—one pro-police and one pro–racial justice. The bipartisan outrage that emerged from seeing the video of George Floyd's murder failed to coalesce into legislative action because a more nuanced position would be seen by one faction as tacit approval of the other's extreme position.

When my team and I put forward ideas on how to address policing reform, we knew three things: First, the way to improve policing is not by defunding the police but by ensuring federal dollars flowing to law enforcement are used in the most effective way to improve training. Second, we should clarify federal law to ensure that law enforcement officers can be held accountable in court for actions violating Americans' civil rights. And third, we have to empower police chiefs to fire bad officers and keep them off the force permanently, which is an action made difficult by pushback from some police unions.

My good friend Pete Aguilar (D-California) had let me know that the Congressional Black Caucus—an all-Democrat organization—was taking the lead for the Democrats in drafting legislation, and they wanted my input.

The White House reached out to me to explain they were moving ahead with an executive order offering new federal incentives for local police to bolster training and create a national database to track misconduct. But there was nothing in it about firing bad cops.

At the same time, House Minority Leader Kevin McCarthy asked me to participate in a Republican-only call to develop our ideas addressing police reform.

On the call, Rep. Pete Stauber, a former professional hockey player and Minnesota police officer, cut right to the point. Police chiefs needed to be able to fire bad cops and keep them off the force, he said. He had an idea—two independent arbitrators had to agree to reinstate a fired police officer. A smart solution to a huge problem that both sides could have agreed on. Sixty leaders of the largest local law enforcement organizations in the United States penned an open letter explaining how contracts and labor laws hamstrung efforts to swiftly rid departments of problematic officers.

I laid out my three points and explained that, as Republicans fighting for civil liberties, we should be on the forefront of this issue because a police officer was taking away a fellow citizen's ultimate civil liberty—the right to live. I added that we should be as outraged, if not more, by what happened to George Floyd than what happened to Carter Page. For months before the George Floyd murder, Republicans were incredibly vocal about the FBI's violation of the civil liberties of Page. He was a former investment banker and foreign policy adviser for President Trump's 2016 presidential campaign who had his electronic communications secretly, and illegally, targeted by the FBI. If you were irate by the spying on Carter Page, then you should be irate about George Floyd's fate.

I spoke with colleagues spearheading both the Senate Republican police reform initiative and the House version. Republicans and Democrats recognized the need to empower police chiefs to fire bad cops. But both Republicans and Democrats were afraid of potential electoral blowback by going against police unions, which are geared to protect labor rights rather than public safety.

The Senate version didn't even include many provisions in the planned executive order, and the Democrat bill, the George Floyd Justice in Policing Act, didn't go far enough to solve problems. But in the House, with the Democrats in power and with more than 218 co-sponsors, they didn't have to take any suggestions from Republicans.

I ultimately voted for the Democrat's bill, one of only three Republicans who did, because I will take something over nothing. It would have banned choke holds, no-knock warrants in drug cases, and made it easier to pursue claims against police officers in civil court. But it didn't empower police chiefs to permanently fire bad cops. A lost opportunity. The bill died in the Senate. There would be no bipartisan nor bicameral police reform bill.

The reality is that no matter who is in office, the only way we can solve problems is *together*. In this polarized age, appealing to the middle and forsaking the edges can seem like a sure way to political ruin. However, appealing to the edges is un-pragmatic because most Americans, and most of the world, are craving solutions to their problems, not just people complaining about them. Most people's idealism manifests in their desire to believe in something larger than themselves. This hunger can only be satisfied when we have leaders who inspire, not fearmonger.

PART II

LEADERS NEED TO INSPIRE, NOT FEARMONGER

CHAPTER 5

BE HONEST AND
DO THE RIGHT THING

My father, a few days away from getting thrown in the same jail as Jack Ruby, got a lesson from a gangster in an Atlanta bar that became one of the best pieces of advice he ever gave me. "The only person you can't fool is the person you see when shaving in the mirror," the dude told my dad. "So be honest and do the right thing."

This Atlanta gangster's leadership tip is an essential element to the Ctrl+Alt+Delete necessary to begin an American reboot. If our country is going to get off the X where we find ourselves dealing with an unprecedented erosion of trust at all levels of our society, we need leaders who will inspire, not fearmonger. This journey to achieve aspirational leadership—whether you are leading the country, a business, or your family—begins with being honest and doing the right thing.

While I was in Congress, whenever we polled my constituents, "lack of leadership in Washington, DC" always came up as their number one or number two concern. This lack of leadership is why I ran for Congress. I had seen the problem firsthand when I was in the Central Intelligence Agency.

In October 2000, shortly after graduating from A&M, I joined the CIA. After taking two journalism classes in Mexico City the summer after my freshman year, I added international studies as a minor. In the first class I took for my new minor, I had a guest lecturer who was a badass former CIA officer named Jim Olson. He told the most amazing stories about the National

Clandestine Service, and I knew I wanted to do what Jim had done. I submitted an application, took a bunch of tests, and was grilled during tons of interviews before I was hired. For almost a decade, I recruited spies and stole secrets all over the world. My responsibility was to stop terrorists from conducting attacks on Americans or our allies, prevent Russian spies from stealing our secrets, and put nuclear weapons proliferators out of business. I was working at CIA headquarters in Langley, Virginia, when the world acted in unison following the attacks on the U.S. Homeland by al-Qa'ida on September 11, 2001; and I was operating on the ground in Kabul in 2009 when debates raged about whether the war in Afghanistan required a "surge of troops."

In addition to collecting intelligence, I was called upon to brief members of Congress. In late 2008, a congressional briefing in Afghanistan changed the trajectory of my life, and that day began with a resonating boom at four A.M.

I shot upright in bed, trying to figure out if the noise was from a dream or real life. When the window rattled so hard that it nearly shattered, I knew it was real. I wrapped myself in a blanket, rolled off the bed and onto the floor.

"Duck and cover, stay away from the windows, seek shelter, and await further instructions," a prerecorded voice blared over the speakers throughout the apartment complex where most of the American employees in Kabul lived.

I was the head of a branch in the CIA station, and I knew the chief of station—the senior-most CIA officer in Afghanistan and my boss—would task my unit to figure out who had carried out this attack.

I verified the safety of the officers under my command and instructed them to assemble in the secure conference room once the all-clear signal was given. I slid my nine-millimeter Glock 19 pistol into a concealed leather holster in the back of my pants, pulled a black sweater over my Kevlar body armor, and left my apartment to get to work.

When the all-clear was sounded, my trusted deputy, Heather, and I met with our team, providing them with a comprehensive summary of what we had learned about the attack. Before outlining a plan of action, we asked each officer whether they had people within their stable of recruited assets and contacts who might be able to provide insights on the morning's events.

I needed information by that afternoon, because I would be asked about it during a scheduled briefing for a congressional delegation from the House Permanent Select Committee on Intelligence (HPSCI) that happened to be visiting. HPSCI (pronounced "hip-see") is one of two congressional committees devoted to monitoring intelligence activities on behalf of the American people.

As I walked into the conference room for the briefing, I overheard several congressmen ask the person handling the logistics for their visit: "Is the CIA going to cut this briefing short so we can get to the bazaar to buy rugs?"

Rug shopping? That's what they were thinking about right now? I was pissed, and the briefing hadn't even begun.

During the ensuing conversation, I was asked why we weren't seeing more cooperation between the Taliban and the Iranian Revolutionary Guard Corps (IRGC). I began explaining how the Taliban was Sunni and the IRGC was Shia.

One of the congressmen raised his hand and asked, "What's the difference between a Sunni and a Shia?"

I assumed he was going to make a terribly inappropriate joke. And who was I to stand in his way? So I played along.

"I don't know, Congressman—what's the difference?" I asked with a big smile.

The congressman's chubby face turned bright red, his eyes widened, and his body stiffened. He had no idea what the difference was between the two main sects of Islam. Not a freaking clue.

It's okay for my brother, Chuck, not to know this, because as a cable company sales manager, this piece of information isn't important for him to know. But this should have been easy stuff for these Washington, DC, intelligence "experts." They were determining how to allocate billions of taxpayers' dollars on national security. They were making decisions on sending our sons and daughters, brothers and sisters, to war zones. But they lacked a basic understanding of one of the greatest global threats facing the U.S. and the rest of the world, and they were more interested in going rug shopping.

My mom would always tell my siblings and me, "You're either part of the problem or you're part of the solution." It was time to be part of the solution.

A year or so before the Kabul briefing, the solution had been introduced to me at a Tex-Mex restaurant in Washington, DC, by Stoney Burke, one of my closest friends, and his best friend from college, a wily political operative named Josh Robinson. Stoney gave me the idea to run for Congress in Texas 23, and Josh gave me the plan. Ever since that first conversation at La Lomita Dos, Josh, an early mentor to Justin Hollis—the guy who would oversee all my successful elections as my campaign manager and political consigliere— gave me the confidence that I could do it.

I was an unlikely congressional candidate. Before I ran, there wasn't a big history of people from the CIA running for office. A rare exception was Porter Goss, a former CIA officer who served in the House for fifteen years before going on to serve as CIA director and in other key leadership posts. Elective office is more of a career destination for former military officers or lawyers. It wasn't considered a traditional path for an A&M computer science major who had been in the CIA and hadn't lived in Texas for a decade.

Stoney and Josh pointed out that serving in Congress would be a way to address problems that had frustrated me in the CIA—including ignorant congressional representatives who preferred rug shopping over doing their jobs. They opened my eyes to the notion that it was a chance to use my CIA skill set to provide a different perspective on national security issues.

Because Texas 23 includes portions of San Antonio, it was a natural place for me to run because it was where I was born and raised, although most people I knew thought I was crazy to leave a job I loved and was good at. But I had to follow my mom's advice to be part of the solution, not part of the problem.

I was unsuccessful during my first go-around in 2010, losing a runoff election by only seven hundred votes, but after a stint in strategic consulting and the cybersecurity industry, I was elected in 2014.

While in the CIA, in addition to experiencing some of our most important national security challenges, I learned a lot about leadership. The best leaders in the organization had character. Or more specifically, good character. The Josephson Institute, which works to improve the ethical quality of society, defines character as "the sum of one's distinctive traits, qualities, and predilections, and amounts to one's moral constitution." Time and time again, I was fortunate to see that character is the foundation of leadership, and developing good character *takes practice.*

In his book *Outliers,* Malcolm Gladwell popularized the notion that it takes ten thousand hours of deliberate practice to become an expert in something. When I speak to students, I relate this concept to being a person of character. I usually show pictures of classical musician Yo-Yo Ma, Microsoft founder Bill Gates, platinum recording artist Beyoncé, four-time NBA champion Lebron James, and comedian George Lopez. I ask what they all have in common, and eventually some kid says they work really hard and practice a lot. I explain that being a person of character takes practice, too. Doing what's right means learning to ignore the intense pressures to follow the crowd or to disregard facts for your own benefit.

I tell these kids that just like playing an instrument or performing on a court or being good at math takes practice, being honest and doing the right thing takes practice, too.

When I was still in the CIA, visualizing what I would be doing when I was in Congress, I thought about plans like improving legislation to help get more resources to our national security community to fight terrorism, or explaining to communities throughout our country why we should have a presence in places like Afghanistan. I didn't think I would be explaining why it was bad for an American president to cry foul after losing an election.

Forty-eight hours after Election Day 2020, President Donald Trump stepped up to a podium at the White House and baselessly questioned the integrity of the vote.

"If you look at the legal votes, I win very easily," Trump said. Democrats "are trying very obviously to commit fraud."

Within a few hours, I spoke up.

"A sitting president undermining our political process and questioning the legality of the voices of countless Americans without evidence is not only dangerous and wrong," I said in a tweeted statement, "it undermines the very foundation this nation was built upon. Every American should have his or her vote counted."

I knew my words weren't going to be popular with some of my Republican colleagues or constituents. But issuing that statement was an easy call. I was being honest and doing the right thing. It's what I had practiced so many times before.

The road to getting to this point, where I was willing to take the consequences of being honest, started when I was eight years old, following a misunderstanding about a cartoon character, a rock, and my dad's car.

My father administered many tough lessons throughout my childhood, several of which he had learned the hard way. When he was a young man, he had embezzled money from a wine company he worked for in Dallas. When the theft was discovered, my dad hid out in Atlanta and worked in a hotel banquet section to make ends meet. One night, after a late shift, he and his buddies were out drinking, carousing, being obnoxious and spending money. That's when the gangster joined the group to encourage my dad and his friends to relocate to an establishment where the gangster would get a cut of the money the group would spend there. At some point, the gangster offered his pearl of wisdom.

My dad ultimately negotiated his return to Dallas, where he was arrested and jailed in the same facility where Jack Ruby was being held for shooting Kennedy assassin Lee Harvey Oswald (authorities had moved Ruby into the Black section, to reduce his visibility). My dad was later released and made good on what he stole.

This incident isn't something he's proud of, but he told my brother, sister, and me that story to impart the lessons that it was important to face up to your mistakes, be honest in word and deed, and do the right thing.

My father supported a family of five on a little over $50,000 a year as a traveling textile salesman. In our house, there wasn't much money, but there was a lot of love. My older brother, Chuck, says we were always broke, but I never realized that. I would have called us lower middle-class. Yes, my mother made a lot of our clothes, but I figured it was because she was a good seamstress. Yes, I knew what it was like to put water in my cereal because we didn't have milk, but I thought it was because we couldn't get to the grocery store. We did have two cars—a company car for my dad, and his first company car that he bought on the cheap. He was proud of those cars.

We didn't have cable, but we had a nice TV, which allowed me to take advantage of the Golden Age of cartoons in the early '80s. I was especially hooked on the *Challenge of the GoBots*, about two warring factions of robots that could turn into vehicles. After one riveting episode in 1985, I decided that I needed a new GoBot toy. My father's blunt response to my entreaty: "You ain't getting a fucking robot."

Indignant at this injustice, I stormed out of the house. For some unknown reason, I came to the conclusion that the only remedy was to pick up a rock and, in clear eight-year-old chicken scratch, etch onto the hood of my dad's company car: "I want Gobot."

When my dad discovered my declaration, I claimed I wrote it with a clump of dirt and was unaware of a rock hidden inside. The incident resulted in the second-worst whipping I'd received in my life (the first was when the collective disobedience of my siblings and I concluded with my sister cutting up the belt that was my father's preferred tool to administer consequences). While my dad was pissed that he was going to have to pay a body shop to fix my handiwork, he was angrier that I lied.

I learned that day the consequences of not heeding my father's advice—physical pain, disappointing someone I loved, and feeling the shame of losing the trust of people I cared about. With that act, my father gave me my first lesson about being honest and doing the right thing.

While being honest should be straightforward, doing the right thing oftentimes requires you to take action that's more difficult, like going against the crowd. I've seen political leaders in Washington who say and do things that are politically expedient, rather than what's right. They worry that someone—their constituents, their colleagues, their president—is not going to like them if they go against those forces.

My job was to understand my constituents and represent them in Washington, DC. But my job was also to do the right thing and be willing to deal with the consequences of my decisions. That was pragmatic idealism. Many of those decisions generated responses that could be categorized as peer pressure or bullying, both of which I had experience with.

I was bullied as a kid. I had messed-up teeth that weren't fixed until high school, when my parents could finally afford braces. Until my late teens, I had a speech impediment. My last name rhymes with "nerd" (back when "nerd" was an insult) and "turd." And I had a huge head—the same size in fourth grade as it is now. Plus, I wore a size 13 shoe in elementary school.

I was made fun of every day. In the first few years of elementary school, I cried three or four times a day. That only made the situation worse. Adding to my misery, in the third grade, my PE teacher, Coach Clark, used to call me "Hurd the Nerd." Coach Clark was the coolest dude at Leon Valley Elementary School. He was tall and lean and the first individual I ever saw in person dunk a basketball. Everyone loved Coach Clark, except me.

One day, I quit speaking to him because of that nickname. As punishment, Coach announced in gym class that the entire class, who were sitting cross-legged on the indoor basketball court, would have to run laps outside unless I spoke to him. I slowly rose at this outrage and announced that I would run all the laps for everybody. I walked outside, tears streaming down my face, and began to serve my sentence. There I was, in my mom's homemade clothes in the San Antonio heat, sweating, gasping (oh, I also had asthma), and crying as I staggered around the schoolyard. Coach Clark came over and got serious.

"Do you know why I call you Hurd the Nerd?" he said.

I probably glared at him and said, "Because you're mean."

He leaned into me and spoke slowly. "No. It's because you shouldn't care about what other people think about you. You should care only about what your loved ones think of you. You are a good, smart kid. Don't let anyone get under your skin." He hugged me and told me to go back inside and join the game of dodgeball.

It took some time, but Coach Clark's lesson stuck—probably the greatest lesson I ever learned from someone other than my parents. I got to a point where I quit caring what the bullies thought of me. When I stopped caring, I stopped crying. When I stopped reacting, they stopped mocking me.

Caring only about what your loved ones think of you doesn't mean callousness toward others. Empathy, the ability to understand another person's feelings, and compassion, the desire to reduce the suffering of another, are critical to becoming an inspiring leader. Sadly, I learned about these twin traits through tragedy while I was student body president at A&M.

On Thursday, November 18, 1999, I had just fallen asleep after watching a meteor shower with my girlfriend. My phone rang at three A.M. It was my best friend, Joni Burke.

"I don't know if you've heard this," she said, "but Bonfire has fallen. Some didn't make it."

I was dressing as I raced out the door. I tried to visualize what the polo fields, where Bonfire was built, would look like. But I was incapable of imagining the chaos.

It's difficult to overstate the importance of Bonfire (always capitalized and without "the") to A&M. An immense three-months-long project run entirely by students, Bonfire was a massive stack of logs burned on campus every fall to symbolize every Aggie's "burning desire" to beat the hell out of the University of Texas football team. Up to five thousand students participated in the construction, and Aggies like to say Bonfire was the largest student-organized project in the nation.

But early that November morning, the massive fifty-nine-foot, five-thousand-log pyre became an avalanche of timber. In an instant, it collapsed on dozens of students working on the structure. Twelve students were killed. Twenty-seven were injured.

I arrived on the scene about an hour later. Some of what happened that night I remember vividly, and some I try not to think about. I remember the lights that rescuers set up to shine down on the wreckage, casting a misty sheen over the horrific scene. I remember the periods of silence that settled over the site when rescuers needed to use sensitive audio equipment to listen for survivors in the tons of logs. I remember cranes moving logs off the stack one at a time. I remember calming desperate students who were trying to rescue buddies, organizing them into lines so they could be ready when Emergency Management professionals needed human finesse to move the rubble.

I ended up serving as A&M's student spokesman to the media, working with university leadership on the crisis response and overseeing my student government staff, who organized a candlelight vigil on campus the evening of the collapse. I did whatever I could to help this shattered community come together.

Out of the twelve funerals held around the country, I attended six. At one of them, a grieving mom approached me. She hugged me and held my hands. Fighting back tears, she looked into my eyes and pleaded: "Don't ever let this happen to another student." It's impossible to understand the grief and pain a parent experiences when having to lay a child to rest, and the only thing I could think to do was hug her back and say, "Yes, ma'am."

From Bonfire, I learned the value of staying calm under fire. Sometimes just being there and hugging someone is all you can do when words won't work. You don't have to try to say something to them to make them feel better. You're not gonna make them feel better. You're there to say, "It's okay. You're not going through this alone." And sometimes, it's sufficient just to say, "I don't know," when there are no answers.

Empathy and compassion were tools I had to use in the CIA—dealing with earthquakes, terrorist attacks, bombings. Then, in Congress, dealing with mass shootings in or near my district—Sutherland Springs church, where twenty-six people were killed and twenty injured in the deadliest shooting ever in Texas; Midland/Odessa (eight people killed, twenty-two injured), and the massacre at the El Paso Walmart in August 2019 that killed twenty-three people and injured an additional twenty-three.

In the hours following these horrifying events, many of my congressional colleagues were heartbroken, despondent, and angry. They were channeling these energies into placing blame and reusing tired talking points that they always trotted out during these incidences.

I was trying to understand whether families, whose worlds were changed forever, were getting the support they needed and whether law enforcement authorities had the necessary resources available to determine if the perpetrator was a lone wolf or part of a broader plot. I wanted to calm emotions, not stoke them. There would be plenty of time to scrutinize steps that should have been taken to prevent these incidents, assess responsibility, and administer consequences.

While we are in the middle of these crises, the right thing to do is to be honest about what we know or don't know. Once we are through the immediate crisis, the right thing to do is work together to protect our constitutional rights while preventing people who shouldn't have guns from obtaining them and addressing the mental health issues that lead to someone believing that killing others is an acceptable and necessary action.

Whenever I become aware of a tragedy, it's hard not to think about those polo fields at Texas A&M. I think about what those twelve Aggies would be doing if that fateful night had turned out differently. I think about how fortunate I am to have had the opportunities that I've had. Taking stock of my blessings makes it easier for me to follow the advice that gangster in Atlanta gave my dad. It's the same advice our national leaders need to heed if we are going to perform an American Reboot in order to successfully tackle the challenges currently plaguing our country.

CHAPTER 6

ENSURE THE AUDIO
AND VIDEO MATCH

"Will, it's like you broke up with ten million people all at once." I had hoped Lynlie was exaggerating her opinion on the response to the speech I had just given on the final day of the Intelligence Committee's November 2019 hearings on the impeachment of President Donald Trump. I was seen by both sides, and the media, as the Republican most likely to vote for impeachment, which would have opened the door for other Republicans to do the same. I had made many Republican colleagues nervous by telling the whip team—individuals responsible for knowing in advance how many people were voting for or against upcoming major legislation—that I was undecided, which I was.

House Minority Leader Kevin McCarthy even asked me to step down from HPSCI, which investigated President Trump's infamous phone conversation in July 2019 with Ukrainian President Volodymyr Zelensky. McCarthy wanted to replace me with a bomb thrower who would more aggressively defend the president. I didn't blame Kevin for trying. He was being a dutiful lieutenant for the president. But I said no. I had an expertise in national security, and I was one of the few people on either side of the political aisle who was seeking facts rather than pushing a predetermined position.

After questioning witnesses, reviewing documents, consulting legal minds across the country, and sitting through hundreds of hours of depositions, I determined there was not evidence to warrant a vote for impeachment.

"An impeachable offense should be compelling, overwhelmingly clear, and unambiguous, and it is not something to be rushed or taken lightly," I said over the buzz of clicking cameras at the final day of the hearing. "I have not heard evidence proving the president committed bribery or extortion."

With that statement, and my vote against impeachment in the House, I crushed the hopes of Trump opponents across the country. And Lynlie was right, social media exploded.

To be clear—I was open to voting for impeachment if I saw a violation of the law. That was my standard for impeachment. But I wouldn't vote for impeachment because I disliked what President Trump said in the call. And I wasn't going to support impeachment because I disagreed with the president on other issues—which I did.

Did the president bungle a series of foreign policy decisions? Absolutely. But he didn't break the law.

What brought me to vote against impeachment were the *facts*. Based on my definition of impeachment, a crime had to be proven, and Adam Schiff (D-California) was alleging the crime was bribery or extortion. The necessary elements of a bribe in a court of law weren't in that phone call where the president asked Zelensky for help in gathering information on alleged misdeeds by Joe Biden and Biden's son Hunter.

Bribery is offering, giving, receiving, or soliciting something of value in order to influence the actions of an official in the discharge of his or her public or legal duties. Among the elements that prosecutors need to prove is *intent*, that the bribe involved something of *value* used to influence the recipient and that an offer was used to *influence* the action or nonaction of the recipient.

At the time of the call, Zelensky didn't even know $400 million in military aid was being withheld. Additionally, no clear evidence was presented during the hearings that President Trump ordered anyone to condition security assistance on investigations into the Bidens. The Democrats agreed with me because they failed to include bribery or extortion in the final articles of impeachment.

The Democrats also claimed the White House was withholding documents and directing administration officials to defy House subpoenas—an obstruction of Congress. White House Counsel Pat Cipollone sent me boxes of documents that had been sent to the Hill. The House had access to all the documents it should have had access to. Regarding Trump administration officials who refused to testify before Congress, Speaker Nancy Pelosi could have turned to the courts to compel them to appear. If she had, and Trump officials had failed to appear, it clearly would have been contempt of Congress. But Speaker Pelosi never did that. She did not use all the tools within her power to force that action.

So, I voted against impeachment.

I had developed my standard of impeachment under President Trump's predecessor, President Barack Obama. Over the course of the Obama presidency, I was approached several times by Republican colleagues and vocal constituents about supporting efforts to try to impeach President Obama. Their justifications for impeachment were the 2012 Benghazi attack—the assault on the U.S. diplomatic post in Benghazi, Libya—as well as the president's executive orders regarding immigration. There was even talk about launching an impeachment over the insane and erroneous claims that President Obama was born outside the United States.

I always said no, for the same reason I voted against the Trump impeachment. I didn't see evidence that laws were being broken. I was being consistent.

My "video" matched my "audio."

That's an expression I've learned from Stoney Burke, who served as my first chief of staff. What you *say*—your audio—has to match up with what you actually *do*—your video. I based my work as a congressman on that principle, and I think it's an important component of leadership. We need to be ideologically consistent. We need to do what we say.

It's easier to do what you say when what you're doing is based on consistent principles. When I lost my first election in 2010, I entered one of the lowest points in my life and was fortunate to receive some well-chosen words of advice from an unexpected source.

In my first Republican primary in 2010, there were five candidates. I came out on top, but I failed to receive 50 percent of the vote. So the other top vote-getter, Quico Canseco, and I went to a runoff. The media and folks who followed elections thought I would easily beat Quico. His staff started looking for jobs because even *they* thought I was going to win. But I lost. The media went from saying that I was this thirty-two-year-old phenom to "How did he screw this up?"

I was devastated. Losing sucked. Even worse, I felt like I had let everyone down. I was so embarrassed that I didn't leave my house for days. I didn't want to see or talk to anybody. There was no plan B—I thought I was going to win. For a short, crazy time, I even considered a serious offer to go fight Somali pirates in the Gulf of Aden. But I actually didn't know what to do next.

So I asked seventy-five people I knew the same two questions. One: "If you were thirty-two again, what would you do?" And two: "If time and money weren't issues, what would you do?"

I got seventy-four crummy answers. "Why don't you go back into the CIA?" "Have you thought about going to law school?" "You could probably get into a management training track at a Texas energy company." It was probably more deflating than losing the election. I thought I was going to learn about the next hot idea, like Google in the 1990s or Instagram in 2010.

But the seventy-fifth answer came from one of my best friends' father—Roger Kramer, a schoolteacher and principal, whom I had known since I was thirteen. He took me to lunch at my favorite Mexican restaurant in San Antonio.

"Well, I don't know what kind of job you should apply for," he told me. "But you should do something that's meaningful and hard."

Meaningful and hard. It was the best answer.

Looking back, the most fulfilling experiences in my life have been meaningful and hard. Serving as student body president in college, serving in the CIA in dangerous places, running for Congress as a Black Republican in a Latino district, helping build a cybersecurity company following my loss before coming back and winning the congressional seat, and then serving the 23rd Congressional District of Texas. They were all super hard but unbelievably meaningful.

I took Mr. Kramer's advice to mean that I should be committed to doing something that was for more noble reasons than my own personal gain, and that this pursuit would at times require overcoming significant challenges. Pursuing higher or more noble principles and purposes is an activity in which one must constantly be engaged, and this activity has a name. It's called idealism. In following Mr. Kramer's words of wisdom, I've discovered that idealism makes it easier to be consistent in aligning your audio and video— matching your words and deeds—because you are engaged in doing things for the right reasons. This logic would be tested during both the Trump and the Obama administrations.

In 2015, I surprised many observers by voting in support of an amendment that would have effectively undone President Obama's 2012 executive action establishing the Deferred Action for Childhood Arrivals (DACA).

DACA shields qualified young people brought to the United States illegally as children from being deported and grants them work authorization. Through no fault of their own, they came to the U.S., and they are now building businesses, paying taxes, or going to school. In San Antonio, there are five thousand DACA recipients, and large swaths of my district support giving Dreamers a permanent legislative fix to their situation. I met with them several times while in office and was always impressed with their energy, drive, and eagerness to contribute to our society, culture, and economy.

My position against Obama's executive action caused an uproar among Dreamer supporters.

When Trump came to office, I also opposed *his* executive order to rescind DACA.

I was being consistent. No matter who is president, immigration law should not be made via executive action. It's the responsibility of Congress to make laws. The 826,000 individuals who have been accepted into the DACA program between 2012 through early 2020 do not need a continual stream of contradictory executive branch actions. They need legal status to stay in the U.S.—a *permanent legislative solution* so they can continue to be a part of the communities they have always called home.

In Congress, I voted for the American Dream and Promise Act of 2019, a bill to provide a pathway to legal status for eligible young people who were brought here as children, who passed background checks, and who completed high school and some college or military service. President Obama had been unable to shepherd an earlier version of this legislation through Congress while he was in office because of opposition by a few Senate Democrats.

I also co-wrote the USA Act of 2018 with Rep. Pete Aguilar (D-California). Along with relief for the Dreamers, it would have improved border security with high-tech solutions like infrared cameras, radar, and lidar (a similar concept to radar that uses light instead of sound). It would also have reduced delays in immigration courts and created a plan to address the root causes of illegal migration to our country. The top reasons being violence, lack of economic opportunity, and extreme poverty in the Northern Triangle—Guatemala, El Salvador, and Honduras. For most of the twenty-first century, illegal immigrants from those three countries alone accounted for 75 percent of Border Patrol apprehensions.

The USA Act received bipartisan support, and we came *so close* to achieving a real solution to the U.S.'s illegal immigration crisis. But Republican Speaker Paul Ryan prevented it from moving forward in the 115th Congress in 2018, and Speaker Nancy Pelosi, a Democrat, blocked it the following year in the 116th Congress.

Hopefully, President Biden learns from the mistakes of his two immediate predecessors and recognizes executive action may provide temporary relief, but alleviating the ambiguity that these individuals and their families live with requires a bipartisan and bicameral solution. The USA Act can still be a starting point.

In addition to immigration, the controversy over Trump and Russia provided plenty of opportunities to show that my audio and video match. I voted to release the infamous "Nunes memo," a 2018 memo by Rep. Devin Nunes (R-California) that questioned the justification for FBI surveillance of Carter Page, the former Trump adviser. I probably received more criticism for voting to release the Nunes memo than I did for the impeachment vote. Anti-Trump sentiment was at an all-time high, and people, including some in the intelligence community, couldn't believe a former CIA officer would vote to release classified information. I did because it was my job to know the difference between information and intelligence and to exercise my duties on HPSCI to inform the public while protecting intelligence operations. I did my job, even though it wasn't popular, because it was the right thing to do.

I supported releasing the Nunes memo not because I had anything against the FBI. I had the honor of working side by side with true American patriots in the FBI who have made tremendous sacrifices for our country. I voted to release the memo because I believed the FBI's warrant request to approve a wiretap on an American citizen was based on unverified information drawn from rumors and circular reporting.

Some might remember hearing about the source of that information from the media. It was the Steele Dossier, a salacious document written by former British intelligence officer Christopher Steele, paid for by the Hillary Clinton campaign and the Democratic National Committee, which contained allegations of cooperation between Trump's presidential campaign and the Russian government during the 2016 election.

Working in the CIA, I learned to watch out for the type of circular reporting that appeared in the Steele Dossier—when a piece of information appears to come from multiple sources, but in fact comes only from one source, even though it is offered through different channels.

To be clear, my vote to release the memo was not about discrediting Special

Counsel Robert Mueller's investigation into Russian interference in the 2016 election—I was fully supportive of the Mueller investigation. But after spending close to a decade collecting intelligence and protecting sources and methods, I knew that it was unverified information masquerading as intelligence.

Trust me, if I had found out from the Mueller report that allegations in the Steele Dossier were true, I would have grilled the intelligence community because then it would mean people had been lying to us. But in fact, Steele is rarely mentioned in Mueller's more than four-hundred-page report.

To me, the biggest contributor to Russian disinformation campaigns was House Intelligence Committee Chairman Adam Schiff (D-California). As a member of the House Intelligence Committee, it became clear to me that Schiff used his position on the committee to knowingly spread a false narrative that there had been collusion between the Russians and President Trump. At various times, Schiff claimed there was "more than circumstantial evidence" of collusion and evidence pointing to signs of cooperation between Russia and the Trump campaign.

Everyone—many House colleagues, the media, the public—was operating under the assumption that Schiff had access to intelligence that other people didn't possess and that he knew something we did not know.

But he didn't.

To be sure, Trump was duped by the Russians about their meddling in the 2016 election, particularly at his shameful July 2018 press conference with Russian President Vladimir Putin in Helsinki, when he contradicted our own intelligence agencies and accepted the former KGB officer's denials regarding that interference. With that performance, the president actively participated in a Russian disinformation campaign that legitimized Russian denials and weakened the credibility of the United States.

Though it was clear the Russians *had* interfered in the 2016 election, according to the Mueller report, there was no evidence that President Trump *colluded* with the Russians. Black's Dictionary defines collusion as a "deceitful agreement or compact between two or more persons, for the one party to bring an action against the other for some evil purpose, as to defraud a third party of his right." That's not what happened here.

But Schiff used his position to further undermine trust in our democracy. "The president's misconduct cannot be decided at the ballot box, for we cannot be assured that the vote will be fairly won," he said during the impeachment proceedings.

I don't know if Schiff was making those claims to create conflict and contrast, but by perpetuating this myth that the Russians actively cooperated with President Trump, he inflicted enormous damage on public trust in the election process. Schiff's audio—wanting to protect the integrity of the election process—failed to match his video—which was taking actions to erode trust in our elections. This became an excuse for President Trump to take a page out of the Democratic playbook to undermine the election results after he lost to Joe Biden. Another appalling effort to destabilize our democracy.

Ensuring the audio and video match, is critical to leadership in Washington. The fact that this principle is so rare to find among both parties may be the reason the American electorate didn't give a mandate to either party. Even though it's hard, the aspirational leadership needed for a successful American Reboot will require leaders whose audio and video match.

CHAPTER 7

DON'T PANDER, BUILD TRUST

Based on the identity of the caller and the fact that he was phoning at noon on a Saturday, I knew my lunch was going to be ruined. I was in the parking lot of Whiskey Cake, one of my favorite restaurants in San Antonio. Even the cell phone ring sounded nervous.

"Hey, Congressman, we really need some help."

It was Maverick County Judge David Saucedo. He was upset. He was tired. He was frustrated.

Two weeks after the July Fourth holiday in 2020, a desperate battle was being waged in Eagle Pass, Texas. Fort Duncan Regional Medical Center was Maverick County's largest hospital; it had been depleted of supplies and lacked sufficient personnel when it was overrun with COVID-19 patients.

As I recall the conversation, Judge Saucedo continued, "We need a mobile medical unit. We need nurses. We need oxygen machines. Honestly, Congressman, we need whatever you can get us. And we need it today."

While the COVID situation in Texas was bad in urban areas like El Paso and San Antonio, the limited medical facilities in rural areas—as we saw in other rural communities around the country—were stretched unbelievably thin during the crisis. By early July, during the first of many waves of the pandemic throughout 2020 and 2021, an average of 48 new cases were diagnosed per day per 100,000 residents in Maverick County. This was double the state average, making it one of the worst-hit counties in the country.

It only got worse.

I remember reading reports of the coronavirus in early January 2020 as it emerged in China. I had become more aware of the potential impact of novel viruses because of Texas's experience with the worldwide Ebola epidemic of 2014 and 2015, when cases broke out in Dallas. One man died, and two healthcare workers tested positive.

I was in Seattle two days after the Centers for Disease Control and Prevention (CDC) diagnosed the Emerald City as having the first case of COVID in the U.S. During my thirty-six-hour trip to discuss quantum computing and artificial intelligence, I had a sinking feeling that this virus was going to be trouble, although, like most people, I certainly didn't anticipate the catastrophe that ultimately developed.

The inability to flatten the COVID curve, despite the efforts undertaken to do so, shook Americans' faith in their leaders. Through the height of the pandemic, trust in the government to deal with COVID plummeted. And COVID was just the latest sign of America's crisis of confidence. Trust in government and its leaders has been cratering for decades (from close to 80 percent in the mid-1960s to almost 20 percent now).

Trust—whether it is in a loved one or a government—is neither a gift nor an inheritance. It is *earned*. The solution to this trust deficit is not Republican leaders pandering only to Republican voters or Democratic leaders pandering only to Democratic voters. Leaders must engender the trust of *all* the people they represent by showing competent action through problem-solving rather than trying to just influence their partisans.

In a country where the political parties are constantly at each other's throats, is this approach unrealistic? No. Because it's the only pragmatic option that will help the greatest number of people possible. I've seen it work in a politically divided district and in Washington, DC, the NBA of partisan fighting.

In my experience, building trust involves two things: First, engaging *everybody*, no matter whether they voted for you, against you, or didn't vote at all. And second, building credibility by solving real problems.

In the last few years, we've seen how *not* to build trust. Announce you have irrefutable evidence of the leader of the free world colluding with Russia but never produce any evidence. Deny a devastating disease and ignore science. Be outraged that poor Ukraine was being extorted for political gain but fail to demonstrate this or even talk about it again after the TV cameras are turned off. Reject and try to overturn the indisputable results of a presidential election and act like sore losers.

These actions have eaten away at faith in our constitutional republic because those entrusted to safeguard it are afraid of the extremist wings of their parties.

I first decided to go into public service because I thought it would be exciting to serve my government in exotic places doing dangerous things. I continued my service in a different way because I believed that while my friends and I were putting ourselves in harm's way to protect our country, some in Washington were being negligent in their duties.

The preamble of our Constitution outlines what citizens want and should get from their government:

- *Establish justice.* Make sure the laws are fairly applied to everyone equally.
- *Insure domestic tranquility and provide for the common defense.* Have a central government strong enough to maintain peace, keep citizens from harm, protect property, and defend our homeland from external attack.
- *Promote general welfare.* Better the lives of its citizens.
- *Secure the blessings of liberty to ourselves and our posterity.* Protect the benefits of being a free country for future generations.

As a representative democracy, we elect legislators to enact laws on our behalf. It's about finding a compromise that is amenable to the greatest number of people possible.

Engendering trust doesn't mean agreeing. Those are two different things. The desired end-state is to be able to *trust* each other without *agreeing* with each other 100 percent of the time. Now, you got to agree sometimes. I've found it's somewhere between 65 and 70 percent. You don't agree with your spouse or best friend 100 percent of the time, so why should that be the standard for your elected official?

This trust deficit isn't just plaguing political leaders. The degradation of trust in our traditional media—newspapers, TV networks, magazines, and the like—has pushed people in our country and around the world to seek "facts" from alternative sources like social media. This transition to sources that blur the lines between facts and opinions has fueled the colossal misinformation crisis we are witnessing. If you watch Fox, you have one set of beliefs. You have another set of beliefs if you tune into MSNBC and read the *New York Times*. If you scroll through YouTube, you can have whatever convictions you want confirmed, depending on which rabbit hole you dive into. Facebook and Twitter operate the same way.

People aren't believing facts because of cognitive bias, defined by the think tank the Rand Corporation as a situation where people "look for opinions and analysis that confirm their own pre-existing beliefs, more heavily weigh personal experience over facts, and rely on mental shortcuts and the opinions of others in the same social networks." We saw the disastrous results of cognitive bias during COVID: People refused to wear face masks, didn't social distance, and declined vaccines because of misinformation they had found on social media.

The chaotic, ignore-the-science COVID response of some within the Trump administration, along with some of our nation's governors, negatively affected the president's reelection chances and prevented Republicans from taking back the House. Some postelection analysis showed 55 percent of voters disapproved of President Trump's handling of the COVID crisis, while an overwhelming 83 percent said the federal government's handling of the pandemic was an important factor in their vote.

Imagine if Republicans hadn't ignored or downplayed COVID and President Trump demonstrated decisive collaborative leadership in dealing with the pandemic. Imagine if the presidential campaign had been waged on the strong economy that existed before an out-of-control pandemic crashed the country. Imagine if the president, instead of pandering to the extremes within the Republican electorate, built trust within those communities that were the largest-growing voting blocs. Would Donald Trump still be president? Would Republicans have taken back the House? Possibly. Or even probably.

Texas 23 was one of the first areas in the U.S. thrust into the pandemic maelstrom when ninety-one American citizens living in Wuhan, China, were evacuated to San Antonio's Lackland Air Force Base for quarantine during early February 2020. They were followed by passengers from the virus-stricken cruise ship, the *Diamond Princess*.

Local residents were panicked over the presence of the evacuees in their community, so I decided to tour the Lackland quarantine facilities. My staff disagreed with my decision to go. They were worried that people would think I would become contagious. Some on my staff were worried that I might catch COVID and die. I believed it was important to show up, see what was going on, help fix any problems, and confirm for my constituents that they were getting correct information. I also wanted to make contact with the knowledgeable staff from the Centers for Disease Control and the Department of Defense who were directly dealing with this issue.

On my visit, I had a sense that the evacuees were being well cared for. The staff demonstrated the kind of compassion for the families' well-being that I would have expected from a pastor at a church, not an overworked government employee. The facility looked like a normal apartment complex—with the exception of buildings surrounded by an eight-foot security fence weighed down by sandbags, and scientists and medical professionals in hazmat suits. To be honest, it looked like a scene from the movie *Outbreak*, where a deadly Ebola-like virus hits a small town in the U.S.

More than anything, that visit, along with the conversations with the professionals dealing with the brewing crisis, impressed upon me the magnitude of COVID's looming threat. When I got back from the base tour, I instructed our staff to call local officials around the 23rd, to start banging on doors and sounding the alarm. Do you have emergency pandemic plans? Have these plans been stress tested? What are your contingencies if your hospitals run out of beds? What will you do if your hospitals are unable to transfer patients to medical centers in El Paso and San Antonio? Some local officials were on the ball. Others shrugged it off. But we gave everyone the same message: "Tell us what you need, and we'll try to get it."

As case counts increased throughout the state, our office went into 24/7 mode. We also worked on building relationships with state and federal officials who could help us. I established contact with Blair Walsh, section chief of the Texas Division of Emergency Management (TDEM), who was incredibly cooperative, unbelievably effective, cool as ice, and as nice as can be. My chief of staff, John Byers, and my district director, Stacy, as well as other staff, burrowed through the state and federal bureaucracies, looking for whoever could assist as we tried to prepare the district for the storm.

I was able to sympathize with the hundreds of thousands of Americans whose families were devastated by COVID because I, too, lost a loved one to the virus. My mom's brother, my uncle Dennis, succumbed in June 2020. When I was a kid, Uncle Dennis, Aunt Jean, and their six kids drove from their home in Indiana to Texas in a Winnebago, which I thought was the coolest thing ever. It became my dream at a young age to travel the country in a Winnebago like Uncle Dennis (that dream was partially realized when we rented an RV for one of our DC2DQ trips). Uncle Dennis was a marathon runner, a kind of quirky guy who was always doing magic tricks, like taking a quarter out of your ear.

Afflicted with Parkinson's disease, he was a resident in a Florida nursing home that the virus viciously spread through. We weren't able to travel to the funeral, and none of his kids could be at his bedside when he died. He and my mom used to talk weekly, and for a while, my family wrestled with whether to even tell her about his death because of her dementia. In the end, we did, and she took it as best she could, though I'm not sure she remembers that her brother is no longer with us.

When the pandemic struck nationally, some communities in the Texas 23rd were among the hardest hit. Wave after wave of major outbreaks occurred in El Paso and San Antonio, and vast stretches of the rural areas of the district were also in crisis. Penitentiary inmates were tasked with moving the bodies of coronavirus victims to relieve medical examiners' personnel, emergency rooms and ICUs were overflowing with patients, children were left orphaned when parents succumbed to COVID, and local companies laid off thousands of workers. My favorite local coffee shop went under, as did many other small businesses. The pandemic decimated so many small businesses that are the backbone of the communities in El Paso and San Antonio.

As the crisis mounted in the early months of March and April 2020, I remember Stacy's daily briefings. First the virus was in five counties. Then ten. Then fourteen, and, like a wildfire, it had spread to twenty-eight out of twenty-nine counties. In the early days, when personal protective equipment for medical staff was in desperately short supply, my staff and I acted fast to connect private companies with the Federal Emergency Management Agency (FEMA) and TDEM, to make sure masks and other supplies got into our communities.

When it came to the crisis at Fort Duncan Regional Medical Center, my staff and I were already aware that the hospital was struggling. Eagle Pass Mayor Luis Sifuentes and Judge Saucedo had been in communication with me for weeks. I told them the same thing every time, "Just tell us what you need."

In Texas, county judges are the elected executive for the county and operate much like mayors, and Judge Saucedo was pretty powerful. He was one of the longest-serving elected officials in Maverick County. When we first met in 2009, he was the kingmaker for Ciro Rodriguez, the former Texas 23 congressman. The first three times I was on the ballot—2010, 2014, and

2016—Judge Saucedo worked hard for all my opponents, to ensure I was defeated. I didn't take it personally; he knew my opponents well, and as one of the senior Democrats in the county, he was going to support Team Democrat.

That never changed my approach to him. When Maverick County needed help to rebuild after a major flood, we helped. When low staffing levels at the border checkpoints were causing unnecessarily long wait times, we worked to right this wrong. When the county library needed help with a grant, we did it. So the judge knew that when he was getting crushed by COVID-19, I would be there for him and the community we represented. Most people wouldn't help a political adversary, but being a true representative means transcending politics.

After hanging up with Judge Saucedo in the parking lot of Whiskey Cake, my staff and I did what we always did—tried to solve a problem. We mined our contacts at TDEM, the Texas Department of State Health Services (DSHS), FEMA, and Health and Human Services (HHS), making sure that Fort Duncan was at the top of their lists for resources.

A Navy Rapid Rural Response Team arrived at the hospital, as well as resources from the state—medics, nurses, and paramedics. In all, thirty-two new staff were deployed to the hospital, easing the immediate crisis.

Did that solve all Maverick County's COVID problems? No. By late October 2020, average new daily cases in Maverick County per 100,000 people were four times higher than the average in the entire state. By March 2021, more than three hundred people had died. And the carnage continued.

Across South Texas, thousands died and tens of thousands were infected. We couldn't fix all the problems our communities were dealing with, but by demonstrating we would engage with everyone to actually solve real problems, we repaired the trust local officials and the community had in their federal partners.

While providing help goes a long way in engendering trust, solving problems is easier when you have an expertise. Expertise creates an opportunity to have instant credibility. When people ask me what they need to do to run for office, I always advise getting experience in something that you will have to work on in the office for which you want to run.

In a fifty-fifty district like mine, establishing credibility is critical, and I was able to do it because I had spent my entire adult life protecting our homeland. My very first bill was aimed at an important group of constituents—U.S. Border Patrol agents. Along the Texas-Mexico border, the Border Patrol is a major employer. Agents work in harsh conditions and oftentimes put their lives at risk. But in 2015, their overtime pay was going to be reduced because of bureaucratic ridiculousness. I passed a bill that fixed the problem.

By the end of my first term, I had seven bills and two amendments signed into law by President Obama—the highest number of bills to become law out of all 435 members of Congress and 100 senators during that term. I focused on issues that I had an expertise in and always had a bipartisan partner before I even began writing the legislation.

Helping Border Patrol was not the only way I leveraged my expertise in that first term.

When I was running for office in 2014, the Islamic terrorist group ISIS was the biggest issue worrying my constituents and Americans around the country. Fellow Texan Mike McCaul (R-Texas), chairman of the Homeland Security Committee, tasked Rep. John Katko (R-New York) to form a bipartisan Foreign Fighters Task Force to counter ISIS's tactics of explicitly encouraging "foreign fighters" who could not make it to Iraq and Syria, to join their struggle in other locations. I joined my buddy Katko, who ultimately introduced the Tracking Foreign Fighters in Terrorist Safe Havens Act, which provides law enforcement with the necessary resources to stop foreign fighters from traveling overseas to fight with ISIS and then return to the U.S. The bill was signed into law by President Obama as part of an appropriations bill.

Solving real problems is hard. So is engaging people who don't agree with you. The difficulty of doing this is why many leaders prefer to pander to their extremes. It's easier. Dealing with an increasingly complicated future that includes a New Cold War with a peer like the government of China, growing inequities across communities, and a technological explosion that is making science fiction science reality, will require making tough decisions as a country. As painful as this will be, we absolutely can't avoid it. Addressing these challenges will require the consent of the governed, which can be earned if the trust deficit is eliminated by leaders having the courage to inspire rather than fearmonger.

CHAPTER 8

WAY MORE UNITES US
THAN DIVIDES US

I thought my staff was trying to use reverse psychology on me when they agreed that livestreaming a sixteen-hundred-mile journey with a Democratic colleague was a good idea.

It was Monday, March 13, 2017, and it was going to be a busy day. I was hosting Rep. Beto O'Rourke (D-Texas) in San Antonio. He had accepted my invitation to meet with several veterans' groups who wanted to visit with someone serving on the Veterans' Affairs Committee. I asked Beto because he was the only Texan on the committee and we had worked together on a number of issues affecting veterans in El Paso, a city that we both represented in Congress. After our three meetings, I was supposed to rush to the airport to catch a flight to DC. I had a dozen or so meetings the following day, and then on Wednesday, Congress was back in session with our first vote series at six thirty P.M.

Upon returning to our cars after our first meeting, I received a notification that Southwest Airlines had canceled my flight. I yelled at Beto before he got in his car, "Bro, that blizzard that's allegedly threatening DC must be real. My flight back to DC just got canceled, and Southwest never cancels flights. They fly in anything."

"That probably means mine tomorrow will be canceled, too." Beto paused in thought. "We can't miss votes. Why don't we drive back to DC together and livestream the whole thing? It could be an epic rolling town hall."

That's how a thirty-six-hour trip—thirty-one hours in the car, five hours of sleep, and twenty-nine hours livestreamed—was born. Over both days, our socials had tens of millions of views, and we were on news outlets all over the world. Beto later revealed that he thought I'd turn him down. Instead, we ended up in a Chevy Impala from Dollar Rent A Car, with a hand-drawn map as our guide.

We kicked off at seven A.M. on March 14 from the iconic San Antonio Mexican restaurant Mi Tierra. Following breakfast, the waitstaff presented us with a donkey pinata for good luck, ultimately christened Willie-berto. We took turns driving and livestreaming, talking with our viewers, our colleagues who called in, and each other about an incredible array of topics, from healthcare, NATO, Trump's wall, sex trafficking, and veterans' mental health issues, to Russian interference in elections, IT procurement, and so much more. We played great tunes—I stuck to mostly '90s and 2000s R&B with a little EDM sprinkled in, and he showed me a range of alternative rock influenced by his days in a punk rock band. We engaged in spirited debate over cake versus pie, and had a "Guess Will's Weight" contest with viewers.

We branded our journey a "Bipartisan Road Trip Town Hall" and hashtagged it #bipartisanroadtrip.

Two lessons came out of the journey. The first was that way more unites us than divides us. I had known this to be true in Texas 23, but the road trip showed me this was true for the rest of the country as well. The recent years of acrimony, hostility, and meanness would have you think we are irreparably divided, but the rapturous reception we received clearly demonstrated that people want to be inspired by their leaders rather than made to be afraid.

The second lesson is that America wants politicians to agree without being disagreeable. They don't expect politicians from across the aisle to always agree. But the country recognizes we have serious problems that need solving, and they want us to have a civil debate on what's best for the majority of our country while protecting the minority's rights. Then they want us to take action, not just blame someone else for inaction.

It may seem like the country has moved in exactly the opposite direction since that two-day road trip. So many Americans automatically believe the other side is going to mess this country up. Like they're twirling their mustaches, hatching devious plans to ruin this experiment we call America. Peter Wehner, a Senior Fellow at the Ethics and Public Policy Center, has written: "Fear strengthens tribalistic instincts, and tribalistic instincts amplify fear. Nothing bonds a group more tightly than a common enemy that is perceived as a mortal threat. In the presence of such an enemy, members of tribal groups look outward rather than inward, at others and never at themselves or their own kind."

But when you are in a car together for thirty-one hours talking about the future of our country, you start seeing the other side's nuances. You realize that we view most of the problems the same way, we just have different ways we want to fix them. The other side isn't trying to ruin the country. They have a different way to solve a problem. That's all.

Beto and I didn't agree on everything we talked about. In fact, we didn't agree on most things. For example, we have vastly different views on the Affordable Care Act—Obamacare. He thought it was great. I saw significant flaws. My friend from El Paso supported significant campaign finance reform. While I believe much of the money in politics is wasted and just makes TV stations and the professional political class rich, my ability to raise money to get my message out allowed me to overcome my modest means and have the resources to win. And Beto had this idea at the time for a mandatory year of service for young people. While I believe broadening one's horizons is important, I wasn't supportive of having the government mandate it.

But what we had was a *real competition of ideas*. It wasn't a competition for attention by yelling at each other or saying outlandish things. It wasn't a competition of making the pithiest remark, because these serious issues require more deliberation than can fit in 280 characters. I believe that's why so many people were glued to their screens and sharing what we were doing with their friends and family.

Even the #bipartisanroadtrip didn't start out with a great deal of bipartisanship. At the start, we were on Beto's socials, and I was reading the comments. We were quickly descending into the kind of social media toxic waste dump that passes for discourse in this country. People were really nasty to me. If those kinds of comments had continued, we would have had to stop, because I wouldn't have put up with that kind of negativity for two days.

However, about ninety minutes in, people changed, and the positivity became infectious. Maybe people at first had jumped to the conclusion that our trip was going to be the usual cable TV mosh pit of insults and slurs. But I kept emphasizing that the trip was to "show what unites us, not just about those things that divide us."

Along our trip, viewers suggested other Republicans and Democrats to do their own distance trips together. The most unlikely idea was super-conservative Louie Gohmert (R-Texas) and super-liberal Sheila Jackson Lee (D-Texas).

No, I don't think solving the Great Divide can be achieved by forcing members of the opposing parties to pair up and drive around the country talking policy. But if I learned anything from my time in Congress, it is that the only way we can solve this country's big problem is by working *together*.

Politicians and citizens alike can't be afraid that our ideas or opinions will not survive being tested. If you are afraid of being wrong, then maybe you don't have a good argument. Instead, we should aspire for a free and open marketplace of ideas, a concept articulated by the British philosopher John Stuart Mill, where the truth or the acceptance of an idea can only be tested against the competition of other ideas rather than some authority like the government.

The challenges we face really do require a debate to ensure the best outcome for all Americans. Representing one of the true swing districts in the country, I always tried to engage groups of people who didn't necessarily agree with all my votes or opinions. This kind of interaction taught me that disagreement is the cornerstone of democracy. If done with honesty and a focus on doing the right thing, then we are a better country for it.

Sadly, we've seen how our culture stokes our biases while affirming our worst assumptions about those who disagree with us, making political compromise and progress impossible. The only way to bridge this divide is to rebuild trust in government by having leaders whose audio and video match.

Over the last twenty years, a misconception has grown in Washington that the only way to get anything done is through "unified government"—when one party controls the White House, the Senate, and the House. But you can't solve problems that way because that unified government usually only lasts for one political cycle—two years. Then, when power shifts and that unified government evaporates, the next folks coming in try to dismantle everything achieved by the previous party. Donald Trump did it, Joe Biden is doing it, and the Republican majority that is likely to take back the House of Representatives in 2022 is likely to do it. It's a shitty and unproductive way to govern, and it prevents us from tackling serious problems that are going to define our generation.

The most impactful pieces of legislation in our recent history have been bipartisan and reached though compromise. The 1964 Civil Rights Act. The Clean Air Act of 1970. The food stamp program in the 1970s. Social Security reform in the 1980s. Americans with Disabilities Act in the 1990s. The 2015 Every Student Succeeds Act, and 2018 criminal justice reform—the First Step Act—to name just a few.

Our road trip livestream viewers and the people we met along the way weren't shy about offering their opinions about our country's trials. Some of these insights were ridiculous, but some were insightful. One of those more insightful moments came only fifty miles into the trip when we stopped at Tantra coffeehouse in San Marcos, Texas, which we found with the help of street-by-street directions from a viewer watching us on Periscope. (We switched to Facebook Live after this stop.)

Beto and I were already jousting over that perennial issue in long-distance driving—go fast and get there (Beto) or take it slow and enjoy the journey (me). Over the protests of his wife and three kids, Beto once tried to drive the family eleven hours straight through from El Paso to San Diego. If he could refuel on the fly instead of stopping at gas stations, he told our viewers, he would.

I wanted to take our time with frequent stops and arrive at the Capitol with a flourish, bursting onto the floor just in the nick of time to cast our votes.

In the end, we compromised. I got a few stops, including South by Southwest—a set of festivals and conferences underway at the time in Austin—and a late-night pilgrimage to the gates of Elvis Presley's Graceland, where I happened to meet some constituents from Texas 23. But, to satisfy Beto, we arrived at the Capitol at a safe (and boring) two hours before the votes would take place.

At Tantra, we met owner-operator Adam Lilley, a skinny, bearded guy with a passion for coffee and a mind that could bend itself around any issue. As he made my vanilla latte and Beto's Americano, he riffed on healthcare policy. At the time, debate over Republicans' proposals to replace Obamacare was obsessing Washington.

"So let me tie this all together," Adam said as he twisted off the steam wand on the espresso machine. "We are everything we put in our bodies. We are everything we consume. It's one of the biggest things that's been left out of healthcare because we are all rightfully waiting for a solution, watching for some type of direction to take us to a new place."

He tapped the milk pitcher on the counter. "So if people are more conscious about what they consume, what they put into their bodies, we'd be a lot less concerned about what the federal government's doing or not doing to ensure our healthcare."

You don't see that kind of perspective on cable news.

Following the trip, Beto and I continued to work together. Two days after we arrived in Washington, we signed on to co-sponsor each other's legislation. I co-sponsored Beto's immigration bill, the American Families United Act, and Beto added his name to my American Law Enforcement Heroes Act, which would make it easier for local police departments to hire veterans. We even won an award, the 2018 Allegheny College Prize for Civility in Public Life.

The trip did have some political ramifications the following year when I ran for reelection and Beto challenged Republican Ted Cruz for his Senate seat. Citing his friendship with me, Beto declined to endorse my opponent, Gina Ortiz Jones, and caught grief from many Democrats who said "party loyalty" had to come before friendship. And I caught it from Republicans for not denouncing Beto.

The media obsession over our stances was ridiculous. I ignored it. In the end, Beto won my district by five percentage points and almost bested Cruz statewide, and I beat Jones. Afterward, Jones blamed Beto for her loss, but what she didn't realize was that Beto's presence on the ticket actually helped her. The results of the 2020 election in District 23 confirmed that I would have crushed her by a larger margin if Beto hadn't been on the top of the ticket that year.

Looking back on that crazy road trip in 2017, what will stay with me—even more than memories of mouthwatering donuts, lack of sleep, and the grinding 1,600 miles of highway as we raced from San Antonio to Washington, DC, in time for votes in the House—are the comments people were inspired to share:

"Thanks for sharing civility in politics."

"There is hope for Congress yet."

"You guys are restoring my faith in politicians."

"This is a sign of Peace."

While the trip didn't change Washington, it did change *me*. It made me inflexible on one of my opinions—that despite what we see daily in Washington and on the news nightly, we have much more in common with each other than we don't. We are faced with so many generation-defining challenges. We are engaged in a geopolitical struggle with China where the winner will control the global economy. Humankind is provoking planet Earth, which will result in a catastrophic response. We've failed to develop a solution to immigration that protects our borders and strengthens our economy. Millions of people struggle to cover an unexpected expense of four hundred dollars; and many Americans wrestle with financial uncertainty because of the rising costs of healthcare, childcare, and senior care. All these problems are *fixable*, and can be addressed with pragmatism—sensible, realistic ways based on practical rather than theoretical considerations. But the competition of ideas necessary to come up with the solutions to these problems requires leaders who aren't afraid to engage in idealism and have the courage to inspire rather than fearmonger.

When we put our hands on our hearts and pledge allegiance to the flag, it's to the *United* States of America, because many generations before us recognized that the only way we achieve the perpetual goal of becoming a more perfect union is when we recognize that way more unites us as a country than divides us.

PART III

PROSPERITY SHOULD BE A PRODUCT OF EMPOWERING PEOPLE, NOT THE GOVERNMENT

CHAPTER 9

KEEP THE BABY, GET RID OF THE BATHWATER

I've been in a number of fights over the years. Fighting the federal government over a wheelchair is one fight I will always remember. There were also fights for resources for people like my mom, whose memory was eroding so fast she couldn't remember how to crochet. There were scuffles that almost became fights, like when my sister tried to wring my neck.

There were fights that I lost, like trying to secure a permanent fix for young men and women who had only known the United States of America as their home, from being deported. And there were fights where the other side denied there was even a fight, like the fight against climate science deniers. Most of these fights stemmed from a complicated domestic policy problem.

I believe the way to solve problems is to empower people, not the government. And the way to help people up the economic ladder is through free markets, not socialism. There are so many ways that quality of life for Americans has improved over the last fifty years. Just one example: According to the U.S. Census Bureau, in the fifty-year period from 1969 to 2019, when adjusted for cost of living, real median family income has increased 48 percent.

Whether you want limited government or bigger government, government should be working on your behalf. Government should give people the opportunity to make their own decisions about where they go to school, where they want to live, which doctors they want to visit, what business they want to start, and, ultimately, who they want to be.

Having a handful of elites in a faraway capital deciding your future just doesn't work, because our global economy is complicated. Individual demand for goods and services changes billions of times around the world every minute, while the supply to meet these demands based on resource availability is constantly in flux.

No matter how good their intentions, a handful of government bureaucrats or socialist cooperatives—a socialist idea for reimagining a com-pany where everyone who works at the company makes decisions for that company—are incapable of managing such a dynamic system.

Our economy is based on supply and demand. It is democratic and capitalist. It is market-oriented and entrepreneurial. It offers incentives for working families in labor as well as management. It rewards work, investment, saving, and productivity. Our system is designed for you, not the government, to have the power to make the decisions on how you achieve your goals.

However, not everyone has benefited. A Pew Research Center study conducted in 2020 showed that while there was more movement up the income ladder than down the income ladder, the wealth gap between America's richest and poorer families more than doubled from 1989 to 2016.

Barriers and structural obstacles like systemic racism and gender discrimination haven't been eradicated, and these impediments are contributing factors to income inequality that prevent some people from advancing his or her economic position. These realities are fueling a trend where a growing chorus of people are trying to delegitimize our economic, political, and social systems by claiming those who haven't benefited from these systems are the norm rather than an unfortunate exception that should be given special attention and focus.

Because of this trend, some folks are looking for ways to replace our political, economic, and social systems with something new. The Democratic Party is increasingly being seduced by the disastrous concept of socialism, which over the past one hundred years has been attempted more than two dozen times around the world and failed miserably. Even the Democratic

Socialists of America, the largest socialist organization in the U.S., admit that no country has fully instituted Democratic Socialism.

In Democratic Socialism, factors of production—inputs needed to produce a good or service like land, labor, entrepreneurship, and capital—are owned and controlled by the workers and consumers affected by the institution. This social ownership could take many forms, such as worker-owned cooperatives or publicly owned enterprises managed by workers and consumer representatives, which are in essence different versions of unions.

Democratic Socialists believe that vital goods and services, including energy, housing, and transit, but not limited to these industries, would be managed through centralized planning (a group of government bureaucrats), while a free-market system based on social ownership would distribute consumer products. German philosopher Karl Marx, who developed his own eponymous social and political philosophy, considered socialism a transition phase between capitalism and communism.

Over the centuries, various forms of socialism have inspired people because of its utopian vision of a better society. However, it has always flopped because it's impractical. Socialism ignores human nature. It ignores the fact that humans are driven by self-interest.

I don't care who you are or where you live, you have the same goals as everybody else—to put food on your table, a roof over your head, and ensure that the people you love are happy and healthy. I saw this reality throughout the diverse communities I represented in Congress, and I saw this to be true in all the exotic locales where I lived and worked around the world.

Democratic capitalism has contributed to making the U.S. the most powerful country to ever exist. To help those who haven't benefited, we shouldn't upend our economic, social, and political system to the detriment of those who have benefited or are benefiting. This would be the ultimate example of throwing the baby out with the bathwater. To help those who haven't benefited, our domestic policy should pay special attention to these Americans and ensure they are empowered to take advantage of the same opportunities as those who have moved up the economic ladder. Let's keep the baby and just get rid of the bathwater.

This shouldn't be hard. I learned the principle that could help us solve this conundrum when I was a kid.

In the summers, my mom kicked my brother, sister, and me out of the house when the game show *The Price Is Right* ended at ten A.M., and we weren't allowed back inside until it started getting dark. Those summer days usually started with me walking over to the house of one of my neighborhood partners-in-crime, Michael Rodriguez, because he was always game for whatever I wanted to do, even when his mom told him he couldn't. One summer, Michael asked me to go to some camp his church was putting on. I had no interest in interrupting my usual summer shenanigans to go to church camp, and even as a kid I didn't like doing things I didn't want to do.

My mother found out about the invitation and chastised me for not doing something Michael wanted to do because he always joined me, even if it got him in trouble. Since I was a momma's boy, a good shaming by my dear mother always changed my behavior, so I went to church camp.

I was immediately angry with Michael because this camp wasn't all fun and games. We had to attend lectures. What the hell kind of camp was this? Summer is for playing, not sitting in a classroom. But in one of these classes I didn't want to be in, we were taught a story from Matthew 25 verse 40.

It was Judgment Day, and the Son of God was on his heavenly throne. All the nations are gathered before him, and Jesus is rendering his verdict on whether folks are getting into heaven or not. There are only two outcomes—salvation or damnation. Jesus sorts the crowd and puts some folks on his right and the rest on his left. He turns to the folks on his right and says—and I'm paraphrasing here—come on in y'all, you made it.

Jesus tells the folks on his right the reason for his decision. "For I was hungry and you gave me something to eat, I was thirsty and you gave me something to drink, I was a stranger and you invited me in, I needed clothes and you clothed me, I was sick and you looked after me, I was in prison and you came to visit me."

The folks on his right were happy, but they asked the Lord, when did we do all this for you? Jesus's reply was simple. "Whatever you did for one of the least of these brothers and sisters of mine, you did for me."

The "least of our brothers and sisters" deserve the freedom to chase opportunities so they can grow and achieve progress. Everyone is anxious about their lives and their futures. Before the economic chaos of the pandemic, nearly 40 percent of Americans said they would struggle with an unexpected four-hundred-dollar expense.

Throughout my congressional career, I saw how this financial uncertainty was exacerbated, especially for the "least of our brothers and sisters," by the rising costs of healthcare, childcare, senior care, and education, as well as anxiety over preparing for the economy of the future, the inability to get immigration right, and the increasing grim effects of climate change.

During my terms in Congress, I was on the frontlines for many of the battles to respond to Americans' concerns—school reform with the Every Student Succeeds Act, because children were still being left behind; my controversial vote against the repeal and replacement of Obamacare; efforts by colleagues and me toward an immigration solution that meets the needs of our economy; the first revision of the tax code in three decades that included provisions to help families deal with the rising costs of childcare; the controversy over President Trump's withdrawal from the Paris Climate Accords; and the early debates over the Green New Deal.

Prosperity is a product of empowering *people*, not the government. And the best first step to empower a person? Ensure he or she can take care of his or her health.

CHAPTER 10

INCREASE ACCESS TO HEALTHCARE WHILE DECREASING ITS COST

"You sound beautiful," President Donald Trump said to me in our first one-on-one interaction.

It was an impromptu phone call as I was walking back from the Capitol to my office on a windy day in the spring of 2017. The call began cordially but deteriorated quickly.

The House was on the eve of an enormous vote on healthcare reform. Republicans' plan to repeal and replace major parts of the Affordable Care Act (ACA)—otherwise known as Obamacare—was being considered by the House. But the Republicans' American Health Care Act of 2017 (AHCA) cut $800 billion out of Medicaid to pay for the plan.

The Medicaid cuts were a major problem for me. Medicaid is the joint federal-state program providing health insurance coverage to millions of Americans, including low-income people and those with disabilities. In my largely rural district, many people worked low-wage jobs and qualified and benefited from the program. About one in every fifteen people in Texas 23 is covered by Medicaid, one of the highest rates in Texas. The AHCA plan also failed to include adequate protections for those with pre-existing conditions—a big concern in a district with a high percentage of chronic health conditions like diabetes and heart disease.

I'd already met with Vice President Pence and a half-dozen of his staff in his Capitol office about my vote. I explained my concerns with the bill, based on the Medicaid needs in my district, and Pence got it immediately. He'd been in the U.S. House of Representatives for twelve years before being elected Indiana governor and understood the needs of members who represented largely rural districts.

"Will, that makes sense," he said. "You're making the right decision for your district."

President Trump's reaction was markedly different. After complimenting me on my "beautiful" voice as I searched for a quieter place that provided cover from the wind gusts, the alleged "ultimate salesman" launched into his pitch.

"Look," President Trump said, "we've been talking about healthcare for a long time. We're poised for a big win here. Big win. We'd really love your support."

"Mr. President, I'd like to be there," I told him. But I explained my problems with the bill and how it would impact my district.

The president, who either hadn't been briefed on my concerns or didn't care, exploded.

"That's what's *wrong* with you Republicans," he said, his voice rising. "You've been talking about this for four years, and we have a chance to do it and you're not going to do it."

Plus, he added, "I *won* your district."

"Mr. President," I interjected, "you actually lost my district by three points."

That didn't slow him down. "Well, I did better than anybody *thought* I was gonna do in your district."

We ended the call with a strange detour into his relationship with Chinese President Xi Jinping.

"He loves me," Trump said, "and I love him."

I voted against the bill—one of only twenty Republicans who did so. It narrowly passed the House (217–213) but died in the Senate.

My vote against the American Health Care Act of 2017 was not an endorsement of Obamacare, because President Obama's signature initiative failed to fix the root problems with our healthcare system. It was promised as a system to make healthcare more accessible and more affordable. While its Medicaid expansion helped some adults who fell into the coverage gap within their state because they had incomes above their state's eligibility for Medicaid but below poverty, Obamacare led to expensive and confusing insurance coverage for American families while adding regulations at the expense of small businesses.

I saw this firsthand in my district, where constituents told me about the doubling of premiums (the amount an individual or business pays to have an insurance policy). A family of four paid an average of $1,200 a month for an unsubsidized benchmark Silver plan through the ACA in 2020. At the same time, their annual deductible (what you pay at the doctor's office before insurance kicks in) could be eight thousand dollars or even higher. If a family is forced to spend their entire savings just to pay for their premiums and deductibles, then that family has neither good insurance nor affordable healthcare.

Compared to other affluent countries, the U.S. spends about twice as much on healthcare but has the lowest life expectancy, even though Americans use roughly the same amount of health services as people in other high-income nations. Cost differences for medical care between the U.S. and other countries are baffling. Why does an MRI cost $1,080 in the U.S. and $280 in France?

Despite all these problems, many Americans (mostly people who get insurance through their employer) are happy with their healthcare. What gets lost in the uproar about efforts to bring health insurance to more people is that *health insurance is not healthcare*. More than a decade after the ACA was signed into law, there are still millions of people who cannot access *or afford* quality healthcare. They may have received expensive *insurance*, but they do not have the financial resources to pay for treatment.

Our healthcare system is flawed, expensive, and confusing. Healthcare is the only industry where the person needing the good or service (the patient), the person deciding on which good or service is needed (the doctor), the person deciding how much the good or service costs (the healthcare system), and the person deciding from where the good or service can be purchased and ultimately paying for the good or service (the insurance company) are all different entities. The entire transaction—from seeing the doctor and getting treatment to paying the bill—takes weeks, if not months, to fully complete.

How do we bring down the cost of healthcare? By using the same principle that brought down the cost of big-screen high-definition televisions—competition. And to have real competition, we need price transparency. People need to know how much a procedure is going to cost before they make their purchasing decision.

Try calling around to surgeons to find out the cost of a knee replacement surgery so you can pick the doctor who charges the least. It can't be done. An essential fix to our dysfunctional system should be price transparency by medical providers and insurers to allow people to shop for healthcare, the way they shop for high-def TVs.

The Trump administration tried to address price transparency by issuing an executive order, referred to as the Transparency Rule. Its goal was to enable insurance holders to estimate how much they were going to have to pay *before* receiving healthcare, by requiring insurers to disclose cost-sharing estimates upon request.

I agreed with the intention of the executive order, but executive orders can be rescinded under a new administration. It needs to be made permanent through legislation and applied to all healthcare services.

The government has saved lives by ensuring that the least of our brothers and sisters have access to healthcare through Medicaid and Medicare. But individuals and families should decide what specific care they need based on their unique situation. The government shouldn't be dictating to them what kind of care they need. Obamacare left decisions on care in the hands of the government, and the progressive plan referred to as Medicare for All would just make these problems even worse by eliminating private medical insurance.

In 2016, I got a tangible example of the dumb things that happen when the federal government is allowed to decide what kind of care an individual should get, rather than giving that person the freedom to decide, when I met a courageous young woman named Stefanie. She had come to a DC2DQ stop seeking help.

Her life had been changed forever when she was diagnosed in 2007 with multiple sclerosis, a disease in which the immune system eats away at the protective covering of a person's nerves. She struggled to find treatment options in the United States.

Relentlessly exploring all treatments, Stefanie resorted to medical tourism and benefited from a stem cell treatment not yet available in Texas. Knowing it could help others like her, Stefanie successfully lobbied the Texas State Legislature to allow patients with terminal illnesses or severe chronic diseases, like MS, access to adult stem cell treatments.

Thanks to Stefanie, the bill was signed into law in 2017.

Stefanie's treatments were so successful that she could put her weight on her legs again and no longer needed a traditional wheelchair. The only problem was that Medicare would not approve a standing wheelchair, which would help her continue to build muscle in her legs and dramatically improve her quality of life.

We pinpointed why her previous Medicare applications for a standing wheelchair were getting denied by the Centers for Medicare and Medicaid Services (CMS) and made the fix. Within a week, she got her standing wheelchair and, in the process, made it easier for people in similar situations to be successful.

Stefanie's experiences point to the consequences of placing the federal government in charge of making medical decisions. Because the case was

unique and the wheelchair was more expensive than the other ones, the bureaucrats at CMS didn't want to approve the expense. You shouldn't need
your congressman to call to get you a piece of equipment that is necessary for
you to function.

Placing additional burdens on everyday families is the lack of *access* to
healthcare. Too many people are relying on hospital emergency rooms for
basic medical care. It's a problem in urban communities, but also a huge challenge in a rural district like Texas 23.

In rural America, doctors' offices are few and far between, so people are
forced into using expensive hospital systems for care or taking long trips to
see the doctor. Receiving treatment for a common ailment at an emergency
room is on average twelve times more expensive than being treated at a physi-
cian's office. If you are an hourly worker who has to take time for a trip to see a
doctor, then you have to sacrifice much-needed dollars out of your paycheck.

During one of my first years in office, I toured a dialysis center in San
Antonio, part of a kidney disease medical practice owned by my friend Reza
Mizani, and I sat with people as they received treatment. One man told me
he drove two hours from Uvalde five days a week for dialysis because the San
Antonio facility was the closest dialysis center. Because of the commute for
treatment, he couldn't keep a job.

Representing rural America, I learned about an innovative model of
healthcare that gives the local community a voice—Community Health
Centers (CHCs). They have a proven track record of success that should be
used in more areas of healthcare.

Started in the '60s to provide medical care to agriculture workers, CHCs
have grown into a national network that serves approximately thirty million
people, close to one in eleven Americans. They are nonprofit private corporations, each governed by a volunteer board of directors comprised of local
citizens from the community. Fifty-one percent of local board members are
required to be patients of the health center.

Community Health Centers are the largest source of comprehensive primary healthcare for medically underserved rural and urban communities, and they save American taxpayers $24 billion a year in healthcare costs by preventing and managing chronic diseases. But these are not ordinary medical clinics—they are also problem-solvers that reach beyond the exam room to address health factors such as lack of nutrition, mental illness, homelessness, and substance abuse disorders.

This model provides integrated care by offering an array of services, including medical, dental, behavioral health, lab X-rays, pharmacy, health education, preventative, and social services. In fact, even though they faced incredible challenges during the COVID-19 pandemic, eight out of ten of CHCs met or exceeded one or more national benchmarks in terms of quality of care in 2020.

From hourly employees and agriculture workers to elected officials, teachers, professors, and police officers, CHCs treat everyone, and sometimes are the only game in town in areas with no doctors or where private doctors aren't seeing new patients. Uninsured patients are charged on a sliding scale based on income, to ensure that care is affordable.

To be clear: Community Health Centers aren't free clinics. While they rely on federal dollars and private funding to close the access gap for the medically vulnerable, the majority of their operating budgets come from money received from services provided. Their mission is an example of idealism—a commitment to changing people's lives—and their approach is pragmatic—help the greatest number of people possible.

CHCs are also economic engines in areas of our country that are most in need. They create jobs and help stimulate the local economy to the tune of one and a half times their operating budgets.

In Texas 23, seven CHC organizations with close to forty healthcare delivery sites provide everything from general medical care to behavioral health to lab testing. One CHC in the district, Community Health Development Inc., serves as the primary healthcare home for about one-third of the population in its service area, and on average, all services included,

Community Health Development takes care of a patient for only *eight hundred dollars a year.*

It will take a lot to fix our health system. But price transparency and having more healthcare systems adopt the Community Health Center model of focusing on prevention would be a good start.

We *can* design a healthcare system where we increase access and decrease the cost. This problem is solvable. The U.S. has some of the greatest doctors, scientists, researchers, healthcare providers, and practitioners to have ever walked the earth. If we put them all in a room, they would be able to design a system based on values that work for all Americans and adapts for an unexpected and unknown future.

Healthcare is an issue that affects every American, and rather than use it to bludgeon the other side in order to score points with the fringes of our political parties, we should be using it to unite our country.

CHAPTER 11

PROVIDE OUR SENIORS QUALITY CARE AND COMPASSION

I was dreading having to talk to my dad about a charge on my credit card from a company I didn't recognize. Like many adult children, my siblings and I help support our parents financially. My dad uses my credit card to buy groceries and medicines, and in early 2020 one particular charge seemed weird.

Sitting in the living room of my parents' house, I confronted my dad about the $250 purchase. He got up and retrieved a newspaper clipping. "Read this while I fix your momma some lunch," he instructed me.

In my hand was an advertisement from the local newspaper for a knee pain cure—$250 for a three-month supply. He pointed to the endorsements in the ad as proof of its effectiveness. The stuff was for my mom, who in addition to being diagnosed with dementia in 2019, has a bad right knee that causes her constant pain. Her inability to commit to rehab makes a knee replacement out of the question.

My mom's health difficulties are a source of deep distress for my dad. He can't stand to see her suffer, so he searches for "cures" and "treatments" from "experts." I did a quick internet search on the product, and of course, there was no scientific evidence proving it could cure knee pain.

"Dad," I said, trying to be as kind as I could as we stood in the kitchen. "This is not medical or scientific analysis. This is an ad for vitamins."

My dad can have a temper, but I didn't see anger on his face. Pointing to my mom in her favorite chair in the front room, he spoke firmly, quietly, and slowly.

"William, I've been married to her for forty-nine years. I'm not going to stop trying to find ways to help her," he said. "I'm not going to stop."

How could I argue with that? In the end, we agreed that he would send the remaining supply back in two weeks if there wasn't a demonstrable improvement. But I knew this wasn't the last time we were going to have this conversation.

My mom is the love of my dad's life, and he is the love of hers. In an era where a biracial relationship was not welcome, they defied bigotry, ran a successful business, and raised a loving family. They are like many of our seniors—for so long, they protected us, and now it's our turn to protect them.

My mother, Mary Alice Knapp, grew up in the small town of Alexandria, Indiana. Her dad wasn't a pleasant man, and her parents divorced when my mom was in high school. Her mother, my grandma Alice, moved to Los Angeles following the divorce. Grandma Alice joined her son, my uncle Lester, and her mother, Blanche. After graduating from high school in 1962, my mom moved in with Blanche, Grandma Alice, Uncle Lester, and his partner "Uncle" Steve.

In L.A., my mom took a job at Bullock's Department Store, where Uncle Lester, Uncle Steve, and Grandma Alice also worked. Lester had moved to Southern California to get as far away from Alexandria as possible. He was a petite, brilliant man. He did what he wanted and didn't care what anyone thought.

Uncle Lester ran Bullock's accounting department, Uncle Steve was a cosmetologist in the hair salon, Grandma Alice was in retail sales. My mom, who could sew, knit, and crochet, worked in Fabrics & Notions (buttons, thread, and sewing tools). In addition to living and working together, they were all registered Republicans.

Mary Alice eventually worked her way up to be the head buyer in Fabrics & Notions. In 1967, she married her first husband, John Estrada, who was thirty-seven years her senior. But he died of intestinal cancer just ten months after they married.

My mom rose in her career to where she was making buying decisions for most of the stores in Bullock's greater L.A. empire. When most salesmen at Bullock's met my mother, they tended to dismiss her as an inexperienced girl, but soon realized she knew more about their products than they did. You didn't tell Mary Alice what to do or what she needed.

One company that sold to Mary Alice's department was Coats & Clark, and its account manager thought Mary Alice was a straight-up pain in the ass. So he handed off the Bullock's account to a new trainee who was the first Black salesman Coats had ever hired—my dad, Bob Hurd.

Bob was divorced, on probation for embezzlement, and had gotten out of Dallas on the advice of his mother, Sammy. One day he had been crying into his beer about his situation, and Sammy gave it to him straight.

"Dallas has been good to you," she told him. "But you ain't been shit to Dallas. It's time to change your friends. It's time to change your attitude. It's time to change your location, and it's time to change your life."

Mary Alice liked going to nice restaurants and watching live music, and Bob had a sizable expense account to pay for the outings. They also spent a lot of time with Mary Alice's family at the Knapp residence. Bob and Blanche drank champagne together (he said Blanche could really "bend the elbow") and sang around the piano. They liked Bob and they saw how the romance was blossoming, but they knew a marriage between a Black man and a White woman in America in the '60s and '70s was going to be hard.

My dad and mom dated for almost two years before getting married in 1971. They were an interracial couple at a time when it was barely legal— *Loving v. Virginia*, the landmark Supreme Court case that declared bans on interracial marriage unconstitutional, had only been decided in 1967.

My dad's job took my parents to San Antonio the same year they married. After the difficulties of buying a house because my dad is Black, the situation didn't improve much when my blond-haired, blue-eyed mom was toting dark-skinned kids around town. She got unwelcoming looks in the grocery store and incredulous comments about why these children were a different race than she was.

When I was born, I failed to sustain respiration, a condition called asphyxia neonatorum. Explaining the alarm in the delivery room, the doctor said I had skin discoloration, but he failed to mention it was because of my lack of breathing. My dad was on the road, and my mom, who had just delivered me by herself, yelled, "He's half-Black!"

If my mom had frustrations about prejudice she experienced when we were kids, she never communicated them to us. Growing up, our mixed race was never an issue. We were who we were. So as far as my mom was concerned, that settled it.

She could be ferociously protective of us. I was a crybaby as a kid—a real momma's boy—and she was always having to comfort me as I clutched her legs and sobbed. She was the only person who understood me through my speech impediment, and I had the sense that I would get through anything with her love.

That same love and caring was present for my older siblings, Chuck and Liz. Just a few years ago, I met the wife of Chuck's eighth-grade football coach, Coach Pipes, at a reception. Mrs. Pipes told me that my mom was the only parent Coach Pipes was ever afraid of.

Chuck, who my father always says was "hyper" as a kid, was always hustling. In elementary school, he would get our mother to buy bags of candy at the grocery store, then he would resell individual candies to his classmates at a significant markup. In middle school, he would purchase wrestling magazines, then xerox the image of the marquee wrestler and somehow get teenagers to buy those black-and-white copies. In college, as the residential assistant in the athletic dormitory, he would be lax in enforcing dorm policy if the athletes gave Chuck a pair of their university-provided basketball shoes so he could ship them home, enabling me to have the latest high-tops despite my parents' modest income.

Chuck, even though he has the biggest and kindest heart, was always up to hijinks. In middle school, when Coach Pipes made him run laps for doing something wrong, nobody questioned whether Chuck was at fault. However,

Chuck, who has serious asthma, started having an asthma attack. Coach Pipes thought the hustling prankster was faking it and made Chuck continue to run. My mom roared into the school the next day and ripped Coach Pipes so bad that, forty years later, he was still afraid of her.

And when my sister, Liz, tore her ACL at a high school basketball game, my mom sprinted down from the top of the arena, shouting "My baby!," side-hurdled the railing, landed ten feet below on the hardwood court, and ran to my sister. It was like she was a ninja.

The first time I realized my parents weren't invincible was when I was in college. My dad and mom had started a business, M.A. Beauty Supply (named after my mom), in 1993, after dad retired from Coats & Clark. My dad saw an opportunity in the billion-dollar Black hair care market. M.A. Beauty Supply sold products such as hair colors and chemical relaxers to beauty salons specializing in serving Black women. Chuck worked in the business as well, and after a few years, they added a cosmetology school to train hairstylists who could style African American hair. My mom, who went back to school to get her cosmetologist's license, conducted training seminars on how to use their products—which led to some strange looks when this White lady showed up to expertly style Black hair.

In 1996, the summer after my freshman year in college, my dad suffered a devastating stroke. I was in a study-abroad program in Mexico, and my family launched a frantic effort to track me down while my dad rapidly declined. It looked like he was going to die. A priest came to his hospital room and gave him the Last Rites.

I got from rural Oaxaca, Mexico, to San Antonio in record time. I walked into the hospital room hours after the Last Rites had been issued. It was late evening, and the doctors let me sit at my dad's side, holding his hand, telling stories of my adventures in Mexico. I relieved my mom and brother so they could go home to shower and sleep in a real bed. When they returned the next morning, my dad opened his eyes. He looked around the room as my mom and brother tried to explain what had happened. But Dad was having none of it. He started pulling tubes out of his nose and removing his IV, and he zeroed in on Chuck.

"Who's opening the business?" he demanded.

Chuck looked at me, half-euphoric and half-annoyed, and offered a dry assessment. "Dad's going to be fine."

While it was clear my dad had dodged the Grim Reaper this time around, it brought home to me a reality that every son or daughter confronts— someday we are going to have to take care of our parents.

For about two decades following my dad's stroke, my parents were in relatively good health. In the months before my second congressional campaign, my mother had a mild heart attack but fully recovered. My brother, sister, and I don't know exactly when my mom's dementia began, but it was probably years before we finally realized it. Our dad likely hid it from us, and maybe from himself, for a while.

From a young age, my mom could sew, knit, and crochet. She was talented. Along with sewing our clothes, she was constantly making all kinds of handcrafted items. As children, Liz, Chuck, and I helped her sew hundreds of puppets for puppet shows she supplied to her friend who owned the Just For You Puppet Company. She'd make clever toys and give them away in bags she had crocheted. At Christmas, she made detailed nativity scenes, with the figures stitched in delicate needlepoint, and her quilts were big money-raisers at the Catholic church she and my dad attended.

As the years passed, she gradually lost the ability to work magic with her hands. The quilts and toys began to look distorted and amateurish. It was the first sign I had seen that there was a problem. Eventually, her memory of how to craft disappeared altogether, and she stopped.

At the same time, my mom was also becoming easily confused, forgetting conversations that just occurred. If she got separated from my dad at the grocery store, she couldn't find her way back to him. In 2019, we got the diagnosis. Microvascular dementia. My mom was seventy-five years old.

Sadly, it's a common diagnosis among the older population. About one out of every six women and one out of every ten men living past the age of fifty-five will develop dementia. About 70 percent of their cases are caused by Alzheimer's. But, of the other cases, vascular dementia is the second leading cause of dementia.

My mom's ability to recognize loved ones is fading. She doesn't remember she has a great-grandson and can't recall the names of Chuck's five-year-old twin daughters. My mom will soon lose the capacity to recognize us and, ultimately, my dad.

Individuals with a family member suffering from dementia lose that loved one twice: once when the loved one's memory goes, and again when that loved one reaches the pearly gates. There are no words to describe losing a loved one. Having to do it twice is unfathomable.

I carried my family's successes and heartbreaks into my life as an elected official, and it informed a lot of what I did in terms of making impactful, meaningful changes to help other families experiencing their own challenges.

Dealing with the destruction my mom's dementia has caused made me glad that I voted for the bipartisan 21st Century Cures Act, signed into law in 2016. The goal of the legislation was to advance medical research, foster a new era of medical innovations, and help find cures to some of the world's cruelest diseases.

While in Congress, I always supported strengthening Medicare. I especially supported Medicare Advantage, an insurance program that provides Medicare benefits through a private-sector insurer. But providing care to our seniors is not enough. We need to be improving care to increase longevity and quality of life. Thanks to the Cures Act, we're able to better prevent and screen cancer, we have a better understanding of the human brain, and we're improving the field of stem cell science.

Through the Cures Act, Congress showed an ability to empower researchers and medical innovators to solve problems plaguing our parents and grandparents by increasing funding for research and streamlining bureaucratic red tape that prevents innovation.

The COVID pandemic showed us that at many levels of government and society, our audio and video failed to match when it came to protecting our seniors. Nursing homes house populations that were the most vulnerable to COVID-19—the elderly and sick. As of September 2021, more than 186,000 residents and staff of nursing homes and other long-term care facilities have died of COVID-19. Why were more people not outraged by these deaths? Why were some elected officials more likely to yell about "You're forcing me to wear a mask" or "You're not closing enough businesses" rather than "People are dying in nursing homes—let's fix this"? There was, and still is, a lack of concern on both sides of the aisle on this issue.

The regulatory system for nursing homes is a mix of state licensure and federal certification, and it appears that state regulators' inability to enforce standards, and nursing home operators cutting corners for years, were the cause of much of the human tragedy that unfolded. The standards that these nursing homes were supposed to be following, weren't being followed. Nursing homes were saying they were doing one thing but, upon being stress tested, we found out that wasn't the case. This was a problem before the pandemic.

The Centers for Medicare and Medicaid Services (CMS) provides quality ratings for the nation's approximately sixteen thousand Medicare and Medicaid–certified nursing homes. Each facility is rated from a low of one star to a high of five stars based on three areas: health inspection results, quality measures, and staffing levels. An overall rating is provided after consideration of five areas: fire safety, health inspection, quality measures, staffing, and penalties. There are ninety-nine nursing homes or long-term care facilities within fifty miles of San Antonio. In 2019, only three received a five-star rating by CMS.

During the pandemic, I held meetings with groups that advocate on behalf of seniors, and even they had a hard time understanding the situation. They did urge requiring the Department of Health and Human Services (HHS) to take action to improve palliative- and hospice-care training of health professionals.

COVID-19 didn't start in nursing homes; it was brought in. The pandemic revealed in the worst way that we need updates to standards of care. Our moms, dads, and grandparents took care of us for most of our lives, and now it's our turn to take care of them. Bottom line, we should throw the book at the regulators responsible for overseeing nursing homes, as well as the healthcare providers who run nursing homes. Nursing homes should be the safest places in our country because they care for the people that made us who we are today.

In addition to providing quality care to our seniors, another way to show compassion and extend the independence of our parents and our grandparents is through consumer protection. This hit home when my siblings and I stumbled across the disturbing fact that my dad had become enmeshed in the network of scams that target vulnerable seniors. While cons are a scourge for all Americans, older adults are especially susceptible, losing an estimated $2.9 billion each year alone to financial rip-offs.

A few years ago, my dad was victimized by a robocaller pretending to be me, who told my dad to buy four hundred dollars in gift cards at Walmart to bail me out of jail. The scammer ordered my dad not to call me, claiming I didn't have my cell phone. I was not in jail and was carrying my cell phone. My dad, willing to go to any limits to help and protect his son, jumped into action, but the scheme unraveled when my dad forgot some of the instructions. Yes, he was told not to call my cell phone, but the caller didn't say anything about calling my trusted deputy chief of staff, Nancy Pack. She has been a valued member of our team since I first won and has been integral to my success. She is part of the family, and she probably gets more phone calls from my father and brother than I do. Immediately recognizing something was amiss, Nancy notified me.

Nancy cut the rip-off short, but "family emergency" robocalls are a major cause of financial cons fleecing the elderly. Individuals impersonating family members generate tens of thousands of complaints annually to the Federal Trade Commission.

Of all calls to cell phones, nearly 50 percent of them are scam calls, and, according to the FTC, the median loss from a successful phone scam in 2020 was $1,170—nearly four times the median loss from all fraud types. To deter criminal, unsolicited robocalls, we passed a piece of bipartisan legislation called the Telephone Robocall Abuse Criminal Enforcement and Deterrence Act (TRACED). It was signed into law in 2019 and addressed robocall scams by broadening the authority of the Federal Communications Commission to levy hefty civil penalties on fraudulent callers and reduce "spoofed calls"— when scammers mask their identity by changing the number displayed on a caller ID.

Robocalls are one of many problems our seniors face. Had I more time in Congress, I would have followed in the footsteps of previous congressional representatives and state attorney generals and investigated deceptive mail practices of companies like Publishers Clearing House and predatory lending practices of so-called financial firms like Worth Financial Service.

As technology evolves and enables us to make our lives better, it will also be used to take advantage of people, and we need to ensure that the regulatory entities designed to protect consumers are up for the task, especially when it comes to our seniors. Technology is not always being adapted for our seniors. My parents sold their business and retired in 2003. Like a lot of seniors, they've struggled to adapt to the modern world.

Whenever I go over to my folks' house, my dad usually has notes he has written to remember topics to bring up with me. One day, there was a note with just a single word—"Irishman."

I was baffled at first. "What's that, Pops?"

"The movie," Dad said. "How do I get it?"

"It's on Netflix," I said. "Let me show you how to do it."

It's an easy maneuver for most of us. But my dad, who didn't know how to type and used my mom for all computer-related things until she couldn't remember, had never navigated how the cursor on the screen and the clicker in his hand worked together.

A major area of conversation in the technology space is the digital divide—that abyss that exists between those who have access to computers and the internet, and those who do not. Usually that conversation is focused on the economic, educational, and social inequalities between those who have computers and online access and those who haven't. But there is another element of the digital divide, and that's our seniors' inability to *use* the technology when they do have access to it.

My dad's words when I confronted him about the fake knee treatment he had purchased for my mom have stuck with me—*"I'll never stop."* As long as he can, he will be looking out for her. Our country has let too many of our seniors down, and we can't stop trying to do better. They deserve it.

CHAPTER 12

INVEST IN
OUR REAL FUTURE

My sister, Liz, a three-sport letterman in high school, leapt across the living room coffee table at me like a coiled puma. Thank God I grabbed her wrists before she wrapped her fingers around my throat like a vise grip.

I was in high school, but I had a PhD in getting under my sister's skin. I had called her a "savage" after I heard her yelling at our mom in the kitchen. As I pulled my sister off me, I repeated the mockery in a cool tone, mustering all the indignation and contempt I could: "You. Are. A. Savage."

Mom charged out of the kitchen. "William," she shouted. "Shut up and leave your sister alone."

"What the hell, Mom," I responded. "I'm defending you!" Then I stormed out of the house to shoot hoops and calm down.

That was nearly thirty years ago, and it's what I regret most in my life. If I could go back, I would've shut my trap, because I was clueless to the emotions my sister was dealing with that day. A junior at the University of Texas at Arlington, she'd just found out she was pregnant, news that could have upended the trajectory of her life and endangered her schooling. Single parenthood, even with the support of the baby's father, was not what Liz had planned.

Liz was able to have Kayla, finish college, and prepare for an incredibly successful career with the help of Kayla's father and both sets of grandparents. Liz went back to school because Mom and Dad were willing to provide child-care during the week. On weekends, Liz made the four-and-a-half-hour drive home to San Antonio to be with her daughter. Of all the people I lived with as a kid, Kayla was the best. She didn't touch my stuff. She didn't call me names or tell me what to do. She didn't use the phone, so I could talk to my girlfriend into the wee hours of the morning without being interrupted.

Mom and Dad's heroic day care duties didn't end there. After Liz graduated and got a job, they watched Kayla during the week and did the same for Liz's son, Jacob, after he was born six years later.

Liz is incredibly grateful for everything our parents did. She is an enormous success because of her determination and hard work, but also because of our parents' willingness to provide an additional loving home to their grandchildren. Almost 60 percent of young children who need childcare spend at least some time in the care of a grandparent. That, however, leaves millions of working parents who must rely on outside help. Before the pandemic, close to thirteen million American children aged five and younger in this country were in some type of childcare.

But the pandemic upended the already fragile childcare infrastructure in the U.S. When COVID-19 struck, 60 percent of childcare providers were forced to shut down, eliminating a lifeline to millions of working families. As the pandemic wore on, some didn't reopen. It has had broader economic ramifications. Parents, especially moms, were faced with working at home *and* providing childcare for young children *and* schooling older ones. This impossible situation forced them to leave the workforce. In 2021, the share of women in the workforce was down to levels not seen in more than thirty years.

Even before the pandemic, state economies lost billions of dollars annually to working parents' childcare challenges. Without reliable childcare, parents can't stay in jobs, companies have difficulty finding and keeping high-quality workers, and there is less tax revenue to bolster states' fiscal health. The economy depends on the availability of accessible, affordable childcare. By boosting worker productivity and improving the chances that children (especially disadvantaged ones) will succeed in life, childcare advances economic growth.

As Rep. Don Beyer (D-Virginia), vice chair of the Joint Economic Committee, pointed out in 2020, childcare also contributes to a more equitable society because parents—particularly single and/or low-income moms—can seek more opportunities in the workplace when their children are cared for in high-quality childcare settings.

Without affordable, high-quality childcare, parents cannot make their American Dream a reality. Childcare is the *foundation* of our workforce. It provides freedom, leading to opportunity and growth, for both individuals and the country as a whole.

As of the writing of this book, I don't have any children. I'm still a bachelor. I was engaged once to a woman from North Dallas whom I had dated on and off for over seven years and with whom I had hoped to spend the rest of my life. But one evening I came home and said, "Hey, honey, I actually work in the CIA, and we are moving back to South Asia." That had an understandably chilling effect on our relationship. But I am an uncle and a great uncle, and I had the honor of representing thousands of working parents.

I've learned about kids' miraculous development up to age five, and how this stage of life forms the critical foundation for the growth of their bodies, their minds, their emotional health, and even their social functioning. A U.S. Chamber of Commerce report points out that "childcare is early education, regardless of the building it occurs in or what we call it. The question is only whether it's advancing or impeding children's learning." But childcare expenses take an enormous chunk out of working parents' paychecks—an average of 23 percent. The average cost for an infant in a childcare center is an astonishing $1,230 per month. For many parents, that's more per year than the cost of a college education.

The government can help ease this financial burden through our tax code. If we truly believe in the idealist notion that our kids are our future, then our policies should reflect the pragmatism of this belief. When I was in

Congress, we doubled the Child Tax Credit to help families bear the costs of raising children by reducing their overall federal income tax bill. (A tax credit reduces the actual amount of tax owed to the government, unlike deductions, which lower the amount of taxable income.)

There are two other tax credits that address childcare. One of these, the Child and Dependent Care Credit, reduces taxes by a percentage of child-care costs, up to a maximum amount. The other is the Earned Income Tax Credit (EITC), which targets low- to moderate-income working households, particularly those with children. The size of the EITC benefit depends on a recipient's income and number of children.

But as is, these tax credits aren't enough. For that reason, I see a lot of merit in proposals to index the dependent-care credit to inflation in childcare costs and expand the Earned Income Tax Credit to help families pay for childcare.

I have seen what my brother, sister, and constituents have gone through to provide a loving environment for their children. I also learned that employers are not always welcoming to working parents

I was going through the hiring process for my second chief of staff, Kristan. In one of our first interactions, she let me know she was pregnant with her third child. I congratulated her and explained that my office offered twelve weeks paid family leave—the maximum for a congressional office. But Kristan brought the fact up that she was pregnant several more times throughout the interview process. I was starting to get annoyed that she kept repeating herself. Did she think I didn't hear her? As I usually do when I don't understand something, I asked Nancy.

"Why the hell does Kristan keep bringing up that she's pregnant. I don't get it."

Nancy knew the answer immediately. "Will, she thinks you won't hire her because she's gonna have to go on maternity leave."

"Shut up, Nancy. Really?" I asked incredulously.

"Yeah, that's a thing. Where have you been living?" Nancy said. "A lot of employers wouldn't have hired her, knowing she was pregnant."

That's outrageous. Your organization has to be pretty inept if you can't handle someone's absence for twelve weeks to be with their newborn. Even though discrimination in the workplace based on pregnancy was made illegal under the 1978 Pregnancy Discrimination Act, it hasn't stopped thousands of employers from passing over, demoting, and firing pregnant women. We need to make it easier—not harder—for working parents to take time off for their children when it's most important, and the federal government can be an example.

I supported the Federal Employee Paid Leave Act, signed into law in 2019, which gave the entire federal government workforce, like my congressional office, up to twelve weeks of paid time off for the birth, adoption, or placement of a new child. But that only takes care of the first three months.

Lessons learned from the pandemic could be adopted to make sure we are focused on our kids. We learned working from home is possible for more employees than we ever could have imagined, and for that reason, the workplace will never be the same. More employers are closing offices and encouraging telecommuting when that's possible.

How can we make it easier for parents to work at home while caring for children if that is what they choose to do? And how can we help workers in public-facing jobs—from frontline medical workers to hotel staff and restaurant workers—who don't have the same work-at-home opportunities with their childcare needs?

These are a few of the hard public policy issues we should be debating, not the dumb things that consume the media discourse. If we are unable to resolve the debate on how to empower our fellow Americans with the freedom and opportunity to choose what's best for their children, then we can forget trying to achieve the thing that is going to make sure we keep this century the American Century.

CHAPTER 13

BUILD THE WORKFORCE OF TOMORROW, NOT YESTERDAY

Our next computer giveaway recipient rolled up in a beat-up sedan. It was a hot August day in 2020, and dozens of idling cars were in a line, wrapped around an apartment complex parking lot on the East Side of San Antonio. The drivers were waiting to receive a refurbished Hewlett-Packard desktop computer from the San Antonio Housing Authority (SAHA). A San Antonio councilwoman and I were busy loading the PCs in the back seats of the cars.

SAHA leadership realized that since their entire staff was working on laptops from home during the pandemic, their 120 or so idle desktop computers could be put to better use. So they gave them to the residents of their properties who earned less than twelve thousand dollars a year and had at least one high school or college student.

It was clear that the kid in the sedan was excited. I leaned into the open passenger-side window and said, "Hey, my man, thanks for coming by today. Make sure the car is in park, but don't turn it off. And unlock the back door if you would, please."

While we placed a monitor, keyboard, CPU, and a bag with cables and a mouse into his back seat, the kid said, "Sir, thank you for doing this. This'll be the first computer we've ever had in our house."

"What?! Seriously?!" I blurted out.

The kid didn't respond. He sat quietly. My incredulity had clearly made him uncomfortable. I went through a mental checklist of the tasks that would be necessary to be successful in school but would be a pain in the ass without a computer.

"What grade are you in, brother?" I asked.

"I'm about to enter my freshman year in college, sir."

"Congrats, man, that's awesome. We're proud of your accomplishment . . . Let me ask you this, though, how did you write your papers and stuff when you had assignments due for class?"

The kid pulled out his cell. "On my phone," he said in a chipper matter-of-fact way.

"*On your phone?*" I said. "You write research papers *on your phone?*" I don't even like to type long texts on my phone. I couldn't imagine tapping out a five-page English paper with my thumbs.

"Sometimes I was able to use a computer at school. But most of the time I did it on this," the kid said, holding up his old phone.

I couldn't imagine being in that kid's situation. My brother, sister, and I got our first computer in 1985 when I was eight. My uncle Steve had upgraded to a Commodore 128, so he gave us his old Commodore 64 desktop. Because of Uncle Steve's donation, we were the first family in our neighborhood with a computer. We also had a modem to access the internet in the early '90s.

I've always had access to a computer at home, and I've had a laptop since I was in college. I was never victim to the three challenges of the digital divide—availability of devices, access to infrastructure, and ability to use. If you have the right device and know how to use it, but you can't access the internet or the cloud, then you're screwed. If you have access to the internet and know how to use a device, but you don't have the right device, you're screwed too. You're also screwed if you are like my dad and have both the right device and access but don't know how to use them.

By 2030, there are expected to be more than 25 billion connected devices in the world for a projected global population of 8.5 billion people. You would think there would be enough devices to go around, but that's far from the case. Schools and local communities are trying to address this device gap.

The Federal Communications Commission's (FCC) most recent statistics from 2019 suggest that 25 million Americans lack access to a broadband connection, but there is strong evidence that closer to 163 million Americans do not have access. And this is out of a total U.S. population of about 330 million.

When it comes to addressing the access gap, it's harder to calculate the exact problem because we don't have trustworthy public data on who doesn't have broadband or high-speed internet access. High-speed internet access matters because, with applications and software requiring increasingly large amounts of data, you need to move that data from your device to its destination and back in nanoseconds. If you can't move data quickly, then your device and the software and applications on that device are worthless.

So why should we care that potentially half the country lacks access to high-speed internet? Because studies suggest that access to broadband has a direct impact on jobs and GDP growth. The lowest broadband access and usage are in U.S. counties with the most unemployment.

This digital divide has compounded another problem. Our economy is losing out on trillions of dollars in economic output because our kids can't keep up academically with kids in other countries. Economists have estimated that the U.S. economy could be almost 4 percent higher than currently projected over two decades if American students' math and science skills were as good as the rest of the world's. Just as worrying: disparities in academic achievement of U.S. students based on their ethnicity, race, family income, and school quality cost billions in unrealized economic gains because a less-educated workforce has difficulty accessing well-paying jobs. In the average school district, White students score up to two grades higher than Black students. On family income, the achievement gap between high-income and low-income children continues to widen. The gap is 30 to 40 percent larger among children born in 2001 than among those born twenty-five years earlier.

These inequities represent a disturbing human and economic cost and point to a larger truth about our economy: We have *income* inequality because we have *education* inequality.

Before the pandemic, less than half of American students could read or do math at grade level. COVID-19 made a tragic problem more so, at a point in time when the stakes couldn't be higher. The U.S. is in a New Cold War with China for global leadership in advanced technology. The economy of the future is going to be defined by advanced technology, and the leader of this race is going to determine whether English and the dollar or Mandarin and the yuan are the language and currency of the global marketplace.

Technology is changing every aspect of our life and every industry. The technological change we are going to see in the next thirty years is going to make the last thirty years look insignificant. We must make sure the seventy-four million kids in our country are ready for this change by preparing them for jobs that don't exist today, or they will be screwed.

Not only is a well-trained and educated society necessary for economic growth, but it is also vital to our safety and security. Education is a national security issue. We need a workforce that can design the next encryption algorithms to protect our military, government, and private sector. We need people who can build the rockets to get us to Mars. We need people who are going to design the algorithms for artificial intelligence, who will chart our future by unlocking the potential of AI's powers, who will accelerate human achievement by transforming industries, governments, and workforces. We need a technologically advanced workforce that can excel in the next scientific breakthrough yet to be discovered. To build the workforce of tomorrow, we start with making sure every kid gets a superior education.

How do we enable our kids and fellow citizens to have the freedom to get an education that helps them move up the economic ladder and ensures America continues to have the strongest economy in the world? By implementing a lesson I learned the second time I almost died on a mountaintop.

During one of my CIA tours, I received a call late one Friday evening from my chief of station asking whether I knew how to ski. I told him I was a mediocre snowboarder, and he said that was good enough and told me that I would be attempting to bump a foreigner of significant intelligence value who was taking his family skiing.

At the ski slope, my strategy was to slide in alongside the target on a ski lift. But each time the target rode the lift, he had his wife and kids with him. Finally, I was at the top of the hill and saw the target below me, headed alone for the ski lift line.

I angled my board down the hill and took off like a bat out of hell. I was moving so fast, you would have thought I was shot out of a cannon. I coul. hear people's exclamations as I whizzed by like a bullet. As I approached the base of the hill and prepared to stop, the fronts of my feet caught something, and I was launched into the air. I did a complete flip and two spins, landing face-first in the snow. I managed to lift my head and spy the target getting onto the ski lift all by himself.

I laid in the snow facedown, disappointed that I had lost my chance, and scanned myself for injuries. I overheard some kid ask his mom whether that man who just flew through the air was going to be all right. My surveillance team lead came over and helped me into a seated position. He leaned into my ear and whispered, "After the target completed his last run, he went into the lodge. He is now sipping cocoa in front of the fire."

I stood up, wiped the excess snow off me, walked into the lodge—and executed a textbook bump.

What I learned that day is that the best solution to a difficult challenge is usually the simplest and the easiest.

Sure, there are hard things that should be done so we can prepare our kids for jobs that don't exist today. Pragmatic actions that will benefit not only kids, but also the future trajectory of our country. States need to figure out how to make it more attractive for people to go into teaching, by significantly increasing salaries for good teachers. We need to encourage educational competition by increasing the number of successful charter schools. School boards and state governments should give school districts and individual traditional public schools the independence to operate the way charter schools do, instead of having a one-size-fits-all solution within districts. While I believe these approaches are straightforward, they have been the subject of complicated debates for years, if not decades.

But here's one strategy that is easy and shouldn't attract controversy: introduce coding into the standard curriculum of every middle school in the United States of America. It's an easy and simple way to ensure our kids are ready for jobs that don't exist today. Coding is the language of the twenty-first-century economy. If our students can't speak it, they will be left behind. Coding teaches kids problem-solving skills, computer literacy, and at the very least, gives them a better understanding of how technology is shaping our world.

In 2017, I learned that Texas universities had graduated only 3,500 students with a degree in computer science, while that same year in Texas alone, there were more than 38,000 open computing jobs (where the average salary was roughly $93,000).

Within this dearth of future employees with necessary computing skills, there is another problem—a lack of women with those skills. Of those 3,500 students who graduated from Texas schools with a computer science degree, only 19 percent were female. Girls Who Code, the international non-profit working to close the gender gap in technology, found that women will likely only hold one in five computing jobs in the U.S. by 2025. An increase of women in the computing workforce from 20 to 39 percent of that population would generate $299 billion in additional cumulative earnings for those women over a decade. This shortage of women in computing is not only a fundamental economic challenge for the U.S. economy, but it also hampers our long-term global competitiveness in advanced technology.

In an effort to do our part to tackle this problem, my team and I worked with a nonprofit called Bootstrap and the University of Texas Center for STEM Education to train middle school teachers how to integrate computer science into their mathematics class.

Because of this initiative, five thousand students at twenty schools in

Texas 23 were exposed to coding, potentially changing their lives. Educational technology integrator Sheryl Sokoler has said, "The earlier we introduce coding to children, the more comfortable they will become with computers and technology, and the more successful they will become when presented with more challenging learning opportunities."

I know this to be true because I experienced it myself.

At Texas A&M, I majored in computer science, but really got interested in technology when I earned an internship at Southwest Research Institute (SwRI) as a sophomore in high school. Created in 1947 in San Antonio, SwRI is one of the oldest and largest independent, nonprofit applied research and development organizations in the United States. SwRI gave me and nineteen other San Antonio area high school sophomores the chance to participate in a National Science Foundation–funded initiative called the Young Engineers and Scientists (YES) program. I can't remember why I was selected, because up to this point in my life, my only real technological talent was the ability to type seventy-five words a minute, but nonetheless I was in the program.

I worked with Dr. Jill Marshall, who received her undergraduate degree from Stanford University and her Ph.D. in physics from the University of Texas. She managed the sensor design and calibration section of SwRI. I didn't appreciate at the time how revolutionary it was in the early '90s for a female engineer to lead a major technological initiative.

Part of the program was to complete an individual research project, and I chose to do mine in robotics. My experience working with Dr. Marshall made me consider a computer science major in college. She exposed me to the possibilities of robotics, while making me understand the disruption this field could cause. The experience helped me understand that humanity can build and control machines that will improve society.

I was lucky to have been exposed to Dr. Marshall and her work at SwRI, and my high school had an amazing computer science teacher, Cathy Sauls. However, as of 2019, only 45 percent of high schools across the U.S. teach computer science. The percentage of middle schools is likely even smaller. While every state should create a state plan for K–12 computer science, let's begin this process with introducing coding in middle school. If a member of Congress can do it within a semester with the help of a couple of innovative companies and the University of Texas, then any state should be able to pull this off.

While not all schools have computer science instruction, many are starting to partner with local tech professionals to increase extracurricular activities available to students. Programs like CyberPatriots, where a guy like Frank Hall of West San Antonio can coach eight teams of students at three high schools in techniques for defending against cyberattacks. A cybersecurity professional by day, Frank devotes almost every afternoon of the workweek to training boys and girls on fighting real-world threats to America's cyber infrastructure. The teams participate in national CyberPatriots competitions (and capture-the-flag contests), with the idea of inspiring them toward careers in cybersecurity or STEM disciplines critical to our nation's future. Every student Frank has coached has gone on to study cybersecurity or computer science in college.

Schools can't train our kids for the future alone. It's going to take professionals in the community like Frank to pitch in when a school lacks capacity. Ultimately, parents still have the biggest role in solving this national security challenge. From an early age, parents need to read to their kids. Even reading to infants leads to improved language skills and cognitive development, like problem solving. A home full of books, studies show, benefits children's educational achievement and job success.

Every child in every neighborhood should be able to go to an excellent school. That involves ensuring that states and local communities are empowered to do what's best for their children because they are most likely to know how to get the best out of their kids. One-size-fits-all federal programs usually designed with the best intentions often limit educational innovation. A fourth grader in Texas should be able to do the same math problems as a fourth grader in California, but the way you teach that Texas student may be different from the way you teach the kid from California.

In 2015 I was proud to have helped a Republican Congress and a

Democrat president sign into law the Every Student Succeeds Act (ESSA). The ESSA built upon and improved one of George W. Bush's signature legislative accomplishments—No Child Left Behind—by giving the states more power to evaluate the performance of schools and decide how to fix them. I learned in Congress that it is difficult to hold someone accountable for an action if that person didn't have all the necessary authority to affect the outcome of events. Congress, in a very bipartisan way, gave states more authority to improve the education of our children; now they need to actually do it.

While we have to prepare our kids for jobs that don't exist today, we must prepare our workforce for disruptions we haven't seen since the Industrial Revolution. The question is not whether this disruption will happen or not. It's coming. The question is how we help today's workforce transition to "new collar" jobs.

We know artificial intelligence will transform the nature of work and affect every aspect of the economy. Grocery store cashiers are being replaced by automated systems. AI-powered virtual assistants are proliferating. Factories are using robots that use AI algorithms and can work alongside humans. Self-driving vehicles will replace truck and ride-share drivers. Machines will interpret X-rays and keep the books at businesses. Automated phone services will replace more receptionists. AI in the workplace will only continue to grow.

These are just some of the reasons that, in 2020, the House passed landmark legislation developed by Rep. Robin Kelly (D-Illinois) and me to pursue a national AI strategy. Robin and I worked with expert stakeholders and the Bipartisan Policy Center with the aim of putting our nation on the path to retain an edge in AI and secure the next seventy years of American-led international prosperity and security.

One of the four pillars of the legislation was Workforce Development, because the proliferation of AI in the workplace doesn't mean a robot revolution will take over. But an AI-driven economy will create the need for a workforce capable of using AI as the tool that it is. Failure to recognize the need to adapt will severely hurt American competitiveness and create unnecessary economic hardship and pain for the average American worker.

Technology will continuously change, which requires lifelong learning and workforce training that will help people develop the skills to adapt as their jobs do. The reality is that in many fields taking advantage of new technologies, employers are begging for workers. In 2019, I served as co-chair of the Aspen Cybersecurity Group, a convening of thirty-eight of the nation's highest-level experts to execute nonpartisan solutions to cybersecurity challenges. We learned that by 2021 there were going to be half a million unfilled cybersecurity positions across government and industry. To expand the pool of candidates to fill these vacancies, we proposed companies expand recruitment beyond applicants with four-year degrees; use non-gender-biased job descriptions that would explain the position without using gender-specific words and phrases; and make career paths clear, understandable, and accessible to employees and job seekers.

Despite these efforts, the U.S. struggles to produce enough high-skilled workers needed to ensure the U.S. economy stays the most important economy in the world. To retain our economy's vaulted status, we are going to have to raise our gaze when it comes to our expectations for the American workforce. As a country we are going to have to take a play out of my mother's playbook that led to me crying the hardest I had ever cried. I was in the fourth grade, and I was sobbing uncontrollably on the bus from school to home. I was minutes away from confessing to my mother that I had done something I had never done before—I got a B on my report card.

In our household, grades below excellent (all As) were not welcome. If I brought home a report card where I dropped from a 98 to a 96, my mom would be on my ass about why I hadn't gone up to 100 instead. She was always loving, but when it came to performance at school—She. Did. Not. Play. Exceptional was the only outcome accepted. My mother's high expectations are why I have such exacting standards now, including for myself, and our country shouldn't settle for anything less than exceptional when it comes to training the workforce of tomorrow.

CHAPTER 14

ENCOURAGE A GLOBAL "BRAIN GAIN" THROUGH IMMIGRATION

It was unusual for Nancy to show up when I was having meetings at the Capitol Hill Club. The Capitol Hill Club, one block from the House office building complex, is a clubhouse where Republicans can fundraise and meet prospective congressional candidates—political activity that is prohibited in our official offices. It was fall 2017, and Nancy's presence meant something was wrong. I excused myself from my meeting and met Nancy halfway.

"What's up?" I asked Nancy.

"There are Dreamers doing a die-in in our office."

Orange T-shirted protesters were trying to take over my office in the Cannon House Office Building. Draping themselves on chairs and lying on the floor of our cramped office suite, they were chanting, "We are the Dreamers, the mighty, mighty Dreamers," livestreaming the event on social media. So many people crammed in that they were spilling into the hallway, blocking the door. The adjoining congressional offices were objecting to the noise.

I was pissed. "Don't they know I'm on their side?" I asked Nancy. "Why are they in *our* offices? I'm one of the few Republicans trying to negotiate an actual solution to their problem."

The demonstrators were protesting because I hadn't become a co-sponsor of the DREAM Act, a sixteen-year-old piece of legislation that allowed young men and women, known as Dreamers, who were brought into this country illegally by their parents, to remain and pursue citizenship as long as they met specific work, school, and background check requirements. This bill had been introduced every year since 2001 and had never passed the Senate.

Even in 2010, when President Obama had Democratic majorities in Congress, six *Democratic* senators killed the DREAM Act from becoming law. Obama's inability to pass the DREAM Act resulted in him taking executive action to create the Deferred Action for Childhood Arrivals program— DACA. DACA was basically the DREAM Act without a pathway to citizenship.

Such protests were going to become louder and more frequent because of opposition to President Trump's decision to make good on his campaign promise to phase out DACA—which preceded the die-in in my office by a month.

While I was finishing my meetings, complaints by my Cannon neighbors caused the Capitol Police to escort the protesters out.

The protestors were correct. I hadn't signed on to the DREAM Act. I generally didn't cosign legislation that I knew had no chance of being signed into law. In sixteen years, the Dream Act had never been signed into law (it passed the House multiple times, including 2020 when I voted for it, but never got close to passage in the Senate), and the legislation as it was written would never be signed into law. While I opposed Trump's executive action, I also opposed Obama's, because a lasting solution to the terrible uncertainty faced by these young men and women, who have only ever known the United States of America as their home, requires a permanent *legislative* fix, not executive action.

Dreamers contribute to our history, culture, and economy. If for some dumb reason they were all deported, our country's economy would lose at least $280 billion over the next decade because hundreds of thousands of people would be taken out of the workforce. Social Security contributions alone could decrease by $31.8 billion.

DACA recipients have the overwhelming support of the U.S. public— that even includes a majority of Trump voters, according to a June 2020

POLITICO/Morning Consult poll. So legislation to allow the Dreamers to stay should be an easy fix that combines pragmatism (these young people contribute to our economy, helping everyone who participates in it) with idealism (a significant majority of Americans think this would improve our country). But immigration reform often ends up being a political bludgeon used by both sides to pander to their edges.

We have always benefited from a global "brain gain"—the immigration of smart, hardworking individuals who contribute to our society into the United States from other countries—because we are one of the few countries that doesn't require you to be born here to be a citizen. This simple fact enables our country to prosper by attracting the best, brightest, and hardest working people from all over the world. The adage that if you aren't growing then you are dying, is true for our country. Our birthrate alone will not be enough to sustain the population necessary to keep our great economic engine humming along. We need immigration to attract the skills necessary to meet the needs of our economy. We should be *embracing* the fact that America is a quilt and adding to it, not preventing additional quilt blocks from being attached.

During my service in the federal government, I received a pretty good education in the byzantine U.S. immigration system. In addition to learning the process of how visas are actually granted, I learned things like how almost half of all Fortune 500 companies have a founder who was an immigrant or the child of an immigrant, immigrants are twice as likely to be granted a patent, and the share of immigrants in high-skill occupations, particularly jobs that prioritize math and science, continues to rise.

For more than two hundred years, smart, productive people have come to our shores as a result of a global brain gain that has significantly benefited America. Entrepreneurs. AI specialists. Software engineers. Researchers. Agricultural workers. Housekeepers. Retail clerks. We need immigrants to join our workforce so the U.S. can continue to thrive. If you're going to be a hardworking member of our society, let's streamline our immigration process in order to get you here as quickly as possible.

We need people like the parents of former representative Mia Love (R-Utah). I worked in Congress with Mia on a variety of legislation, including immigration bills. She was the first Black Republican woman and the first Haitian American to be elected to Congress. Her parents, Maxime and Marie Bourdeau, fled Haiti with ten dollars in their pockets. Her dad worked up from the very bottom to become a paint-company manager while her mother was a nurse's aide, and they worked hard to make a life for their family, insisting their children not be burdens on society.

But when I was in office, I was routinely approached by constituents who claimed that immigrants "take our jobs." I always quizzed them.

"Was your job taken by an immigrant?" I'd ask. The answer was always no.

I would dig a little deeper.

"Did somebody in your family have a job taken by an immigrant?" Again, I always got a shake of the head.

I'd try one more time.

"Do you know *anybody* whose job was taken by an immigrant?" The answer was always the same: "No, but I saw something on Facebook."

Social media: the ultimate source of real facts.

Instead of "taking our jobs," abundant research has found that immigration has overall *boosted* wages and income of Americans.

We need businesspeople like Reza Mizani, who founded and runs South Texas Renal Care, a practice that employs more than one hundred people and cares for thousands of kidney patients in twelve locations around San Antonio. Reza grew up in Iran, but during the brutal Iran-Iraq war in 1985, his desperate parents sent him to Turkey, where he lived on his own at the age of twelve until he was able to emigrate to the Dominican Republic and then on to the U.S.

Homesick and fending for himself in Istanbul, Reza recalls a very "dark time" as his family sought to find him a home away from Iran. Each day he went to a library where he found books to teach himself so he wouldn't fall behind when he could return to his schooling. When he finally got to the

Dominican Republic, he graduated from medical school and then did his residency when he moved to the United States.

In San Antonio, Reza launched his practice because he wanted to care for the whole patient while dealing with a brutal sickness that is the source of misery to patients and their families. Coming from a background of significant struggle and suffering, Reza has used his experiences to build a practice that cares for each patient with patience and respect.

This country also wouldn't thrive without immigrants who have dedicated themselves to public service, like my friend Ambassador Sichan Siv, who escaped Cambodian slave labor camps and arrived in the U.S. in 1976 with just two dollars. The Khmer Rouge killed his entire family. From his start picking apples in Connecticut, Siv rose to serve in the White House as deputy assistant to President George H. W. Bush and served at the State Department before becoming a U.S. ambassador at the UN under President George W. Bush.

As we consider changes to our immigration laws—such as moving to a merit-based system of immigration, which uses a points system based on attributes like labor-market skills and education—we need to ensure our definition of "merit" would allow for people like the Bourdeaus, Dr. Mizani, and Ambassador Siv. They would not have benefited from a "merit-based" system because they did not have the high-level skills and top-tier educations that we traditionally assume lead to automatic success in this country. However, each one of them, and the families they built, contributed greatly to our economy and our culture and made their American Dream come true.

But we need to remain aware of the people who came before us, and the value and impact they have had. The great equalizer is someone's ability to work hard, and the Bourdeaus, Dr. Mizani, and Ambassador Siv exemplify that.

Just as my experiences with our visa issuance system informed my understanding of immigration, my time in the NCS, where part of my job included traveling in alias and entering into countries illegally, gave me a perspective on the weak underbelly of an issue intimately connected to immigration—border security. This unique mix of experiences allowed me to bring a point of view, forged in real-world experiences, to the challenges of the U.S.-Mexico border.

When a lot of people think of the U.S.-Mexico border, they conjure images of illegal immigration and drug smuggling. And, yes, both are serious problems. But the U.S.-Mexico border—two thousand miles with fifty-five active land ports of entry—is critical to the economic health of the U.S. economy. The Border or *La Frontera* is not just a line of demarcation between the U.S. and Mexico. It's a region where the people and the economies of the U.S. and Mexico meld, with commercial, cultural, and family ties that have an enormous impact on the rest of the country.

Mexico is the top U.S. trade partner, with trade in goods between the U.S. and Mexico totaling more than half a trillion dollars a year. Nearly five million U.S. jobs depend on trade with Mexico, and Mexico is the first- or second-largest trading partner for twenty-seven American states.

Hundreds of thousands of people cross the border legally each day, and up to 1.5 million U.S. citizens live in Mexico. It's not uncommon for people to work in the U.S. and live in Mexico, and vice versa.

To correct misconceptions about the border, I brought congressional colleagues and administration officials down for tours of the border. Some were nervous when I took them into Mexico. Many were expecting the Battle of Mogadishu in 1993, with shootouts in the streets like *Black Hawk Down*. But the reality is that 80 percent of the extreme violence in Mexico happens in 20 percent of the country, and very little of that violence spills over into the U.S. The border cities of El Paso, Laredo, Eagle Pass, and Del Rio are among the safest cities of their size in the U.S.

When President Trump came to office, immigration became a signature issue. He branded illegal immigrants as rapists, drug dealers, and criminals, expressed support for limiting legal immigration, issued the order to rescind DACA, imposed a travel ban that severely restricted travel to the U.S. for citizens of seven largely Muslim countries, and pledged to build a wall all along the U.S.-Mexico border.

I knew these positions were going to be disastrous to *La Frontera* and the rest of the country. So, I began to think of an immigration and border security solution—something I could fight for, rather than just talking about what I was against. The first step in this process was to find a willing Democrat to partner with on this difficult task.

All my Democratic colleagues with whom I consulted said the same name—Rep. Pete Aguilar (D-California). Pete and I, as well as our staffs, had months of thoughtful debates over contentious issues. We held consultations with immigration groups and experts across the political spectrum. Most of our colleagues thought it would be impossible to come up with a truly bipartisan plan, but Pete and I shared the same goal of solving an important problem. In early 2018, Pete—who had become one of my best friends in Congress—and I introduced the Uniting and Securing America (USA) Act.

Instead of sprawling legislation that tried to fix everything at once, which only drives everyone into their partisan corners, the USA Act was highly pragmatic—it was *targeted* and *bipartisan*.

With sixty co-sponsors across the political spectrum, it had four aims, all with strong support on both sides of the aisle: First, protect DACA recipients from deportation. Second, implement operational control of the border though increased manpower, technology, as well as physical barriers where it made sense. Third, fix the immigration backlog keeping families in limbo. And finally, advance reforms in Central America to address the root causes driving unlawful migration to the United States.

Of those four provisions, allowing the DACA recipients benefiting from the program at the time to remain in the U.S. and offering them a pathway to U.S. citizenship should have been the biggest no-brainer. It certainly was a big issue in Texas, which is home to more than one hundred thousand DACA recipients.

Dreamers are our classmates and our co-workers: 97 percent are in school or working. They start new businesses at a rate almost double the American public. They are paying taxes as well as purchasing homes, cars, and services from American businesses—creating jobs and contributing to our economy. During the height of COVID, an estimated two hundred thousand Dreamers worked on the frontlines fighting the pandemic.

The USA Act was also the only bipartisan bill dealing with DACA recipients that also included measures on border security. In fact, it was the first time the Congressional Hispanic Caucus had agreed to support pairing a DACA-related solution to border security. Safeguarding the homeland and limiting the flow of illicit drugs is an essential component of any immigration bill and any immigration policy, because it's critical to garnering Republican support and important to the country's security as a whole.

President Trump's approach to border security was, of course, his wall. But the smart solution to border security isn't building a thirty-foot-high concrete structure from sea-to-shining-sea. At $33 billion, that was the most expensive and least effective way to create border security. It was a third-century solution to a twenty-first-century problem. If Border Patrol takes hours to respond to certain parts of the border, then a wall is not going to prevent anyone from doing anything, since nobody will be there to apprehend someone who goes over or under the wall.

There's a notion that the people of *La Frontera* don't care about border security. That's ridiculous. For them, "border security" means "public safety." They want to keep drug mules, cartels, and human traffickers off their land. They want to be able to move back and forth across the border safely, securely, and quickly.

Effective border security should be evaluated by how much illegal drugs and immigration is being stopped rather than how many miles of wall we have built. True security can't be achieved with a one-size-fits-all solution.

Each section of the border has unique geographical, cultural, and technological challenges, and each section should be addressed with a specific approach.

At the beginning of President Biden's first term, he exacerbated a crisis at the border because he lacked a real plan. His unwillingness to clearly condemn illegal immigration encouraged illegal immigration. The crisis diverted resources from those with legitimate asylum claims and rewarded kingpin human smugglers. President Biden's own secretary of homeland security, Alejandro Mayorkas, explained that America was "on pace to encounter more individuals on the southwest border than we [had] in the last twenty years."

A physical barrier may be an effective tool in the densely populated areas where there is urban-to-urban contact, like in cities and towns. But gaining operational control of our entire southern border, meaning we know everything that crosses it, requires a smart, flexible approach based on technology and manpower, which I like to call a "Smart Wall."

The USA Act included language from a bipartisan piece of legislation I had previously introduced called the Secure Miles with All Resources and Technology (SMART) Act. The SMART Act directed the secretary of homeland security to perform a mile-by-mile examination of the border to determine the best tool needed for that section to achieve operational control of the border.

Innovative solutions to usher in a new era of border security are being deployed along portions of the border by companies like the California start-up called Anduril. The company is installing a technology-based barrier that uses day- and night-time cameras mounted on thirty-three-foot portable surveillance towers powered by solar panels and equipped with radar. The towers are networked, feeding information to an artificial-intelligence system that distinguishes among drones, human figures, animals, and vehicles, sending location and mapping information to the cell phones of U.S. patrol agents.

The system allows agents to monitor hundreds of miles and respond strategically. As an added benefit, at roughly $100,000 a mile, it costs a fraction of the $24.5 million per mile it would have cost to build a contiguous physical wall.

I first took Anduril's co-founders, Palmer Luckey and Brian Schimpf, to the border in 2017. We humped through walls of bamboo-like Carrizo cane along the Rio Grande in hundred-degree weather to witness some of the conditions that Border Patrol agents face. We talked to local law enforcement and local landowners.

I introduced Palmer and Brian to a rancher who was using do-it-yourself technology to monitor the interlopers, cartels, and drug smugglers that plagued his property. The rancher agreed to host three of Anduril's test towers, and he saw immediate results—a significant decrease of illegal activity happening on his property, and the arrests of those that continued. By the end of 2022, more than two hundred of these towers will be protecting our border and giving Border Patrol agents the intelligence they need to achieve effective border security.

Along with a DACA solution and enhanced border security, a critical component of the USA Act was aimed at fixing our broken immigration court system. Immigration courts, a branch of the Justice Department that conducts removal proceedings and adjudicates asylum claims for immigrants, are hopelessly logjammed. Between 2009 and 2019, the case backlog quadrupled. But resources to the courts have not kept pace, and the backlog continues to grow. In June 2021, there was a 1.4 million-case backlog, the highest ever.

There are too few judges for the cases flooding in. The average wait time to get in front of an immigration judge has soared to close to two years, causing people to languish, unable to earn a living or contribute to society. The USA Act required the attorney general to add 165 immigration court judges and beef up their training, including in skills like interviewing children and handling cases involving survivors of sexual assault and trafficking.

The Trump administration's inhumane family separation policy, announced in 2018, had its roots in the dysfunctional immigration court system. With epic waits for court appearances, all illegal border crossings were referred for federal criminal prosecution, leading to children being separated from their parents when their parents were sent to jail.

One night in June 2018, while I was on a layover in the Dallas airport on my way back to San Antonio from Washington, DC, I received word that the family separation policy had hit my district. Tyler Lowe, my district director, advised me that in the outskirts of El Paso at the Tornillo Port of Entry—the same port of entry we had renamed for Marcelino Serna—a makeshift tent facility to house unaccompanied minors, including those separated from their parents, was being erected.

The facility was destined to become the largest shelter for migrant children in the country, ultimately holding children who had crossed the border unaccompanied by their parents, while other facilities around the country would hold children separated from their parents.

After learning about the Tornillo facility, I switched my flight to El Paso so I could do what I usually did when there was a breaking situation—show up so I could listen and gather on-the-ground intelligence. I knew I would get questions from my constituents and the media, and I wanted to see firsthand what was happening, and how the children were being treated.

I ran into headwinds—the Department of Homeland Security wasn't approving congressional visits to the site. But I didn't take no for an answer when I was a kid, and I definitely wasn't going to take no from a department tasked with implementing a policy that went against our ideals as a nation. Besides, I knew the individual running the facility wouldn't refuse entry to a congressman if I showed up unannounced.

I arrived at the Tornillo facility a little after ten P.M., knocked on the door, and was let in. Floodlights illuminated the facility, which was composed of several tents, each one housing about twenty children and two adult chaperones. I talked with several officials overseeing the care of the kids, who explained that the biggest complaint about the facility itself they were getting from the kids was that the AC units were set too high, making them super cold.

At this point, there had been about two thousand separations at the border, and from what I had seen at Tornillo, the individuals tasked to execute a terrible policy were trying to do their jobs with humanity. But how the hell did we get to this point? Our immigration policies should reflect our country's values, and our values are not snatching children out of their mother's arms, even if that mother crossed the border illegally.

Public outrage at the policy, including among Republicans, was starting to mount until Democrats started the movement to "Defund ICE" (U.S. Immigration and Customs Enforcement). Republicans were driven away from working with Democrats when calls to abolish the agency revealed that many Democrats were more interested in grandstanding than working with Republicans on correcting an executive branch policy that many in both parties disagreed with. This hypocrisy was further illuminated when some of the most vocal Democratic representatives in Congress failed to hold the Biden administration to the same standards as the Trump administration when it came to the ongoing crisis at our border.

Our government must treat all people humanely, even ones who come here illegally.

While having more judges is a fix to an acute problem of streamlining immigration courts, the solution to the chronic problem of illegal immigration is to address the root causes of why people flee their home countries in the first place. To address this chronic issue, the USA Act provided foreign aid and economic development dollars to the countries of the "Northern Triangle"— El Salvador, Guatemala, and Honduras.

Among the poorest countries in the Western Hemisphere, the Northern Triangle nations have historically made up the vast majority of illegal immigration coming across the southern border of the U.S. Their citizens seek to escape brutal violence, lack of economic opportunity, and extreme poverty. These three evils are fueled by the lack of trust that citizens living in the Northern Triangle have in their governments, primarily due to political corruption.

In the decades following the end of World War II, the Northern Triangle served as a backdrop to the intrigues of the Cold War and had faced
decades-long civil wars. Honduras served as a staging point for the training
of the Contras to counter the USSR-backed Communists in Nicaragua, the
Sandinistas, who were trying to destabilize El Salvador and the rest of the
region. The CIA was influenced to support the overthrow of the first demo-
cratically elected government of Guatemala at the urging of the United Fruit
Company—the folks that provided the Chiquita banana to the world. Decades of conflict prevented the growth of strong legal institutions, which led
to an inability to prosecute crime and the expansion of corruption through all
levels of the government.

Corruption is politicians taking bags of money to do something or not do
something. But corruption is also a bureaucrat or low-level public official who
won't provide a public service without compensation in return. This kind of
corruption has eroded trust in all levels of the governments of the Northern
Triangle. An entrepreneur can't get a building permit unless there is a bribe. A
business can't import or export a product without paying a bribe to a customs
official. A citizen who is lost can't even get the police to give them directions
unless they pay a bribe. If the police won't give directions, then how do you
get them to prosecute a crime or prevent a murder?

In El Salvador, Guatemala, and Honduras, homicide rates are among
the highest in the world. Women and girls are in particular peril: El Salvador and Honduras have the greatest rates of murder of women and girls in
Latin America. In the 2000s, in response to the persistent violence issues, the
governments of the Northern Triangle implemented controversial anti-crime
policies, like expanding police powers and enacting harsher punishments for
gang members, that failed in their intention to reduce crime and likely indi-
rectly led to a growth in gang membership by placing an increased burden on
prisons that were already overcrowded and oftentimes run by gangs.

Imagine how bad a situation must be when you think the best option
you have is to put your family through a treacherous 2,300-mile trek with no

guarantee of success—or even survival. If we were faced with those circumstances in our country, I have no doubt we would undertake the same terrible journey if we believed it was the only way to secure our children's future.

After a trip that involved meetings with government officials, anti-crime units, and humanitarian groups throughout the Northern Triangle, it became clear that there were programs that *could* improve the underlying conditions causing the flight. Foreign aid programs that strengthen the rule of law could go a long way to fixing the root causes driving people north. For example, rebuilding police departments on the principles of community policing reestablishes trust between the community and those tasked with protecting and serving that community. Additionally, digitizing government services (like allowing citizens to pay for services online, whether it's a driver's license or a business permit) promotes transparency and reduces opportunities for corruption by expanding a citizen's access to public services. These foreign aid programs cost a fraction of what it costs the U.S. government to deal with the illegal immigration situation within our borders.

But the Trump administration went in the opposite direction and cut off aid to these countries. Instead of that approach, we need a Marshall Plan for the Northern Triangle to coordinate federal and international efforts to strengthen the rule of law and economic prosperity in Central America— much like the U.S. rebuilt the war-torn European nations after World War II.

One of the reasons for the success of the Marshall Plan was that it called for the European countries we were trying to help, to conduct a detailed self-assessment of their needs. They then made a multi-year commitment to take actions like deliver on production commitments, create internal monetary and financial stability, and reduce trade barriers.

We need this same commitment from El Salvador, Honduras, and Guatemala, as well as an agreement from them to work together as one region. With this commitment, the U.S. should develop a ten-year National Economic Security plan for the Northern Triangle that coordinates the foreign aid initiatives throughout the federal government.

It should specifically detail how the U.S. International Development Finance Corporation's plans for debt financing, equity investing, and development of investment funds will work in concert with State Department and USAID grants, while supporting the poverty-reducing investments made by the Millennium Challenge Corporation. This group is an independent agency that provides grants to countries that have been determined to have good economic policies and potential for economic growth. That ten-year plan should be developed in partnership with the ongoing efforts of American and international philanthropies operating in the Northern Triangle.

This is the kind of change Pete and I thought the USA Act could inspire.

In addition to outlining ideas on how to solve this decades-long crisis, our work had an added urgency to it. When President Trump announced he was scrapping DACA, the potential deportation clock began to tick for the young men and women already in the DACA program. Speaker Ryan promised to bring a bill up to fix the problem so there wouldn't be any unreasonable deportations. But Speaker Ryan's deadlines came and went.

Finally, in May 2018, Pete and Rep. Jeff Denham (R-California) came up with the idea of using a rare legislative tactic called a "discharge petition" to force Speaker Ryan to schedule votes on four immigration bills, including the USA Act.

If the USA Act had come up for a vote in the House, we knew we would have well over 235 votes for passage, and it likely would have won approval in the Senate. In the previous year, an earlier version of the USA Act co-sponsored by Senator John McCain (R-Arizona) had received fifty-four of the sixty votes needed for the legislation to move, and we thought we had a way to get those remaining six votes.

We introduced the petition on May 9, and to be successful we needed the signatures of 218 House members by June 12. We had thirty-four days to pull off something that had been done successfully only twenty times in more than ninety years. Assuming all 193 House Democrats supported the petition, we needed just 25 Republicans to join the rebellion. Pete Aguilar led the Democrats working on this effort, while I worked with Jeff and Carlos Curbelo (R-Florida), who were spearheading finding other Republican representatives looking for a deal.

Six days before our deadline, we had 215 signatures—three signatures shy of our goal. We had the entire Democratic Caucus signed on, save one, my good buddy Henry Cuellar (D-Texas). But he had promised me early that he would be a yes, so we just needed two Republicans.

GOP leaders, however, were also mounting an opposition. Majority Leader Kevin McCarthy (R-California) warned us that forcing a bipartisan vote on immigration would cost us the House, because conservatives would be pissed off if we saved DACA without building more wall than what the USA Act would likely produce, and also if we didn't restrict *legal* immigration. Speaker Ryan played "good cop," urging us to work within the party to find a Republican solution.

Days before the deadline, we'd turned over every rock and twisted every arm, landing on two realistic candidates: Reps. Dennis Ross (R-Florida) and my friend Dan Newhouse (R-Washington).

The day before the deadline, during a meeting with leaders of the Republican rebellion, Speaker Ryan called. If we would stop pushing Dennis and Dan, Ryan promised votes on some agriculture bills that were important not only to Dennis and Dan but to many of my colleagues in the room.

I was mortified that my battle buddies were contemplating taking Ryan's deal. We had leadership where we wanted them, and we didn't have to settle for some bullshit vote on legislation we knew would go nowhere in the Senate. But reading the room, I could tell things were not moving in the right direction.

"I'm fine with that," one member of our group finally said to Ryan.

"So am I," said another. I was the lone objection.

It was over. The discharge petition, and ultimately a vote on the USA Act, would not happen. Solving four of our biggest national security challenges failed because of some vague promise over an ag bill vote. I abruptly walked out of the meeting to save my friends from an eruption. We had come *so close.*

I often get asked if there was something I regret not doing while I was in Congress. My answer is easy—not getting the USA Act passed. Its failure reflects all the problems with Washington—appealing to the fringes rather than the middle, the lack of willingness to be honest and do the right thing, the failure to get audio and video to match, and the inability to recognize how more unites us than divides us.

Through a pragmatic idealist point of view, the issues of immigration, border security, and foreign aid could be a clarion call rather than a weapon to exacerbate political contempt. The practical reality is that our economy needs two things to keep growing: a fresh supply of people to contribute to it, and additional markets around the world to trade with it. Our economy has been successful because our country has been built on the noble principle that despite the circumstances of your birth or your position in life, you can achieve a better, richer, happier life if you work hard and obey the law. Recognizing these realities is the first step to solving these challenges, which is necessary for keeping this century the American Century. Having leaders who are willing to inspire rather than fearmonger is the subsequent step.

There are many issues we could solve with real leadership in Washington, DC. While DC has consistently shown an inability to muster the convictions to solve a problem like immigration, when it comes to another national security issue involving an opponent that is undefeated, we have to change our ways.

CHAPTER 15

PREVENT PLANET EARTH FROM
TEACHING US A TERRIBLE LESSON

Receiving my first standing ovation in the middle of a speech was unexpected. I was speaking to an audience involved in agriculture and land conservation. I clearly remember how shocked I was that a simple comment had incited such a response. All I had said was, "Climate change is real, and man is having an impact on our environment."

This is the basic fact I learned in the summer of 1996 when I studied journalism abroad in Mexico City. One morning I left my host family's home on my way to class, and everything seemed different. It was like I was walking in a different neighborhood than I had all the previous weeks. I stopped. I looked around. I tried to orient myself. *Wait a minute, are those mountains? Mexico City is surrounded by mountains?* The smog that had covered Mexico City during the duration of my stay had lifted. I was able to see the Sierra Madre mountains that encircle the city.

I didn't know anything about Mexico City before I showed up. Prior to my freshman year in college, I had only been outside of Texas three times: Alexandria, Indiana, for Grandma Alice's funeral; Langston, Oklahoma, for a high school engineering seminar; Santa Clara County, California, to visit Stanford.

I was unaware that the most populous metropolitan area in the Western Hemisphere was in the base of a massive bowl formed by the meeting of two mountain ranges. Those mountain ranges could be seen from the city on a clear day, and this was one of those rare clear days.

Mexico City had been designated in 1992 by the United Nations as "the most polluted city on the planet." Six years later, it earned the infamous honor of "the most dangerous city for children." By 2020, through herculean effort, Mexico City had dropped to 926 on the list of most polluted cities. Having traveled back to Mexico City many times since studying there, I'm amazed at how much cleaner it is.

The pollution in the '90s wasn't a naturally occurring phenomenon. It was the product of humankind. The improved air quality wasn't the result of inaction, it was the result of thinking big and taking local action.

In my speech, I was simply trying to communicate this understanding, but I realized the applause was a result of the perception that I was an outlier in the Republican Party. I'm not an outlier, most GOP members *do* believe that climate change is real and believe we need to take steps to address it. But these Republicans have been overshadowed by the outspoken GOP, elected officials, and conservative writers who have questioned inaccurately the science of climate change and humanity's role in it. The number of climate deniers who identify with the Republican brand is more than I would like, but it's far from the majority.

We need to reframe the conversation around climate change. It's not a matter of "protecting the Earth." Mother Nature is not going to lose a fight. Dealing with climate change is about humans changing our behaviors to prevent a response from Mother Nature that will ruin *us* and the rest of the biological ecosystem of which we are a part. Mother Nature is undefeated.

Biologists have determined that about 99 percent of species that have ever existed on Earth have gone extinct. While the vast majority of species died from what was essentially old age, the planet has gone through five mass extinction events. The worst of these, 250 million years ago, wiped out 96 percent of marine life existing on Earth and three of every four species on land. The Earth kept spinning on its axis and it kept circling the Sun. Our Earth is going to stay undefeated, because time is on *her* side, not ours. Planet Earth doesn't need us. We need Planet Earth.

Unfortunately, because conflict sells advertising on television and garners clicks on social media, the conversation around environmental issues is defined by the fringes—extreme environmentalists versus climate deniers. This is a dangerous choice. The question we should be asking ourselves is how we maximize human advancement while sustaining harmony with our home.

The air pollution I witnessed in Mexico City is part of a much larger crisis. Every year, more than seven million people die from air pollution. Reducing air pollution saves lives. But climate change is an existential crisis that threatens to cause the sixth mass extinction, extreme weather events (which we're seeing already), widespread hunger, and mass migration. An overabundance of carbon dioxide (CO_2) in the air is exacerbating the warming of the Earth. Carbon dioxide helps our planet hold the energy from the sun so that it doesn't escape back into space. Plants take in CO_2 and give away oxygen, which we breathe in then exhale CO_2. A circle of life. Once a carbon dioxide molecule escapes into the atmosphere, it can hang around for hundreds of years.

When this cycle of carbon outputs and carbon absorption is balanced, we are all good. However, the Industrial Revolution began to affect this balance, and this imbalance has only been exacerbated in recent history. More than half of all the industrial carbon dioxide emissions released into the atmosphere since the Industrial Revolution have occurred in close to the last thirty-five years. And we can't deny that much of it is the result of human activities, such as how we make things, power things, and grow things.

I think of it this way. We have a 10-gallon barrel catching water from a faucet. There is already 9 gallons of water in this barrel, and the goal is to not let it overflow. We can address this problem two ways: ensure the least amount of water goes into the barrel, as well as figure out how to get water out of the barrel.

In this metaphor, what we do in the present and the future to address CO_2 and other greenhouse gas emissions is addressing the water going into the barrel. How we absorb the CO_2 already in the atmosphere is dealing with the water already in the barrel. The result of water overflowing? More and worse human calamity due to heat waves, droughts, wildfires, famines, and flooding.

Preventing further provocations of planet Earth is a balancing act, and our challenge is staggering. According to the United Nation's Intergovernmental Panel on Climate Change, net human-caused emissions of carbon dioxide worldwide have to fall by 45 percent from 2010 levels by 2030 and reach *net zero* by around 2050 to prevent a global catastrophe.

Here is what will happen if we stay on our current trajectory and allow global temperatures to increase 1 or 2 degrees Celsius (this is 1.8 to 3.6 degrees Fahrenheit). Storms will get worse. Hurricanes and floods will destroy homes, roads, and critical infrastructure that took time to build and will take even longer to rebuild. While some places will see more rain, other places will experience worse drought. When air gets hotter, it sucks up more water from soil and plants. Droughts will threaten water supplies, severely reducing drinking water and irrigation of crops responsible for feeding and hydrating tens of millions of Americans.

Drying plants and trees makes everything more prone to burning, so we will see more fires. While some places are getting drier and others are burning more, our coasts will witness rising sea levels. The extra heat caused by increased CO_2 will restrict the livable habitat of plants and animals, leading to a reduction in crop yields and animals that produce less milk and live shorter lives, which ultimately drives up prices of food at the grocery store.

Dealing with COVID-19 shows us how not to deal with climate change. The economic destruction brought on by a global economic standstill reduced greenhouse gas emissions by less than 10 percent (some estimates suggest around 5 percent), but hundreds of millions of people lost their jobs and hundreds of thousands of businesses failed.

COVID-19 showed us that we can't close down the economy. To combat climate change, we must *modernize* our economies. We need governments, trade alliances, and innovators to make clean technologies the most affordable option for continued human advancement, and we need a market that encourages the development of tools we don't yet have or are too expensive today. This is how we decarbonize to the extent that we can in the most economically responsible way to achieve "net zero" emissions or "carbon neutral"—a state where emissions are balanced by absorbing an equivalent amount from the atmosphere.

Net zero versus zero emissions is a big difference. Having 100 percent of our energy needs coming from renewables is impossible, especially in the transportation sector, based on our current understanding of science. Fossil fuels will still play a role in our world, and the oil and natural gas boom in places like my home state of Texas has led to American energy independence. Energy independence is an important tool in foreign policy, and innovation in the oil and gas sector has led to the use of artificial intelligence to drilling less wells, using no fresh water, and storing the results of carbon capture.

Additionally, we still have 940 million of the least of our brothers and sisters around the world who still don't have access to electricity and three billion without access to clean cooking.

When I speak to schools, I show pictures from my travels around the world, and the last image I display is a picture of a traditional village in South Asia. I ask the kids what's missing from the picture. Nobody guesses correctly, and I reveal the answer is no power lines, meaning no electricity. This always elicits cries from the audience: "No Xbox!" then "No TV!"

I always add: "What about no refrigerator?" The room goes silent because these kids' minds are blown, having never considered a life without something we accept as a basic necessity. Having a refrigerator and lights at night dramatically improves quality of life across the globe, and people are in dire need of affordable energy right now—not just in 2050.

We know which industries, like the transportation sector, need to be transformed. The U.S. Environmental Protection Agency has broken down the five industries that produce greenhouse gas emissions: transportation

(29%), electricity production (25%), industry (23%), commercial/residential (13%), and agriculture (10%). But this has to be a partnership between government and the private sector—either one can't do it alone.

We know what tools we have in our tool kit—tools like renewables (wind, solar, and nuclear), efficiency measures, reforestation, afforestation (planting trees in an area where there was never a forest). We know some of the tools we need to develop—carbon capture and energy storage technologies. But we must remember the United States is not operating in a vacuum.

In 2019, nearly 90 percent of the two hundred most polluted cities in the world were in China and India. China was the largest emitter of greenhouse gas emissions in 2018, responsible for 28 percent of global emissions. The United States was second, with responsibility for 15 percent. But another quarter of greenhouse gas emissions was made up by the European Union nations (13%), India (7%), and Russia (5%).

The world must work together on this shared problem through international agreements that make sense. There has been a lot of debate around the Paris Climate Accord. It is a legally binding international treaty adopted by more than 190 world leaders in Paris that set specific targets for limiting global warming to achieve a climate neutral world by mid-century. President Obama signed it, President Trump withdrew from it, and President Biden got back into it. The international community has criticized America for its inconsistency, but this is what happens when international agreements are joined through executive action rather than Senate approval. Regardless, the Paris Accord allows the Chinese, the Russians, and the Indians to produce *more* carbon dioxide emissions.

Instead of letting countries like China, Russia, and India produce more CO_2, we should be using trade deals and foreign aid to help countries modernize their economies faster than what the rest of the industrialized world has done so they don't have to go through a period of increased CO_2 production. Parts of India where they still burn dung for heat don't have to transition to electricity powered by coal like many in the industrialized world did. With the help of the international community they can transition to electricity provided by natural gas with carbon capture or nuclear energy.

Some countries are turning to nuclear power as a path to a low-carbon future. So let's ensure they do it with American-developed technology. Our success in the commercial nuclear energy sector not only grows the largest carbon-free source of energy in the U.S. but also enables us to stop the spread of nuclear weapons. We can't solve climate change without nuclear power, so proposals like the Green New Deal are dead on arrival if nuclear power is excluded as a solution.

While authoritarian regimes like China and Russia are increasing their nuclear energy capabilities, we are seeing trends where America's use of nuclear energy is on the decline. A viable commercial nuclear energy industry in the United States is a national security imperative.

Preventing our planet from ruining us can't be accomplished by national governments alone. We need to see a boost in climate cooperation at subnational levels—states, counties, and cities. Subnational governments and local stakeholders should further their local-level cooperation with non-state actors and the private sector—from investing in smarter energy infrastructure to increasing the use of public transportation and microtransit.

But stopping planet Earth from teaching us a lesson is going to be hard. An increase in deaths around the world may not be enough to convince people that climate change is real and action is urgently needed, especially if the deaths climb gradually rather than suddenly and dramatically.

Even the significant deaths resulting from COVID-19 were met by a surprising callousness by much of our population. Some political leaders minimized the lethality of the disease and used it to appeal to their fringes rather than coming together to confront the foe. Unfortunately, some among us may react to climate change as we did to the pandemic deaths: by simply learning to live with it, especially since those most harmed by climate change are people who inhabit the poorest, hottest parts of the world. Sadly, they are the ones least responsible for causing it.

Climate change is one of the most urgent issues confronting us. Failing to act will result in disaster, and it's going to take all of us—citizens, government, industry—to develop creative, doable solutions that keep our country economically healthy while addressing this existential crisis.

That means, even in these times of uncommon partisanship, it is especially important to find common ground. When it comes to the environment, we need to all recognize we live in a city surrounded by mountains.

PART IV

ENEMIES SHOULD FEAR US, FRIENDS SHOULD LOVE US

CHAPTER 16

UNDERSTAND THE REAL SOURCE OF AMERICAN POWER

We were halfway to Islamabad on a Chinook helicopter when the orphan I was holding laid her head on my shoulder and relaxed. It was October 2005, my fifth year in the CIA, and I was leading an expedition to Azad Kashmir—the Pakistani-administered portion of the region over which India and Pakistan have been fighting since 1947. While considered one of the most beautiful parts of the subcontinent, it is also home to Pakistani terrorist groups like Lashkar-e-Taiba ("Army of the Good") and Jaish-e Mohammed ("The Army of Mohammed"), which prevented few Westerners, let alone government officials, from traveling there.

The area was suffering from the aftermath of a devastating earthquake that claimed the lives of eighty thousand people. Ryan Crocker, the U.S. ambassador to Pakistan, wanted updates on how the U.S. government could aid the Pakistanis as they grappled with the disaster. Three colleagues and I loaded up an armored SUV and made the journey from Islamabad to Muzaffarabad, the capital of Azad Kashmir.

The destruction was unbelievable. The number of people displaced was staggering. It was the height of winter, falling to 20 degrees below zero at night. Following our first reports, the ambassador directed the U.S. military to provide helicopters to help move the inhabitants of entire villages to safety, and we were helping direct the airlift.

We were packing CH-47 Chinook helicopters with one hundred to one hundred fifty people each trip. On day three or four of our expedition, I was about to jump on one of these helicopters to take me back to Islamabad to brief Ambassador Crocker when we got a report that a village had been without food, running water, shelter, and electricity since the earthquake. We decided to make an additional stop.

As we landed, the crew slung open the bay doors of the helicopter and folks began pouring in. The officer manning the door was in full flight gear, which made him look like he was from outer space. A little girl, who couldn't have been more than five or six years old and had lost both her parents in the earthquake, saw this whole scene and froze in fear. She started crying and refused to get on the helicopter.

A village elder picked her up and thrust her into my arms. I held her tight while gripping a hand strap with the other hand. With a throaty roar, the massive aircraft took off. About fifteen minutes before arriving in Islamabad, the little girl settled down and rested in my arms.

When we reached our destination, everyone piled out. I put the little girl down, and she started to walk away. After taking a few steps, she whipped around, ran back to me, and gave me the biggest hug I've ever gotten in my life. She then walked over to the crewman who she first thought was from outer space and kissed him on the hand. He patted her on the head and gave her a thumbs-up. She smiled real big, returned the gesture, then raced off.

The face of that little girl is forever seared into my brain. What we did over those few days in those Himalayan mountains is an example of how America is one of the few countries with the resources and willingness to help those in need, even if they are seven thousand miles away. America has become a world power not because of what we have *taken*, but because of what we have *given*.

We have become a world power not just by helping a village respond to a disaster, or helping countries rebuild after a world war. We have become a world power by being an example of how to turn values into reality. The source of American power is our *values*. We have shown the world for well over two hundred years that a government's legitimacy and ability to use the powers of the state flows from the consent of the governed. "We the people" are sovereign. Not the government. After the United States, it took more than sixty years for the next country, Switzerland, to attempt this experiment in democracy. Only fourteen countries have been practicing democracy for more than a century.

We take being a democracy for granted. Since most Americans only have experience with democracy, the idea that other forms of government exist is such a foreign thought experiment that it's not even contemplated with any seriousness. But taking democracy for granted is especially dangerous at a time when around the world it's in retreat and many societies are doubting whether a democracy is the most logical way to ensure prosperity for a people.

Freedom House, established in 1941 to support and defend democracy around the world, has been producing an annual report for almost fifty years assessing the condition of political rights and civil liberties in 195 countries and fifteen territories. In its *Freedom in the World Report* covering 2020, it outlined how 2020 marked the fifteenth year of decline of global freedom and the greatest net decrease in freedom over the last fifteen years.

This decline has been fueled by the claims of those who are against freedom that democracy is incapable of addressing the needs of the people. We have to push back on this narrative because democracy keeps citizens safer by putting limits on the power of the government and allowing citizens to choose their own leaders. Authoritarian leaders and regimes demanding blind submission to authority and attacking democratic institutions, like voting laws and the protection of minority rights, claim to act in the national interest, but in reality are trying to stay in power indefinitely. If America is not making the case for democracy, who will? America's matching of its audio and video is the best way to demonstrate to the world and its own people how democracy makes citizens safer, happier, more financially secure, and better able to determine what happens in their society.

The American experiment has been dominated by our quest to ensure our government encourages and protects, rather than restricts our rights to life, liberty, and the pursuit of happiness. This endeavor has made freedom, opportunity, and growth core American values. These values have guided our domestic policy. Our foreign policy should, first, extend the inalienable rights of our citizens, and second, strengthen these rights for all humanity. We can accomplish this through a foreign policy governed by achieving a state of affairs where our enemies fear us, and our friends love us.

Despite going through a recent period when American leadership failed to reflect American values and the U.S. image plummeted internationally, there are millions of people around the world who still believe that America is the land of the free and the home of the brave. Over the long arc of our history, we have consistently striven to achieve our foundational idea that all of us are created equal and endowed with unalienable rights.

Foreign policy and national security strategy are most effective when they are based on clearly articulated national interests. They're even more effective when those national interests are reflections of national *values*.

Since 1987, each president is required to submit a report on his National Security Strategy to Congress. These documents define the U.S.'s national interests, articulate national security objectives, outline obstacles to achieving these objectives, and enumerate a strategy to achieve these objectives while dealing with the threats we face.

What's surprising is that, despite the vast political divides that have erupted in this country, the National Security Strategy Reports' explanation of U.S. national interests have stayed largely the same, no matter who was president, from Ronald Reagan to Joe Biden.

Each report has explained that the U.S. seeks:

- The survival of the U.S., our allies, and our partners,
- A healthy and growing economy,

- A rules-based international order advanced by U.S. leadership,
- The growth of free markets, acceptance of the rule of law, and re-
  spect for human rights, and
- A stable and secure world.

As a CIA officer for nine years, I was on the frontlines of American conflicts in the Middle East and Southeast Asia in the 2000s, a time when our foreign policy was being reshaped and put to the test. I began my move from my hometown of San Antonio to the Washington, DC, area on October 12, 2000—the day that Al-Qa'ida attacked the USS *Cole*, a Navy missile destroyer being refueled in the Yemeni port city of Aden. Just a few weeks later I was detailed to the office responsible for tracking down the perpetrators.

The end of my tenure for the CIA was in Kabul, Afghanistan, just six months before the Camp Chapman attack—the most lethal attack against the CIA in more than a quarter of a century.

In all my work, I dealt with our adversaries up close and personal. I lived in places where I witnessed the consequences of corrupt governments, unaccountable political leaders, weak or nonexistent justice systems, and few fundamental rights. And while defending companies from cyberattacks while at the cybersecurity firm FusionX, I saw our opponents get more technologically advanced. In Congress, I observed how our rivals' attempts to undermine our power have grown in size and scope.

Through all of these experiences, I came to one conclusion: Our enemies are as determined as ever to undermine the peace and prosperity American leadership has fostered since World War II.

U.S. economic and military dominance is no longer guaranteed. The increasing strength of our adversaries, primarily a resurgent China, and the degradation of the ability of U.S. leaders to get things done at home, jeopardize America's primacy in the international order.

General Jim Mattis put it in stark terms in 2013. He warned that the failure of political leaders to work together is a risk to U.S. security.

"The dysfunction in Washington right now shows a country unable to govern itself," he said in a speech. "And [a functioning political system] is worth more than ten battleships to us."

When I was in the CIA, I viewed China as a regional powerhouse rather than a global superpower. For more than forty years, the U.S. has encouraged China to develop its own economy and take its place alongside the U.S. as a central player on the world stage. But while attending a 2018 HPSCI public hearing on China, I learned they don't want to join us. They want to replace us.

One of the witnesses for this hearing was Michael Pillsbury, a former Senate staffer and Department of Defense official and director for Chinese Strategy at the Hudson Institute, a Washington, DC–based think tank.

Pillsbury provided stunning insights into China's not-so-secret strategy to replace America as the global hegemon. He talked about the Made in China 2025 Plan—the Chinese government's ten-year plan, released in 2015—to update China's manufacturing base by rapidly developing ten high-tech industries. The plan set specific targets: By 2025, China would achieve 70 percent self-sufficiency in high-tech industries. And by 2049—the hundredth anniversary of the founding of the People's Republic of China—it "seeks a dominant position in global markets," Pillsbury said.

His statements weren't his opinion or conjecture. It was what the Chinese government *said about themselves.* After the hearing, I read Pillsbury's book, *The Hundred-Year Marathon,* and digested passages like, "Chinese leaders have persuaded many in the West to believe that China's rise will be peaceful and will not come at other's expense, even while they adhere to a strategy that fundamentally rejects this."

Every president since Nixon—except for President Trump—has held the belief that China is going to participate in the international order as an honest broker. But China's leadership has no interest in taking on that role. For years it has threatened global supply chains, stolen American intellectual property, and economically bullied smaller countries. In November 2018, a bipartisan commission tasked by Congress to review America's National Defense Strategy issued a report that determined that the U.S. "might struggle to win, or might lose, a war against China or Russia."

But we are in uncharted territory. This New Cold War is occurring with a "frenemy." The economies of the U.S. and China are intertwined in a way we never were with the former USSR or Russia. China is a major customer for U.S. businesses, and it is integral to the supply chains of American industry. Despite these interconnections, the government of China is absolutely an adversary. We must coexist, but from a position of strength.

This power competition with China is happening at a time when technological change is affecting all domains of conflict—land, air, sea, space, and cyberspace. We are at the beginning of the Fourth Industrial Revolution, where technological change over the next thirty years is going to make the advancements over the last thirty years look insignificant.

And with technological change comes economic power to those who can seize the lead. Largely due to its growing technological might, China is expected to become the world's largest economy by mid-century, while the U.S. will have sunk to third place in global GDP ranking, behind India. This has enormous implications for our foreign policy and our national security. Those who write the checks write the rules.

Technological change in this rapidly advancing landscape has brought another significant global threat to U.S. national security: the global pandemic of misinformation, disinformation, and lies that travel faster than the truth. In 1787, British dramatist Thomas Francklin wrote, "Falsehood will fly, as it were, on the wings of the wind, and carry its tales to every corner of the earth; whilst truth lags behind; her steps, though sure, are slow and solemn, and she has neither vigor nor activity enough to pursue and overtake her enemy." While this was true more than two hundred and thirty years ago, it is especially accurate in the twenty-first century.

One 2018 study at MIT's Media Lab of the spread of false and true news stories circulated on Twitter found that falsehoods traveled "significantly farther, faster, deeper, and more broadly than the truth." This infodemic is fueling domestic terrorism and radicalizing elements of societies across the globe. *Truth Decay*, a book from the Rand Corporation, points out that the infodemic is "eroding civil discourse, causing political paralysis at the federal level, increasing alienation and disengagement within the electorate, and increasing uncertainty in national policy that is having domestic and diplomatic implications."

The ability to easily weaponize information coupled with game-changing technologies—like AI bots that can proliferate falsehoods and misinformation globally in nanoseconds—getting more powerful and cheaper, have developed into a danger to U.S. national security. Asymmetric dangers— threats not originating from the governments of nation-states like terrorists, nuclear weapons proliferators, and cyber criminals—are metastasizing. These entities are trying to destabilize America and disrupt the international order—the rules, norms, and multilateral institutions that govern the interactions between countries on the international stage.

The growth of these persistent asymmetric threats is increasing concerns from our allies about America's commitment to leading an international order that is being challenged by rogue nations who believe the international order is against their interests.

Edward Fishman, a former U.S. Department of State official and nonresident senior fellow at the Atlantic Council, has explained that "International orders seldom change in noticeable ways. Just as Rome wasn't built in a day, Pax Romana was not a passing phase: it persisted for centuries." He points out that the world order resulting from the 1815 Congress of Vienna, which remade Europe after the fall of Napoleon, didn't fully unravel until the outbreak of World War I in 1914. "But at rare moments," Fishman adds, "confidence in the old order collapses and humanity is left with a vacuum. It is during these times that new orders are born."

One of the rules of power is that if there is a power vacuum, it will get filled. Since President Reagan, one of the recurring national interests of America has been a rules-based international order advanced by U.S. leadership.

Doubt in America's commitment to international leadership is fueling rogue nations' opposition to the international system they believe doesn't and won't benefit them. If North Korean leader Kim Jong-Un believes that the only way to hold on to power in the current international system is to develop intercontinental ballistic missiles with the ability to reach the U.S. mainland with a nuclear weapon, then he's going to pursue nuclear weapons.

Syrian President Bashar al-Assad believes that draconian measures, like killing half a million of this own people, are the way to remain in power in this international order.

I'm not advocating for regime change in these countries by the United States. But until rogue nations realize that their participation in the international order is to their benefit, then they will continue their negative behavior. This realization can only come through pressure from the rest of the world *and* an entirely new generation of leaders, supported by populations desiring that current leaders change their ways, in these rogue countries.

Values plus national interests and a recognition of the threats we face shape the objectives of our national security strategy:

- Prevent a catastrophic attack against the U.S. homeland,
- Limit the security consequences from failing states,
- Stop the proliferation of disinformation,
- Cease the spread of weapons of mass destruction (chemical, biological, and nuclear),
- Ensure American energy independence while getting the world to commit to addressing climate change,
- Avoid a global economic crisis, and
- Prevent global infectious diseases from debilitating the world.

We can boil down all these objectives into that simple governing philosophy—our enemies should fear us, and our friends should love us. To enact this philosophy and achieve these national objectives, most national security *practitioners* would say we have four tools to do so. I would add a fifth element to these levers of national power, known by the acronym of DIME: Diplomacy (embassies, ambassadors, treaties), Intelligence/Information (agencies like the CIA, the NSA, as well as public diplomacy), Military (guns and tanks), and Economic (foreign aid, bilateral trade agreements, and multilateral pacts like the World Trade Organization).

The fifth lever I would add is C for Cyber. Cyberspace is a domain, just like air, land, sea, and space. Cyberspace as a domain of conflict is man-made, growing at an exponential rate and contested. The tools, tactics, techniques, and procedures used in the digital world are unique and distinct, and a skilled practitioner is required for their use. To exercise national power effectively, the state needs to understand what's happening, make a decision on what to do, and take action that results in the desired effect. Since the information revolution, all three of these activities are increasingly being affected by, or happening in, cyberspace. We fight our enemies in the air. We fight them on land, we fight them on the seas and in space, and we are currently fighting them in cyberspace.

The Military and Intelligence levers of national power get the most focus, but as Ambassador Crocker once told me: "If we have more wingtips and pumps on the ground, we can prevent the need for boots on the ground." Meaning, if you have more diplomats or distribution of foreign aid, like USAID, then this "soft power" prevents the need for "hard power"—the most expensive tool in our tool kit—our military.

The U.S. became a true global superpower when we joined the Allies and won World War II, then helped rebuild Europe from the ashes. We stood up to despots and tyrants and helped our friends stand on their own. We didn't take spoils after that war, but instead gave Europe a hand. We saw the number of democracies in the world quadruple from 1945 to 1989, and then continue to increase dramatically after America and our Allies were successful in bringing down the Iron Curtain.

This made the middle of the twentieth century the beginning of Pax Americana. Our foreign policy was based on our values, which not only led to economic prosperity in America, but it also led to more of humankind being able to enjoy the rights that America proved were inalienable.

If we want this long peace—where the United States is the world's dominant economic and military power—to continue through the twenty-first century, then we need a national security strategy based on a doctrine that has two simple parts that reflect how to treat others.

CHAPTER 17

BE TOUGH WITH TOUGH GUYS

Almost all 450 seats in the Congressional Theatre in the Capitol Visitor Center were taken—a first. The facility was uncharacteristically quiet before the all-Congress briefing by Secretary of State John Kerry, Energy Secretary Ernie Moniz, and Norman Roule, the National Intelligence Manager for Iran. It was 2015, and they were briefing us on the infamous Iran Deal that President Obama was about to sign.

In the briefing, Secretary Kerry was getting all the attention from my colleagues, but to me, the most important person on stage was Norman Roule—whom I had known as Norm. As the National Intelligence Manager for Iran, he oversaw all aspects of our national intelligence policy and activities regarding Iran, but I knew him because we had served together in the CIA.

Norm had been a brilliant case officer, incredibly successful at recruiting spies, and was the agency's foremost Iran expert. In short, a legend. I couldn't think of anyone who understood Iran better.

When I was recognized for my few minutes of questions, I directed my inquires at Norm.

"Norm, it looks like you lost weight since I saw you last."

"Thanks for noticing. It's good to see you, Will."

"My first question for you, Norm, is this. Has the Iranian government ever lied to or misled the IAEA?" I was referring to the International Atomic Energy Agency, the UN's global atomic watchdog.

Norm nodded. His reply was unequivocal. "Yes, a number of times."

I continued. "Has the Iranian government ever lied to or misled the Security Council of the UN?"

Again, Norm briskly nodded. "Multiple times. They did it recently."

"Is the Iranian government supporting groups that are killing Americans, right now in places like Iraq?" I asked.

"Yes. Absolutely," he said. This admission coming from President Obama's senior-most adviser on national intelligence matters concerning Iran.

My final question: "Can we trust the Iranian government?"

Norm didn't hesitate. "No."

Norm's blunt responses still hold true. Understanding that the Iranian government has been lying to us for more than forty years and has no intention of changing must be key to any engagements we have with them. The government of Iran has and always will act like a tough guy. We should be tough in response.

The first plank in our national security strategy should focus on being tough with tough guys. Being tough means delivering consequences in response to negative behavior that goes against the international order. When China agreed to join the World Trade Organization, they agreed to follow a certain set of rules. So when China breaks the rules, there should be consequences. If Russia violates the Law of War and invades Georgia and Ukraine, then there should be consequences. If there are not consequences to negative behavior, then negative behavior will continue.

The second part of being tough is a commitment to deterrence—being so clearly capable of winning a fight that an adversary decides against using violence to get its way. This means we must constantly be seeking a clear competitive advantage to impose consequences in whatever domain of conflict—land, air, sea, space, or cyberspace—is being employed, and maintain our military as the most dominant fighting force in the world. Our adversaries should fear us.

At the same time, we should be strengthening alliances with our friends, building on existing coalitions and making new alliances when needed—be nice with nice guys. Military power combined with soft power, economic and development aid, can improve the lives of people around the world.

To be tough with tough guys or nice with nice guys, we need a clear understanding of who are our allies and who are our adversaries.

Presidents Trump and Obama got this concept mixed up. The Trump administration, at times, treated Mexico, Canada, South Korea, and Japan as enemies and Russia and North Korea as friends. The Obama administration treated Israel as an adversary and Iran as an ally.

The government of Iran has been at war with the U.S. since it stormed our embassy in Tehran and held fifty-two Americans hostage for 444 days. It is still the world's top state sponsor of terrorism and has killed hundreds of thousands of people, including U.S. troops and more than 1,500 of its own people for peacefully protesting.

The Iranian regime, not the U.S., is responsible for escalating tensions around the world. And President Obama's 2015 Iran nuclear deal—under which Tehran claimed it would accept limits on its nuclear program in exchange for sanctions relief—failed to realize this fact. The Obama administration treated Iran like a victim instead of the culprit.

The Iranian economy was on its knees, which would have forced the Iranian theocracy to change its nefarious ways. However, the Iran deal helped prop up the tyrannical regime by giving it billions of dollars of aid at the beginning of the deal rather than after Iran met stringent requirements on compliance with international norms on nuclear weapons. Additionally, the deal had nothing in it about the Iranian government stopping its support to terrorism. By trying to revive the Iran deal as it was written under President Obama, President Biden is aiming to repeat history.

Despite having signed a deal, the Iranian government has never stopped its drive to.produce nuclear weapons. In 2018, the Israeli government provided intelligence gathered from inside Iran whose authenticity was verified by the U.S. intelligence community that conclusively proved that Iran had been lying about having a nuclear weapons program.

The end goal with the government of Iran is not just signing *any* deal. The end goal is getting Iran to rejoin the international community by undertaking a few simple actions: stop killing American citizens and allies; stop lying about its nuclear program; stop using terrorism and coercion to prevent the people of Iraq, Yemen, Lebanon, and Afghanistan from choosing their future; and stop murdering its own citizens.

Another perennial tough guy is Russia. Since the crumbling of the Berlin Wall in 1989 that precipitated the fall of Communism in central and eastern Europe, Russia has stopped being the other pole in a bipolar world. However, it has become a kleptocracy run by a dictator who looted his way to power, operates like a regional thug, and anointed himself the leader of a movement to fight a decadent West. Vladimir Putin is here to stay and won't end his assault on Western democracy and multilateral institutions anytime soon.

While possessing nuclear weapons and cyber tools, Putin's Russia is trying to reestablish the territorial integrity of the USSR. Its ongoing cyber warfare continues to disrupt the politics, governments, and economies of neighboring states. Russia's continued aggression toward its neighbors, including Ukraine and Georgia, has served as a destabilizing force in Europe. Its autocratic regime, humanitarian abuses, and pervasive culture of corruption have rotted the Russian government to its core.

Presidents George W. Bush, Obama, and Trump all tried to "reset" relations with Russia. But it didn't work. Without radically new leadership that rejects Putin's dictatorial ways, Russia isn't going to change, and it has no interest in being a productive member of the global community. The West needs to penetrate Russian society with Western ideas and values that could provoke challenges to the regime. One way to do this is to help former Soviet republics like Moldova, Georgia, and Ukraine be firmly committed to and welcomed inside the Western alliance and to support credible journalists who are countering Russian disinformation inside these countries as well as those facing the risks of operating in Russia.

A tough guy who we should be even tougher with is Syrian President Bashar al-Assad. In the late '90s, foreign policy observers hoped the Western-educated ophthalmologist would usher in democratic reforms in Syria when he succeeded his father as president. But Assad's murder of half a million of his own people shows his blatant disregard for human life. A peaceful, prosperous Syria can only exist with a government in place that does not include al-Assad, who has conducted a systemic genocide against his own people.

Resetting relationships with tough guys like Assad is an impossible task because normalizing relations with such a leader would validate the use of sadistic behavior. We saw this phenomenon in 1938 when Britain and France thought the Munich Agreement, which gave legitimacy to Hitler's annexation of the German-speaking region of Czechoslovakia, would stop Hitler's reign of terror against Germany's neighbors. We've now seen this play out similarly in recent times with Assad. Appeasing our adversaries will only make future conflict and bloodshed more likely.

The kind of fear that we want to instill in our enemies is the realization that we will deliver consequences for negative behavior, not reward it. This means we can't make a threat that we aren't willing to follow through with. President Trump's response to the Iranian Quds Force General Qasem Soleimani is probably the best example of appropriately following through on consequences. President Obama's infamous unwillingness to enforce his own red line in Syria—Assad's use of chemical weapons against his own people—is the worst example.

In August 2012, President Obama said the use of chemical weapons by Syrian leader Bashar al-Assad would cross his "red line." A year later, Syrian forces killed more than 1,400 people with sarin gas, a lethal chemical weapon that leads to a horrifying death. Obama failed to respond. He struck a deal with Russia to destroy six hundred metric tons of Syria's weapons stockpile. But that didn't stop al-Assad. He continued to use chemicals on his own people: Between 2013 and 2018, the Syrian regime was responsible for the majority of eighty-five chemical attacks in the country.

In Iran, Qasem Soleimani's Quds Force was roughly equivalent to U.S. Special Forces. He oversaw the equipping and training of proxy militias to attack U.S. military forces. These extremist fighters have killed more than six hundred American soldiers. Within Iran, the Quds Force worked with the Ayatollah to suppress freedom, imprison those who speak out against the government, and kill innocent protesters in their own streets.

In 2020, President Trump had determined that the U.S. would retaliate against Iran if its aggression resulted in the deaths of Americans. Iranian-backed militias attacked American troops in northern Iraq, killing an American civilian contractor and several U.S. service members, and attempted to storm our embassy in Baghdad. Soleimani's cumulative actions brought about the drone strike that killed him.

Soleimani headed the most dangerous and well-armed terrorist organization in the world, and his death removed a major terrorist leader from the battlefield. Taking him out was an appropriate response after all the hostile acts the Iranian government and its proxies have committed against the United States.

At the time of the attack on Soleimani, some of my Democratic colleagues claimed President Trump's decision to remove him was a dangerous one, making us less secure. But the reality was the opposite. President Trump followed through on his warning, making it clear to our adversaries that the U.S. was to be taken seriously, and the Iranian government became more cautious in its military operations for the remainder of Trump's term.

Being tough with tough guys includes non-state actors. Since 9/11, the U.S. government has gotten effective at delivering consequences to terrorist organizations. The reason why terrorist groups like al-Qa'ida and ISIS are shells of their former selves is because the U.S. intelligence community has gotten better at collecting intelligence on the plans and intentions of these groups. This increase in intelligence production has made the U.S. military more efficient in destroying terrorist networks.

A similar level of focus needs to be placed on transnational criminal organizations such as drug traffickers, cartels, human smugglers, and human traffickers.

Every year, Americans spend nearly $150 billion on illegal drugs, much of which are illegally smuggled in. To give some comparison of how large that number is, Starbucks' yearly revenue is about $23 billion, and McDonald's takes in close to $30 billion a year. In other words, the value of illegal drugs sold in the U.S. is close to triple the value of all those venti lattes and Big Macs.

Human traffickers enact a devastating toll on hundreds of thousands of men, women, and children coming across our borders, including forced labor in the sex trade, domestic servitude, and working under prison-like conditions. Human smuggling is slightly different; it is the illegal transport of someone across an international border with their consent following payment. Both are sources of great suffering and danger.

The United Nations has declared human trafficking and smuggling among the fastest-growing international crimes. It's tough to put precise numbers on the extent, but the U.S. Department of Justice estimates that between 800,000 to 900,000 people are trafficked globally each year, with up to 18,500 trafficked into the U.S. Figures on the volume of human smuggling are also hard to come by, but it is believed that smuggling into North America generates close to $7 billion a year in revenue for smugglers.

Traffickers in people, human smugglers, and drug trafficking organizations are benefiting from the humanitarian crisis on our southern border, and they should receive the same level of focus that the U.S. government puts on foreign terrorist organizations. The individuals and organizations taking advantage of human suffering endanger the security of the United States and the entire Western Hemisphere. Understanding and disabling these smuggling and trafficking networks should be a national intelligence priority.

These transnational criminal organizations are different from terrorist groups. A terrorist is generally looking to conduct one operation, a suicide attack, and that terrorist may be by himself or operating with a handful of individuals and only need a modicum of supplies. There is no public element of a terrorist organization. Their recruiting, training, and plans are secret.

Kingpin human smugglers, cartels, and drug trafficking organizations have to replicate operations over and over and are literally moving tons of product. A human smuggler has to promote his or her services. They have to notify their clients where to meet to start their journey and they need an infrastructure of drivers, safehouses, and guides. The drug trafficking industry has manufacturers, wholesalers, retailers, transportation infrastructure, and security organizations. Because of the number of moving parts within illicit trafficking networks, the surface area of attack (the various points at which an intelligence organization can focus its efforts) is much larger than that of terrorist organizations.

But we aren't using our intelligence resources in the same way against illicit trafficking as we are terrorism. While I was in Congress, I partnered with another former CIA officer turned member of Congress, Rep. Abigail Spanberger (D-Virginia), to try to address this issue with the Trafficking and Smuggling Intelligence Act of 2019, signed into law by President Trump. This bill required the director of national intelligence to produce regular assessments based on intelligence collection of drug smuggling and human trafficking in the Northern Triangle and Mexico and review the current intelligence operations in the region. The first assessment was conducted before I left Congress.

Almost a quarter of the way through the twenty-first century, we should have been able to eliminate human trafficking, which is modern-day slavery. But being connected to the U.S. intelligence community for more than two decades, I've learned the world is still a dangerous place filled with dangerous people. Whether it's international criminal organizations, non-state actors, rogue nations, or terrorists, there are plenty of bad actors who will continue to prey on the weak and take advantage of the helpless. While pragmatic idealism doesn't mean the U.S. should be the policeman of the world, it does mean we must realize that in this interconnected world, a problem allowed to fester abroad will eventually touch us here at home.

Being tough with tough guys will make our enemies fear us, but so will having a posse. This reality is what should inform the second part of our doctrine governing our national security strategy. It's a concept whose value I recognized on the day the U.S. Air Force began bombing Taliban-controlled Afghanistan.

CHAPTER 18

BE NICE WITH NICE GUYS

When the senior special operations command officer handed me a thumb drive after explaining its contents, I asked "What's a 'lat long'?" I thought it was a reasonable question. I was halfway through a twelve-hour shift at the Counterterrorism Center Special Operations Division (CTC/SO) in the basement of the Old Headquarters Building at CIA's campus in Langley, Virginia.

"You better figure that out real quick, kid," he snapped, "because those are the locations we are going to start bombing in a few hours."

I was still a trainee. I hadn't even gone to the Farm (the CIA training facility for the National Clandestine Service) yet. The officer needed someone to ensure none of our intelligence assets were near the latitudes and longitudes of the targets of the upcoming Air Force bombing campaign in Afghanistan. Thank God there were other people around who knew how to do that.

It was October 7, 2001, less than a month after the horrific attacks on America on September 11. Al-Qa'ida and the Taliban were about to get first-hand experience in what air superiority really meant and what a posse really looked like. Five days earlier on October 2, after a half century of focusing on deterring Soviet aggression in Europe, NATO members committed tens of thousands of allied forces to suppress terrorism in Afghanistan. This was a follow-up to NATO's decision on September 12 to invoke, for the first time, the Article 5 commitment of the NATO charter—an agreement that an armed attack against one or more NATO members in Europe or North America shall be considered an attack against them all.

Also on September 12, the UN Security Council passed a resolution calling on all countries to cooperate in bringing the perpetrators, organizers, and sponsors of the attacks to justice and that those responsible for supporting or harboring the perpetrators, organizers, and sponsors would be held accountable.

By early November, the Afghanistan capital of Kabul fell, and exactly two months after the start of that bombing campaign, in December 2001, the last Taliban stronghold in Afghanistan, the southern city of Qandahar, was secured by allied forces.

In three short months the Taliban was pushed out of Afghanistan and about 75 percent of al-Qa'ida had been killed. This successful operation was conducted by the most lethal air force the world had ever seen and about four hundred Americans on the ground in Afghanistan—a mix of U.S. Special Forces and CIA officers—supporting Afghan tribal forces.

America helped create NATO and the UN. We developed and sustained relationships with the member countries in times of peace. The U.S. intelligence community continued relationships with Afghan tribal leaders after Communist forces were kicked out of the country in the late 1980s. For decades, we maintained friendships both bilateral and multilateral—we were nice to nice guys. If you want friends in times of conflict, you must cultivate friends in times of peace.

The Afghanistan campaign was one of the most successful operations in history because we worked with allies. It was successful because Americans and Brits merged with Hazaras, Tajiks, Uzbeks, and Pashtuns—the predominant Afghan ethnic groups—against a common foe for compatible interests. We were clear about who our friends and enemies were, and we were able to leverage old alliances to counter a global threat.

In a global battlefield, American national security needs to be based on *strengthening* alliances with our friends, not weakening them.

Famed Duke basketball Coach Mike Krzyzewski uses the analogy of a fist to illustrate the power of working together.

"If you hold your hand out with all five fingers flexed out and try to punch someone, you will cause yourself an extraordinary amount of pain and possibly break some fingers," he explains to his players. "However, if you make a fist with all five fingers, you can really make a powerful punch."

While Obama got being tough with tough guys wrong in Syria, President Trump got being nice with nice guys wrong in the Arab Republic. In 2019, I voted for a bipartisan resolution that opposed his disastrous decision to remove U.S. forces from northern Syria because it meant abandoning one of our oldest allies in the Mideast, the Kurds, who have been vital U.S. partners in our war against terrorism. Not only did we let our friends down and make our country less secure by creating a power vacuum in northern Syria, but we also ceded leadership in the region to our adversaries Russia and Iran.

President Trump's America First foreign policy, which was really an America Alone policy, was the equivalent of trying to punch with your fingers flexed out. Trump showed little appreciation for the power of international agreements. He attempted to pull out of the World Health Organization, criticized the World Trade Organization, scuttled the Trans-Pacific Partnership, and declared that the U.S. would go at it alone on defense issues if NATO members did not increase their military spending. In the early months of Joe Biden's presidency, he talked about how America is back to playing leadership roles in international organizations. However, his actions, such as not cooperating with allies in the withdrawal of military forces from Afghanistan, haven't always reflected this sentiment in early tests of his foreign policy decision-making.

The end goal with international organizations is not just to participate in them. The end goal is to provide *leadership* in these organizations, so they can achieve their missions. This includes ensuring our partners are pulling their weight. NATO nations, for example, are expected to devote 2 percent of their gross domestic product (GDP) to national defense budgets, and many members were not hitting that mark. President Trump made this issue his singular focus, and now NATO nations are spending close to that 2 percent mark. But Trump's rhetoric and actions—being tough with nice guys—toward our most important allies eroded trust rather than improved confidence in us.

The WHO plays an important role in responding to global crises like COVID-19. However, throughout the pandemic, valid concerns about the WHO's handling of the pandemic were raised. The organization developed a perceived unwillingness to hold the Chinese government accountable for the conduct expected of a WHO member. In response to these concerns, the Trump administration tried to take its ball and go home by vowing to pull out of the WHO. The correct response in that moment would have been working with our allies to get answers, and reforming the WHO. Anyone can complain and point fingers, but it requires real leadership to reveal to people a problem, and then get everyone committed to fixing it. This is what is required of American leadership in the international order.

Trump's foreign policy, emphasizing isolationism, wasn't brand-new. President Obama worked to reduce the U.S. defense budget and curb overseas entanglements—not just because he saw that as advantageous foreign policy, but also because he viewed that as a way to win elections. President Biden doubled down on this isolationism with his disastrous decision to withdraw U.S. forces from Afghanistan while abandoning hundreds of American citizens and thousands of Afghan nationals who had risked their lives to help us over the last twenty years.

President Biden witnessed and participated in a similar debacle when he was vice president. President Obama, correcting what he perceived to be the error of the Bush Doctrine, which was unilateral preemptive war in Iraq, withdrew American combat troops from Iraq at the end of 2011, an action that created a power vacuum, enabling ISIS's rise to power. President Obama entered office pledging to end the U.S. occupation of Afghanistan as well, and so did President Trump, but President Biden was the one to pull us out. While he has the distinction of overseeing the debacle that was the American withdrawal from Afghanistan, the seeds of this disaster were sown when the Trump administration negotiatied directly with the Taliban without the involvement of the Afghan government.

There was bipartisan opposition to America having a continued role in

Afghanistan. Our activity in Afghanistan was referred to as a "forever war." According to the Costs of War project at Brown University, when you add up the expenses of the Departments of Defense and State, the cost of caring for the conflict's veterans, and the interest on the money borrowed to cover it all, the price tag of our activity in Afghanistan from 9/11 through FY2022 was more than $2 trillion.

As of September 2021, a total of 2,461 U.S. military personnel had paid the ultimate price by giving their life in Afghanistan since the events of September 11, and at least 20,066 members of our armed forces had been wounded. This also means the lives of thousands of families have been irrevocably impacted forever.

This sacrifice of treasure and blood was for two reasons. The first was to respond to the attacks on our homeland on September 11, 2001, when 2,977 Americans died and thousands were injured in New York City; Shanksville, Pennsylvania; and Arlington, Virginia. This was the worst attack on our homeland since 1941, when 2,403 Americans were killed and 1,143 were wounded during a surprise bombing at Pearl Harbor which prompted the U.S. to enter World War II. The Institute for the Analysis of Global Security estimates that the loss of life, property damage, and economic volatility resulting from the attacks on 9/11 cost America more than $2 trillion.

The second reason for the twenty years of American sacrifice was to prevent another attack like 9/11. Many observers critical of American involvement in Afghanistan often ask the hypothetical question as to whether the trillions of dollars expended on the war in Afghanistan could have been better spent on things like healthcare, infrastructure projects, or education. I answer that hypothetical with another: How many similar 9/11-style attacks on our homeland did those trillions of dollars prevent? Having spent the first half of my adult life in the Central Intelligence Agency, I know the answer—many.

I find the use of the term "forever war" offensive because I think it devalues the sacrifices that have been made. Not just the sacrifices by the people who gave their life or limbs, but the sacrifices endured by the tens of thousands who spent time away from their families and toiled in a faraway place to protect us here at home. Many still have nightmares about what they had to witness to do their job.

Following the successful Afghanistan campaign in 2001, many mistakes were made. We failed to have clear goals on how to assist our friends, who helped us achieve our goal of nearly eliminating al-Qa'ida, rebuild their country. We failed to involve reasonable elements of the Taliban who hadn't committed human rights abuses in that rebuilding. We diverted our attention away from Afghanistan in 2003 with the invasion of Iraq, and in 2006 when the Taliban began their slow ascent to where they are now, we failed to treat them with the same ferocity that we did al-Qa'ida. Instead of turning Pakistan into a steadfast ally, we bungled several opportunities to encourage them to distance themselves from the Taliban. As brilliant author and war correspondent David Halberstam, as well as many others, has noted: We failed to learn a lesson from the Vietnam War and were unable to adapt to the reality that our adversary controlled the pace of war depending on its needs at any moment.

I agree with the late senator John McCain, who said, "War is far too horrible a thing to drag out unnecessarily." President Biden's complete withdrawal from Afghanistan led to the Taliban having more control of the country than they did in the '90s. Immediately after capturing the country, the Taliban claimed their rule would be different than their previous reign; however, within weeks of taking over they passed edicts forbidding women from playing sports, executed the families of opposition figures, killed girls who were in an orchestra, and selected a terrorist and close ally of al-Qa'ida for minister of interior affairs. A second Taliban reign will eventually create the same conditions that lead to al-Qa'ida having the capacity and ability to plot their deadly attack on America.

When we withdrew from Vietnam after nineteen years of engagement there, which saw the loss of more than fifty-eight thousand American lives, our allies, the South Vietnamese, ultimately surrendered to the North Vietnamese. Within a year of our departure, Vietnam became a unified country—our goal all along; however, it became unified under a Communist flag, which is what we spent nineteen years trying to prevent. Not only is our departure from Afghanistan creating a severely more unstable world that will eventually produce something that touches our shores, but our departure from Afghanistan tells our friends, and reminds our enemies, that our friendship can't always be counted on, even when its ultimately in our best interests.

Continuing to have a small footprint in Afghanistan of around 3,500 troops would have been enough to conduct counterterrorism operations in the region and provide the necessary support to the Afghan military to repel the Taliban. Having this small of a force isn't nation-building but what is necessary to deny a safe haven for terrorists and to prevent another attack like the one that happened on 9/11. To put this number in context, the United States spends roughly $8.5 billion a year maintaining 28,500 troops in South Korea and 55,000 troops in Japan. A review of our decades-long presence in Japan and Korea by the Government Accountability Office (GAO) found this forward-deployed presence enables regional stability and security, defense capability and interoperability, emergency response, denuclearization and nonproliferation, and strong alliances. Basically, it makes the region more free and safer.

Since President Biden has taken this option of a small counterterrorism footprint off the table for the foreseeable future, to prevent Afghanistan from becoming a failed state he now must work with the international community, including Russia and China, on two issues: preventing a humanitarian crisis from taking over a country where more than half the population depends on foreign aid for their daily needs while also convincing the Taliban to go against their instincts and refrain from committing more human rights abuses. Being nice with tough guys is rarely a winning strategy.

Until World War II, the political leaders of the United States heeded George Washington's warning in his farewell presidential address, "steer clear of permanent alliances with any portion of the foreign world . . . in my opinion it is unnecessary and would be unwise to extend them." This guidance was no longer relevant after the Second Great War, because in the 149 years between Washington's farewell presidential address and the end of World War II, the world had become interconnected.

American leadership in organizations like NATO has enabled seventy years of peace and prosperity for hundreds of millions of people. The U.S. and our allies created a better world from the ashes of World War II. It's been a period of overall peace and prosperity almost without precedent in the history of the world.

This peace has allowed our economy to become the world's most important, because we had stable trading partners. The U.S. is a whole lot richer because of trade with Europe. Our combined economies make up half of all the goods and services produced in the world, and Americans enjoy a life the rest of the world envies. To continue this run at a time when the government of China is trying to replace us, we need to continue to collaborate with our friends. America leading, not America alone. America has a unique ability to form alliances, one that Russia and China have never been able to demonstrate. China and Russia don't have alliances, they have dependents.

Building on alliances with our neighbors and pursuing trade pacts not only strengthens our ties with our friends, but it's also good for our citizens. Trade pacts like the North American Free Trade Agreement (NAFTA), which was between the U.S., Mexico, and Canada. It was negotiated by Republican President George H. W. Bush in 1992, then passed in the Democratic-controlled Senate and House of Representatives with a majority of votes in both chambers provided by Republicans. NAFTA took effect in the beginning of 1994 after being signed into law by Democratic President Bill Clinton.

NAFTA was responsible for tripling trade between the U.S., Mexico, and Canada, creating one of the largest and most important trade areas in the world—home to more than 480 million people (7 percent of the world population). It generated 28 percent of global gross domestic product and accounted for 16 percent of global trade.

Obama, not Trump, was the first to express skepticism of NAFTA. On the campaign trail, Obama pledged to open it up to renegotiations but dropped that promise once he took office, blaming the global economic meltdown. Critics of NAFTA failed to realize that the U.S., Mexico, and Canada are not competitors. *We build things together.*

The global economy has changed drastically since NAFTA was signed in my hometown of San Antonio a quarter century ago. So it needed to be updated. The United States Mexico Canada Agreement (USMCA) reflects the modern demands of our economy, while boosting North American competitiveness against China. It sets a framework for digital trade in goods and services that bans customs duties on digital products and improves protections for intellectual property. Its aim is to prevent non-USMCA countries, like China, from unfairly taking advantage of liberalized trade in North America. Overall, the pact will generate jobs in America and grow our posse to prevent China from achieving its aim of displacing the U.S. as a global superpower.

The United States must also work with our international allies to counteract abusive Chinese practices that hurt the entire global trading system. This includes competing with China's Belt and Road Initiative, the colossal state-backed economic campaign seeking global dominance. It is the most ambitious global infrastructure plan ever conceived.

The brainchild of Chinese President Xi Jinping, this "New Silk Road" developmental plan spans countries from East Asia to Europe. New roads, railways, power grids, oil and gas pipelines, ports, airports, and conference centers are being constructed—mostly funded by loans from China to developing countries. The "Belt" refers to economic and overland routes for road and rail transportation, while the "Road" refers to sea routes connecting through Southeast Asia to South Asia, the Middle East, and Africa.

As of 2021, 139 countries are participating in the Belt and Road Initiative. Including China, this group of countries accounts for 40 percent of global GDP and 63 percent of the world's population. But the project has left many countries in debt as China lures developing nations into taking on unsustainable loans for the projects, enabling China to seize the assets when countries encounter financial difficulties, thus expanding Beijing's military and extending its global influence. Just as ominously, it allows China to export to other governments surveillance technology that can be used to extend authoritarian abuses like curbing free speech and restricting civil liberties of their own citizens.

To counter the Belt and Road Initiative, the United States needs a National Economic Security Plan. The Marshall Plan for the Northern Triangle can be one element of a National Economic Security Plan that can be used to coordinate with our allies. However, when there is a lack of trust in America's commitment to providing leadership, taking on challenges like the Chinese threat becomes more difficult. Our allies become more likely to go at it alone, while smaller countries become more apt to trust the Chinese than the U.S.

These types of economic threats to our national security don't get the attention they deserve. With a more robust economic national security strategy, we can improve economic strength at home by increasing access to trading partners and deal with national security challenges before they reach our borders and shores.

Another way to solve problems before they get to our shores is to be deliberate in the use of our soft power. Harvard University's Joseph Nye defines soft power as "the ability to get what you want through attraction rather than coercion or payments." The most important tool to leverage this soft power is public diplomacy—informing and influencing public opinion in other countries to further our interests and promote our foreign policy objectives.

In the traditional sense, governments engage in public diplomacy through activities like educational exchange programs, language training, and hosting cultural events.

When I served in Pakistan, I would hear stories about the popular

American Centers, affiliates of U.S. Consulates in Lahore, Karachi, and Islamabad. In the '70s, '80s, and '90s, Pakistanis flocked to them in order to listen to American music, peruse American magazines, and absorb the latest in American culture. They were the equivalent of community centers. However, the security safeguards put in place after the September 11 attacks severely curtailed local populations' access to the centers, and an important tool used to leverage our soft power atrophied.

But in this interconnected world, public diplomacy is not just limited to governments. Our cultural assets and political views are owned by our entire society, so cities, non-governmental organizations, civic groups, and even private companies are engaging meaningfully with foreign publics and are participating in public diplomacy whether they recognize it or not.

The Russians are extremely skilled at exporting their culture for the purposes of disinformation. For example, the people of Moldova love Russian TV soap operas. So when the Russians beam them into this politically fragile former Soviet state, the shows are embedded with false data and destabilizing propaganda—for example, depicting Moscow and pro-Russian separatists in eastern Ukraine as valiant crusaders for justice.

Beijing has also gotten into this game, using culture as a political weapon to soften its image abroad. This is why the Chinese government has endorsed the financing of some of America's biggest movie blockbusters, buying theater chains and teaming up with Hollywood producers, who are relying more and more on the Chinese markets to make profits. Which means the Chinese are increasingly turning up as the "good guys" in all sorts of flicks. For example, in *Gravity*, Sandra Bullock survives by getting herself to the Chinese Space Station.

Additionally, American filmmakers are coming under pressure that, if they want to enter the Chinese market, they can't cross certain red lines of the Chinese state—like Taiwan is not its own country. This is what led to a situation in 2021, when *Fast and Furious* actor John Cena made a public apology for referring to Taiwan as a "country." To understand the current history of Taiwan we have to go back to a time when it went by another name.

In 1895, the island of Taiwan, referred to as Formosa by Europeans until the twentieth century, was ceded to the Empire of Japan by the Chinese Qing Dynasty at the conclusion of the First Sino-Japanese War. A little over forty years later in 1937, the Japanese invaded mainland China where the government, the Republic of China (ROC), was led by Nationalist leader Chiang Kai-Shek.

During this occupation Japan controlled roughly 25 percent of China's land and more than a third of its entire population. Following the Japanese defeat in World War II, Taiwan was given back to the official government of China—the ROC. By 1949, after years of civil war, Chiang's ROC was pushed to the island province of Taiwan by Mao Zedong, the leader of Communist forces, and Mao created the People's Republic of China (PRC).

Until the 1970s, the US recognized the ROC as the true government. In 1971, during the presidency of Richard Nixon, the United Nations sat the PRC as the official representative of China and expelled the ROC representative. Then in 1979, during President Jimmy Carter's administration, the U.S. government recognized the PRC as the sole legal government of China; however, the U.S. did not recognize Chinese sovereignty over Taiwan (the preferred official name for the island government after deciding to de-recognize the ROC). The Carter Administration did *acknowledge*, rather than recognize, the Chinese position that Taiwan was part of China. In response to the Carter administration's moves, Congress passed the Taiwan Relations Act in 1979 to protect American security and commercial interests in Taiwan. This legislation provided a framework for continued relations in the absence of official diplomatic ties.

In 1982 under Ronald Reagan, the United States government stated it had no intention of pursuing a policy of "two Chinas," but added six assurances attempting to clarify the U.S. position on Taiwan. This "one China" position where the U.S. recognizes the PRC as the sole government of China but only *acknowledges* the Chinese position that Taiwan is part of China, has been America's official position since the '80s and has allowed the U.S. to maintain formal relationships with the PRC and unofficial relations with

Taiwan. While Taiwan is the eleventh largest trading partner of the U.S. and the twenty-second largest economy, only fifteen countries have recognized it as a sovereign nation, not including its most important ally, the United States. Complicating a complicated situation even further is that the Chinese government understands that if it wants to surpass the United States as the global superpower, then Chinese culture will have to spread faster and farther than America's. As part of this effort, the Chinese government has extende 1 its censorship and control over American movies over the last decade. Hollywood producers, script writers, and directors are increasingly making cre ative decisions to avoid antagonizing Chinese officials.

Our popular culture is a manifestation of our values, and throughout the world, it is admired and emulated. Our movies, our food, our style, and our music—all are eagerly consumed worldwide. When our global public image takes a hit, it makes it harder to use all our tools of national power.

An old Swahili proverb says, "If you want to go fast, go alone. If you want to go far, go together." In a world that is shrinking because of constantly evolving technology, and an adversary who is bigger than us and wants to replace us, we will be unable to continue our success without allies and partners. If we want our enemies to fear us and our friends to love us, then we need to be tough with tough guys and nice and with nice guys. Adopting a foreign policy strategy that distinguishes between our adversaries and our friends, and treats them accordingly, is a strategy we can adopt *now*.

But our eyes also need to be on the future, to look where our enemies and our allies will be headed *tomorrow*.

Hockey legend Wayne Gretzky once had a smart observation about his goal-scoring strategy—skate to where the puck will be, not to where the puck has been. But too often, when it comes to developing a national security strategy, the U.S. skates to where the puck *was*. We rely too much on the past being prologue to the future, rather than preparing for new, dangerous challenges ahead.

CHAPTER 19

PREPARE FOR THE WARS OF TOMORROW, NOT THE ONES OF THE PAST

In a spacious, book-lined private office, I asked a senior former national security official: "Which day are we going to celebrate as the end of the Global War on Terrorism?" When I was in Congress, I asked this question of anyone involved at a high level in national security. Usually, the responses failed to answer the question with any specificity.

I added, "We need to understand the preconditions for victory. We aren't going to be able to kill every terrorist."

This senior national security official wrinkled her brow and fixed me with a stare. "No, but we can kill a lot of 'em."

Her response was so unexpectedly coarse that I almost spit out the tea I'd been served. While I agreed with part of the sentiment—we do need to deliver consequences to those trying to do us harm—we can't kill our way to victory unless we kill the ideas that power extremism. Terrorism is a tool used to extend a warped extremist worldview. The targets of the terror are preventing the terrorist from actualizing their belief.

The best observation I've learned about how we deal with terrorism came from my former CIA boss and business partner, Hank Crumpton.

"Extremism is like influenza," he told me. He explained that you can inoculate communities from it, but it's always going to be there. When there is growth in one area, you surge there and pay special attention to it. But it's never going to totally go away.

Prior to the world being rocked on September 11, 2001, neither al-Qa'ida nor Usama bin Laden were household names. The CIA Counterterrorism Center (CTC) and FBI counterterrorism specialists had been tracking al-Qa'ida and bin Laden in the mid-1990s, but terrorism wasn't the national security issue then that it became at the turn of the new century.

Similarly, the devastating consequences of the COVID-19 pandemic have come as a huge shock to many. Off and on over the years, the prospect of a global pandemic surfaced in national security strategies, but even though the U.S. had seen outbreaks of zoonotic diseases like Ebola, West Nile Virus, Zika, and novel coronaviruses like SARS and MERS, the American public and most national security practitioners did not believe a virus could bring the global economy to a standstill.

Unfortunately, our national security experts fall into the trap of preparing for the last crisis or conflict and failing to understand wars of the future. Whether it is combatting extremism or cyber warfare, dealing with state actors like our "frenemy" China, battling health crises, or dealing with crises we can't even imagine, it's important to remember that the wars we will face in the future will *not* be the same as the wars of the past. We can't afford to be ill prepared.

Even while experiencing the devastating global COVID-19 pandemic, the world is still unprepared for the next deadly virus, and even less prepared to defend against a weaponized virus.

In future wars, our adversaries will not offer their unconditional surrender. There will be no General Robert E. Lee surrendering his Confederate troops to Union General Ulysses S. Grant at Appomattox Court House. There will be no V-E Day as in World War II, when Great Britain and the United States celebrated their victory over the Nazi war machine. Nor will there be a Potsdam Agreement, signed by the United Kingdom, the United States, and the Soviet Union after the surrender of Germany, which laid out the military occupation and reconstruction of the defeated country.

Unconditional surrenders are relatively infrequent in world history. But the United States and our allies have grown accustomed to thinking in those terms. We expect to wave flags, hold ticker tape parades, and kiss each other in the street to celebrate victory in Afghanistan or in Iraq. Some assume that China's economy needs to become subservient to the U.S. for the U.S. to "win," or that cyber criminals will one day be driven out of existence. Despite experts' warnings, many even expect diseases like COVID-19 to be wiped out of existence.

To succeed in future conflicts, we need to define what "victory" over our adversaries, whether governments, terrorists, hackers, or viruses, looks like.

With terrorism, as Hank points out, extremism is always going to exist in some form. We need the ability to search it out and strike back when we see an outbreak.

The same goes for a virus: Victory in the fight against COVID-19 (and whatever virus comes next) isn't going to be zero deaths and no illness. Victory likely looks more like our annual battle against the flu, where deaths and illnesses are inevitable, but effective public health measures and vaccines keep diseases from devastating the world.

What does success look like in a New Cold War with China? Success means that the American economy remains the most important economy in the world. It means that China becomes a destination for American goods and services and a competitor in industry, while also following the norms of the international order. The end goal is an entity that we can work and compete with.

We'll be able to predict some of the wars of tomorrow. Others will be unforeseen. One reality that will be true, regardless of the type of conflict, is that it will happen within an *infodemic*, where a mixture of disinformation, misinformation, and lies spread like an epidemic, offline and online, eroding our democratic society and institutions.

This infodemic is weakening our information ecosystem because, when we are overloaded with information, we resort to mental shortcuts influenced by our biases. Misinformation only worsens polarization and confirmation bias by driving social media users into silos that further cement their belief in dangerous falsehoods and deceptions.

Disinformation is more than just the Russians trying to erode trust in our electoral process. It comes in many forms. Cybersecurity specialist Camille François, who studies how people and organizations leverage digital technologies to harm society and individuals, provides a helpful framework for describing and analyzing disinformation: There are manipulative *actors* using deceptive *behaviors* to push harmful *content*.

Based on François's research, the EU DisinfoLab, a nonprofit organization for disinformation activists and experts, sorts the use of disinformation into four categories—foreign, political, issue-based, and lucrative.

The first is *foreign influence*—the use of disinformation by foreign actors to disrupt societies over certain issues and/or to push an agenda. This includes China's false claims about the origins and spread of COVID, ISIS's online recruitment campaigns to radicalize vulnerable young men, and Russian efforts to destabilize Eastern Europe and erode trust in the U.S. electoral system. Other forms are Iran's anti-Israel, anti-American propaganda campaigns, Taliban falsehoods about the frequency of civilian deaths resulting from the actions of U.S. troops, and North Korea's mass lies to its own people.

In the U.S., we see our foreign adversaries launching social media campaigns that try to erode trust in our democratic institutions—politicians, political establishments, the press, and the scientific establishment—by sowing divisions on social and political issues, including the results of our elections, race, religion, immigration, police violence, Southern heritage, and gun rights. For instance, according to a 2019 bipartisan report by the Senate Select Committee on Intelligence, entities backed by the Russian Government created a Facebook group called "Blacktivist," signing on more than five hundred thousand followers and engaging with 11.2 million Facebook users, in a bid to stoke racial divisions before the 2016 presidential elections by targeting African Americans in key metropolitan areas and trying to suppress their vote.

A stunningly effective incident that sowed disinformation by a foreign state didn't involve social media but did involve Russia and the president of the United States. This disinformation effort occurred when President Trump stood by President Vladimir Putin's side in 2018, after closed-door talks in Helsinki, Finland, as Putin denied that Russians were meddling in our election and pushed lies about his country's destabilizing and illegal actions in Ukraine.

President Trump even repudiated his own intelligence agencies on the issue of Russia's election interference, saying, "President Putin says it's not Russia. I don't see any reason why it would be."

For Vladimir Putin, spouting many of his usual lies while the leader of the free world stood next to him nodding and providing no rebuttal was priceless imagery. It was used to try to convince the world that Putin was right.

Over the course of my CIA career, I saw Russian intelligence manipulate many people. Disinformation and chaos, after all, is a Russian art form developed during the Soviet era and adapted to leverage modern tools. But I never thought I would see the day that an American president would be one of those to fall for such disinformation.

Aside from foreign disinformation, EU DisinfoLab identifies domestic *political* types of disinformation aimed at undermining adversaries.

This has long been known as old-fashioned dirty politics. Like the Democratic Congressional Campaign Committee's use of misleading talking points during the 2018 congressional elections in videos and advertisements. That effort spread inaccurate information about Republicans' stance on pre-existing conditions in the healthcare reform debates. Or in the 2014 election cycle, when the National Republican Congressional Committee actually created websites that looked like news websites critical of Democratic opponents.

Political disinformation can be *issue-based* as well. Extreme environmentalist groups went from supporting natural gas a decade ago—when the price was sky-high and it wasn't a feasible alternative to oil—to opposing natural gas when it became a more viable energy source. Why? Because they needed a boogeyman to scare people in order to raise money.

Finally, disinformation can be *lucrative*—used to make a profit. Like supporters of QAnon, the movement based on false conspiracy theories, who peddle hats, T-shirts, bumper stickers, and even jewelry and pet collars online.

Both foreign and domestic players—terrorists, hackers, countries—are trying to erode trust in our institutions, and they have been incredibly effective. As a result of disinformation campaigns, Americans have declining trust in the U.S. government at all levels, societal institutions—the media, law enforcement, and technology companies—and each other. Even the medical community is not immune, as seen by false pandemic rumors that hospitals were making money by artificially jacking up their COVID patient loads. Lack of trust exists at every level of society.

For some, the only trusted "experts" are those on YouTube and social media who spout crazy conspiracy theories and false claims about government officials, the media, and other bulwark institutions. Unbeknownst to some of those "experts," some of their content is boosted by foreign-owned bots aiming to create conflict.

Seeding mistrust of our institutions is classic misdirection. If Americans are consumed with fighting among ourselves, then we can't focus on problems around the world. If Russia's goal is to reestablish the territorial integrity of the USSR, which institution is preventing this from happening? NATO. But if Russia can undermine confidence in NATO, then Eastern European nations will be less apt to view the West as a reliable ally, and Russia wins. If you erode Western European countries' belief that America has their back, they are less likely to be firm with an aggressive Russia, and Russia wins again.

Similarly, the Chinese Communist Party's (CCP) false claims, echoed by Russia and Iran, that COVID-19 originated from a U.S. Army base in

Italy helped distract the world from Chinese culpability for the spread of COVID-19. The CCP's claims also saved face at home with a Chinese populace devastated by this deadly epidemic and discredited the U.S. pandemic response in an effort to drive a wedge between the United States and our international allies. At the same time, the CCP's lies supercharged Chinese General Secretary Xi Jinping's campaign to become the world's superpower.

But in an environment of disinformation and digital theft, the concept of "war" can become muddled, and the potential response uncertain.

What *is* a digital act of war? It's easy to describe a physical war: Specific examples as defined by the United Nations are an invasion or attack by armed forces of a state, military occupation, bombardment against the territory of another state, blockade of ports or coasts, and the sending of armed bands, groups, irregulars, or mercenaries to carry out acts of armed force against another state.

We all know what that war looks like, and we all understand how nations react. If North Korea were to launch a missile into San Francisco, both sides would know our response: We would launch a hundred missiles at Pyongyang. A missile attack on buildings in a city is an example of a physical attack on physical resources. It's the kind of warfare that most countries have been accustomed to since the beginning of recorded history.

But a *digital* act of war is far less clear-cut. What if foreign hackers gained access to important parts of the digital infrastructure of U.S. federal, state, and local agencies? What if they retained that access for months, reading confidential emails and reports? That's exactly what happened in 2020 when Russian intelligence services gained access to the software of a U.S. company called SolarWinds that was deployed across the U.S. government. This Solar-Winds hack was one of the worst cyber espionage incidents ever in the U.S.

How should the U.S. respond to an unprecedented act of espionage like this? If we caught someone physically stealing this information, then that individual would be arrested, and diplomats from the country that coordinated the theft would be kicked out of the U.S.

But what if, instead of theft of the information, all the equipment through-out the federal government was made inoperable, but there was no loss of life? This would be considered a digital attack on digital resources. How do we respond? If they steal our stuff, do we blow them up? This is the uncharted environment the U.S. is operating in now. Deterrence—being so clearly capable of winning a fight that an adversary decides against using violence to get its way—doesn't exist because we haven't defined what constitutes a digital act of war. We haven't outlined if, and how, we would respond.

Formulating a response to digital-on-digital attacks is hard because of the difficulty of attribution—determining who conducted the attack. Let's say a cyberattack is launched against the American power grid. The perpetrator doesn't launch the assault from his or her personal laptop in his or her home. Instead, the perpetrator is digitally cloaked, and the attack pathway bounces around the world, hijacking digital infrastructure not owned by the culprit and appearing to come from, say, a Moldovan hospital. If we can't identify the attack's origin, it's not obvious how we counterattack.

Cyberattacks without a known perpetrator could also include malware that infiltrates traffic control systems resulting in plane crashes, wipes out vital data from the federal government that brings the government to a standstill, or wrecks our financial system with massive shutdowns of critical computer networks. We have already seen cyberattacks that turn off a community's power, manipulate a water-treatment plant in an attempt to poison a town's water, and prevent multiple states from having fuel to power their vehicles for multiple days. In 2021, we saw the cyberattack on the Colonial Pipeline take out nearly half the East Coast's fuel supply. The attacks can also be less catastrophic, though extremely disruptive, such as holding a hospital's patient data for ransom or stealing emails containing confidential trade secrets from corporations. San Diego–based Scripps Health was forced to cancel medical procedures and divert some critical care patients to other hospitals after it was the target of a cyberattack in 2021.

These are just some of the challenges that digital wars of the future will present, and we need to work through these issues now. If we are going to reduce the probability and impact of cyberattacks of significant consequence, then the public and private sector will need to significantly improve collaboration. This operational collaboration usually occurs when we are responding to, or recovering from, an attack, but it needs to happen in the period where an organization is trying to prevent and prepare for an attack.

In 2019, I was proud to support an initiative in Congress that established a commission to develop a consensus on a strategic approach to defending the United States in cyberspace against cyberattacks of significant consequences. In early 2020, this Cyberspace Solarium Commission produced a clear-eyed report that outlined three ways to achieve this end state of defending against and reducing the amount of significant cyberattacks.

The first plank in the strategy is to *shape behavior*—the United States must work with allies and partners to promote responsible behavior in cyberspace. The second plank is to *deny benefits*—we must deny benefits to adversaries who have long exploited cyberspace to their advantage, to American disadvantage, and at little cost to themselves. This new approach requires securing critical networks in collaboration with the private sector to promote national resilience and increase the security of the cyber ecosystem. The third plank is to *impose costs*—the U.S. must maintain the capability, capacity, and credibility needed to retaliate against actors who target America in and through cyberspace.

Another war of tomorrow we will have to fight is driven by disease—the next global pandemic. COVID-19 is far from the last pandemic the world is going to reckon with. The World Health Organization has determined that, starting in the sixteenth century, there have been, on average, three pandemics per century occurring at intervals of ten to fifty years. This analysis was based on what has been naturally occurring throughout the world. What if COVID-19 were actually designed in a lab specifically to affect the population of the U.S.?

The technology of bioengineering can turn this thought experiment into reality. Scientists are getting to a point where they can program cells the way computer software can be programmed. The ability to isolate specific DNA patterns to bioengineer a virus so that it affects one group of people more than another already exists. Manipulating a virus is cheaper than building a nuclear weapon, and we have witnessed the devastating affects a deadly virus can have on the world.

The only way to confront these global health issues is with a global approach, such as the worldwide scientific effort to develop vaccines for COVID-19 in record time. It was one of the greatest examples of international cooperation in recent history. The entire world joined together to share resources and information for the common goal of creating vaccines.

Every country needs to have pandemic plans, better surveillance of viruses circulating in humans, increased diagnosis of infections when people get sick, and a proactive strategy for developing vaccines and therapeutics. We must cooperate as a community of nations, and the U.S. must be an integral part of international health organizations.

There are already stellar examples of effective international partnerships with active American leadership.

The Global Fund is a collaboration of governments, the private sector, nonprofit organizations, and affected communities that has been fighting the worldwide epidemics of AIDS, tuberculosis, and malaria. Since 2002, the Global Fund's work has contributed to extraordinary improvements in global health with programs in more than one hundred countries, saving thirty-eight million lives and providing prevention, treatment, and care services to hundreds of millions of people. It has strengthened communities and improved economies worldwide.

In 2019, governments, NGOs, and philanthropic organizations got together in Lyon, France, to pledge $14 billion over three years. It was the largest amount ever raised for a multilateral health organization, with the goal of saving sixteen million lives and ending the epidemics of AIDS, tuberculosis, and malaria by 2030. One thousand adolescent girls are infected by HIV every day, and without the work enabled by the Global Fund, seven million more children would have died of malaria.

People shouldn't be dying from preventable diseases, and the Global Fund is an example of how international commitment can solve global challenges. When it comes to preventing future pandemics, preparedness and international cooperation are critical. We can't drop the ball next time. We are at war with communicable diseases, and we must build an infrastructure in partnership with other nations to be successful in this conflict.

A consequence of not preparing for the wars of tomorrow is an overreaction when they actually happen. When people are scared, they are more willing to sacrifice liberties in search of security. It happened in America during World War II with the internment of Japanese Americans, and the debate resurfaces every time there is a terrorist attack in the U.S.

In times of crisis, people are willing to give up some of their freedoms to feel safe. During the pandemic, for example, surveys consistently found that people agreed the government should be able to place restrictions and requirements on businesses and people to protect public health, even if they undermined civil liberties. Immediately after significant terrorist attacks like 9/11 in the United States and the November 2015 Paris attacks in France, Americans showed a willingness to accept more invasive law enforcement surveillance in their private lives.

There are examples around the world and over the ages of how a desire for safety, when taken to its extreme, creates the preconditions for a population to be intoxicated with the idea of an authoritarian government offering a false promise of safety. But I believe we *can* have ultimate security *and* ultimate liberty. It requires us to strengthen alliances, not weaken them. It requires us to be prepared for the wars of tomorrow, not the ones of the past. It requires us to define what success means in new wars, where guns and tanks can be enhanced or replaced by computers, hackers, disinformation, and diseases.

One of President Dwight D. Eisenhower's most popular speeches was his

1953 inaugural address, where he said: "Whatever America hopes to bring to pass in the world must first come to pass in the heart of America."

America can, and should, be an example for the rest of the world—that shining city on the hill. America needs to achieve in our own country the values that undergird our foreign policy. We need to practice what we preach. If we're criticizing the Chinese government about its human rights, we can't be separating children from their parents on the border or seeing our citizens being murdered in police custody. Our individual freedoms are what allow for the opportunities that have made our country grow into a global superpower.

As we work to keep our place on the world stage, we'll need to confront a major challenge—technological change accelerating at an unprecedented speed. We are already locked in this must-win race for technological dominance. The U.S. absolutely must win or face an inexorable decline of its power and influence. In this race, there is no second place.

PART V

TAKE ADVANTAGE OF TECHNOLOGY BEFORE IT TAKES ADVANTAGE OF US

CHAPTER 20

REALIZE WHAT "MADE IN CHINA" REALLY MEANS

When I woke up on July 22, 2015, I didn't think my second meeting of the morning would upend my view of the new world order.

Senior leaders from Silicon Valley Bank came to my office to talk about entrepreneurship, venture capital, and the start-up ecosystem. As with many presentations of this sort, it started out a little boring and vague.

But then they mentioned that Chinese companies were starting to get an increasingly larger amount of the worldwide venture capital market. They explained that 80 percent of global venture capital deals had been directed at U.S. firms in 2006, but the amount invested in U.S. companies dropped to just 55 percent of total deals in 2015.

In 2006, the biggest venture capital deals were dominated by investments in American companies. But by 2015, the landscape had undergone a radical change. The biggest venture deals were in *Chinese* companies.

When I was at the Crumpton Group, the strategic advisory and business development firm I joined after leaving the CIA, I advised businesses seeking venture capital. I knew that venture capital is the pointy end of the financial spear because it's money going to start-up companies and small businesses— mostly technology—that have long-term growth potential.

This change was a grim sign for the U.S. If venture capital was increasingly flowing to China, it indicated China was focused on future technology in a way that the U.S. was not. This meeting with Silicon Valley Bank was three years before I learned from Michael Pillsbury at that HPSCI hearing about China's goals to replace America on the world stage.

For most of my life, the phrase "Made in China" had a negative connotation. It meant poor quality or a knockoff. The Silicon Valley Bank presentation made me realize that my understanding of this phrase was naive. "Made in China," especially in the technology sector, means something radically different than in the past. Increasingly, "Made in China" means high quality and advanced.

A critical factor in America's economic and military success has been the achievement of global leadership in advanced technology; however, the U.S. and our allies are at our most tenuous position in this area since World War II. In this Fourth Industrial Revolution we are currently in, where technological change over the next thirty years will make the last thirty years look insignificant, we are dealing with a dramatically shifting global landscape. This environment is influenced by the long-term effects of the COVID-19 pandemic and a Chinese government that is trying to rapidly erode American technological advantages through legal and illegal means.

We are talking about technologies like aerospace, 5G, artificial intelligence, and quantum computing, which can change the world for the better or worse. These technologies in the wrong hands have the capability to misinform populations, extend authoritarian grip over civil society, and widen the equity divide within disadvantaged communities. Winning this generation-defining struggle for global leadership in advanced technology will not just affect the American economy but will shape the rest of the century for the entire world.

We can take advantage of technology before it takes advantage of us, but America needs a comprehensive technology agenda that spurs innovation, leverages innovative technologies within government to better serve citizens, mitigates the challenges posed by technological disruption, and is compatible with our allies to ensure our democratic values of the free world, not autocracies, drive development of these new tools.

America's future hangs in the balance, and we're not prepared for the battle to save it. Many in the U.S. are oblivious to the fact that we are locked in a winner-take-all "New Cold War" with China, which could be described as starting in May 2015 when Chinese Premier Li Keqiang issued the first Made in China 2025 strategic plan. In place of bombs and planes, this war is being fought with supercomputers and algorithms.

The government, private sector, and broader society are still dragging their feet when it comes to making this country technologically "combat ready" for the war that is already raging. The first step in making sure we are successful in this New Cold War is recognizing China is a peer adversary who can beat us.

Since my meeting in 2015, China has continued to see a rise in VC funding. The changing landscape of VC funding is an early warning sign of a new world order. In China's relentless drive to replace the U.S. in advanced technology, it is directing all its resources—manpower, raw materials, government funding, and private capital—to participate in this colossal initiative.

The United States needs to match this focus. We need to coordinate data strategies across the public and private sector to get better and more data to train algorithms that drive AI. We need to invest in digital infrastructure. We must drive innovation by empowering users of these twenty-first-century tools with the ability to control their own data. We must encourage accountability in the technology sector to ensure technology increases equity not decreases it, and we must defend our digital infrastructure from attacks.

The Chinese Communist Party has orchestrated some of the largest data breaches in U.S. history and is conducting a decades-long aggressive campaign to steal American intellectual property. China has been implicated in stealing the personal information, including Social Security numbers, of nearly half of U.S. adults from the credit-reporting agency Equifax, data on eighty million people from healthcare giant Anthem, and passport and credit-card information from up to five hundred million customers of Marriott. Not to mention a hack into the files of the Office of Personnel Management in the mid-2000s, which victimized me and hundreds of thousands of other federal workers when our personal data was stolen.

The sheer scope of China's larceny is breathtaking. Bill Evanina, former director of the U.S. National Counterintelligence and Security Center, warned in 2021 that Beijing has stolen personally identifiable information from 80 percent of Americans.

China's theft of U.S. intellectual property is just as audacious. During the pandemic, federal law enforcement warned that China-backed hackers were working to steal U.S. research on coronavirus vaccines, treatments, and testing.

John Demers, head of the National Security Division at the U.S. Justice Department, said in 2020 that China is the nation most responsible for the theft of U.S. intellectual property. He said China steals American intellectual property, copies it, replaces the U.S. company that owns the intellectual property in the Chinese domestic market, then supplants the U.S. in the global market.

Chinese telecom giant Huawei, with deep ties to the Communist government, is dominating the burgeoning 5G tech field, which is an industry that will make our mobile phones even more powerful than they are now. As of 2019, Huawei's 5G global market share was as large as the combined global market share of its chief rivals, the Finnish company Nokia and the Swedish business Ericsson. However, U.S.-inspired bans of Huawei initiated by the Trump administration and continued by the Biden administration enabled Huawei's rivals to gain more market share outside of China.

China is also pouring billions into quantum computers—technology potentially allowing the decoding of encrypted communications from classified reports stored on NSA and CIA computers to emails stored in commercial servers to financial transactions performed by your bank. Its ambitious space program includes laser weapons that can take out our satellites and sensors. And in facial-recognition technology, China is forging ahead with its campaign to create a mass-surveillance state, using new data-vacuuming and privacy-busting technologies that could set dangerous precedents for human rights around the world. The number of surveillance cameras in China was expected to reach 626 million units by 2020 in a population of 1.4 billion.

From the start of the century to 2018, the government of China had increased its research funding to support the development of innovative products or services by 140 percent, while the United States had only increased its research funding by 7.5 percent.

In the 1960s space race, the Soviets were consistently ahead, achieving notable firsts like the first satellite into space (*Sputnik*), first man into space (Yuri Gagarin), and the first spacewalk (Alexei Leonov). Ultimately, we surpassed them. In 1969, *Apollo 11* enabled Neil Armstrong to take one giant leap for mankind by walking on the moon.

But the new technological wars make the space race pale in comparison. This time, there is no second place when it comes to perfecting technologies that will revolutionize the world. The country in second place will be unable to catch up to the leader.

The Chinese have made their intentions clear: By 2049, "Made in China" will mean the gold standard in technology. The only way to achieve this goal is to displace the United States off the throne we have held since World War II.

This New Cold War will still have—and be fueled by—old battle lines like human rights abuses, Tibet, Hong Kong, and Taiwan. The government of China has also committed genocide against the Uyghurs, its Muslim minority population in Xinjiang region—the largest of China's administrative regions. This includes forced sterilizations and the placement of well over one million people in an estimated 500 to 1,400 internment and "reeducation" camps, where people are subjected to brainwashing techniques and torture, including waterboarding. The Chinese government is using its social and technological surveillance systems to control Uyghurs' daily life and suppress their identity. The government is going to great lengths to hide the nature and extent of its crimes by restricting outside access to Xinjiang.

We can't engage in battle if we don't know our foe. That's especially critical with China. We need to understand its history, cultural fault lines, and internal and external tensions. Because, even more than with many other countries, the past is present in China.

Tibet, for example, is one of the many enduring sources of friction between the U.S. and China. Some Tibetans advocate independence from China, but the Dalai Lama, the exiled Tibetan Buddhist spiritual leader, has proposed a "middle way approach" of genuine autonomy without independence. China's leaders have rejected this approach as "independence in disguise" and fueled the conflict with draconian measures like restricting the religious freedoms of Tibetan Buddhists, encouraging the migration of ethnic Chinese, and refusing to negotiate with the Dalai Lama.

Hong Kong's legal autonomy has been undermined by the Chinese government failing to respect its own commitments to the treaty it signed with the British in 1984. As China tightens its grip on Hong Kong, tensions between the U.S. and China continue to rise.

And Taiwan, the island democracy across the Taiwan Strait from mainland China, is the place most likely to ignite a hot war between the U.S. and China. It is one of the only places where Beijing claims sovereignty but fails to control. Chinese leaders believe that without reunification, China can't re-emerge as a great power. If China was successful in their reunification plans, in addition to recapturing territory that was lost in the seventeenth century, they would end up owning 70 percent of the world's manufacturing capacity of semiconductors—the building blocks of the information revolution.

American political scientist Graham Allison has explained that Chinese President Xi Jinping "has increasingly portrayed the party as the inheritor and successor to a five-thousand-year-old Chinese empire brought low only by the marauding West." A Chinese phrase, he said, "that translates into 'never forget our national humiliation,' has become a mantra that nurtures a patriotism grounded in victimhood and infused with a demand for payback."

While posted to another part of Asia when I served in the CIA, I learned

the importance of how centuries of culture impact an individual and a population. I would meet with a warlord who was one of the members of the original mujahideen, the guerilla fighters who fought the Soviets in Afghanistan
in the 1980s. This warlord who introduced me to the nectar of pomegranates
was somewhere between the ages of sixty and one hundred and twenty years
old—he had lived a hard life, and every wrinkle and scar on his face reminded
you of this fact.

We would sit cross-legged on an ornate carpet, and he would select an
unblemished pomegranate from his private stock. He crushed the juicy crys-
tals of flesh inside the fruit without perforating its rind. After twenty minutes
of this, the fruit looked like a dark pink water balloon. The warlord slipped a
straw into a small incision made with a large knife that he always carried with
him, and we sipped the sweet juice straight from the fruit.

I never spoke first. After staring at me enjoying the results of his labor,
he said, "Mr. Willy," (he would always call me this), "I've been a citizen of my
country for fifty years."

The region where he was born had only been an independent country for
several decades.

"I've been a Muslim for one thousand four hundred years."

The Islamic calendar begins in 622 AD, when Muhammad traveled from
Mecca to Medina on the Hijra.

"But I've been a Pashtun for three thousand three hundred and thirty
years."

The majority of Afghanistan and the border region of Pakistan is dominated by complex tribalism, and the Pashtuns—the ethno-linguistic group
that dominates this area—is a society consisting of many tribes and clans.

It's hard for Americans to understand how centuries of culture impacts a
society or individual. When we say "American," that adjective reflects a unified land, affirmation of basic cultural practices and acceptance of religion or,
more specifically, the absence of the religious conflict we see in other parts
of the world. Even with our problems of race resulting from our original sin

of slavery, it's hard for us to understand how deeply ethnic, religious, and tribal differences can influence a country's national interests. Although the late 2010s and early 2020s will be defined in American history as extremely hyper-partisan times, Americans have generally been united around the ideals codified in our founding documents.

As we engage in this New Cold War, we must recognize how the power of China's motivating factor aimed at righting the perceived wrongs of a five-thousand-year-old civilization affects this new line of conflict in advanced technology.

Every American should care about this struggle with China to be the global leader in advanced technology. We face a potential future where Mandarin and the yuan—not English and the dollar—dominate the global economy. The economic impact is clear—Americans will be poorer because the dollar will purchase much less, our economy will be weaker, creating less opportunities for good-paying jobs, and our debt will take up a greater percentage of federal spending, which means fewer federal dollars for infrastructure and programs to help those most in need.

We won't be able to travel as much because our dollars won't go as far. Our money will buy less food at the grocery store. When we go to our favorite theater in our hometown, the movies will be in Mandarin with English subtitles. If we work in a company that has any international operations, we will be forced to learn Mandarin because it will be the de facto language of business.

You only have to look at the fate of empires and superpowers throughout history to see the disastrous consequences of losing this New Cold War. Did a Roman in 475 AD ever believe that the Western Roman Empire could fall the following year because of the invading Goths? What about a Spanish or Portuguese citizen in the seventeenth century? Part of both Portugal's and Spain's global maritime empires in the fifteenth and sixteenth centuries was built on the trade in gold and slaves to become major players in the spice trade.

Did a Spanish or Portuguese citizen ever think the Dutch city of Amsterdam would become more important than Madrid or Lisbon?

But empires are empires—until they aren't. We know too well what happened with the British. In the eighteenth century, the United Kingdom of Great Britain became a global superpower after becoming the dominant colonial power in North America and subjugating the Mughal Empire in India. Even in the early parts of the twentieth century, a Briton would never have thought that New York and Washington, DC, would one day replace London as the financial and political epicenters of the world.

If America loses this contest, we will join the ranks of the Western Roman Empire of the fifth century, the Spanish and Portuguese empires of the sixteenth century, and the United Kingdom of the early twentieth century. Our military and political leaders, as well as the general public, need to anticipate the unimaginable—the "black swan" events that we think won't ever happen. We must understand that these black swan events usually occur at some point. In 2020, few believed a virus could bring the global economy to its knees. In 2021, few thought that an ill-prepared electric grid could bring the world's ninth-largest economy, the state of Texas, to the edge of collapse during a winter storm that we knew about a week in advance.

It's easy to dismiss potential black swan events. But when it comes to national security, we need to prepare for the things we think can't happen. Because they do. And they will.

Estonia is a continent away from Beijing. But what happened there in 2007—when it was the target of the first known cyberattack against an entire country—is an example of what could occur in the U.S. if the Chinese turned all their resources toward us.

Estonia is on the Baltic Sea and, with a population of about 1.3 million people, shares a border with Latvia and Russia. It was forced to join the USSR in 1940, an action the U.S. never recognized diplomatically. When the Soviet

Union collapsed in 1991, Estonia regained its freedom and eventually joined both NATO and the EU. A country literally on the front lines of conflict with Russia, Estonia has a sizable ethnic Russian minority.

In early May 2017, Mike McCaul, the chairman of the Homeland Security Committee and a fellow Texan, invited me on a congressional delegation trip to Poland, Estonia, and Ukraine. I was five months into my second term in Congress, and the purpose of the trip was to examine Russian cybersecurity threats and aggression toward both Eastern Europe and the U.S., as well as explore the prospects for increasing regional cooperation against these threats.

What I learned there informed my opinion about the existential threat we face from China. And it all began with a statue.

In April 2007, the Estonian government planned to move the Bronze Soldier—a six-foot-tall soldier in a World War II Red Army military uniform set against a stone structure—from the middle of the capital of Tallinn to a military cemetery on the outskirts of the city. The Bronze Soldier was unveiled in 1947, and for Russian speakers in Estonia, it represented the USSR's victory over Nazism. But for ethnic Estonians, the meaning was different: Red Army soldiers were occupiers, and the Bronze Soldier was a painful reminder of fifty years of Soviet subjugation. The decision to move the statue sparked outrage in Russia, and Russian-speaking citizens in Estonia took to the streets for two nights of rioting and looting.

During our briefings, four Estonian cyber officials explained that for weeks following the rioting, Estonia was the target of major cyberattacks. Online services for banks were taken down, media outlets were prevented from uploading articles, and the government couldn't issue paychecks. In every area of Estonian society, massive amounts of spam overwhelmed servers.

As a result, Estonian citizens found they couldn't get cash from ATMs or access their online accounts, government employees went without pay, and newspapers and broadcasters had difficulty reporting on what was going on.

These Bronze Soldier cyberattacks, performed by the Russian government and hackers sponsored by the Russian government, were the first use of wide-ranging cyberattacks on a nation state, and this nation state was a member of NATO.

The Russians proved that it's possible to cripple a country with cyberattacks. The Chinese have the same, if not better, technical capabilities than the Russians. We should assume that Beijing can replicate to an even greater extent what the Russians did in Estonia.

We are failing to recognize the threat from the Chinese government. We are woefully underprepared. For decades, we've been naive about China's intentions.

As we look at the history of the U.S. and China relationship, we have a clear picture of actions that failed to produce the desired results. Economic interdependence with China and encouraging China to become part of the global economic structure did not create a genuine market economy. Nor did it reform China's political system. The Trump administration's aggressive use of the sanctions policy failed to change the behavior of Chinese Communists and made them more entrenched and threatening toward their neighbors.

For the U.S., China is a formidable competitor on every front, and the implications of trailing an authoritarian regime that will one day surpass the U.S. as the world's largest economy are dire. Meeting the unique challenge of head-to-head economic and technological competition requires a new approach to ensure American competitiveness and protection of our interests.

CHAPTER 21

ACHIEVE TECHNICAL FITNESS FOR CYBER WAR

Five months after getting sworn into office, I opened a letter from the Office of Personnel Management (OPM) explaining that the extensive personal data I had provided when I joined the CIA was now in the hands of a foreign adversary.

I knew that OPM, the agency that manages the government's civilian workforce, had been the target of one of the most devastating cyberattacks in U.S. history. Personnel files containing what are called "SF-86 forms," filled out by millions of federal workers as part of our applications for security clearances, had been stolen.

I was one of those federal workers. Like millions of others who'd had their data taken, I was pissed.

An SF-86 data theft was way more extensive than the typical credit card account hack, where card information is used to make unauthorized purchases. The SF-86 forms ask individuals for deeply personal stuff, like where they've lived, how much money they've saved, where it was kept, the home addresses of their kids, parents, siblings, foreign contacts, whether they sought help for a mental health problem, or had gotten into money trouble.

If *narcotraficantes* in Mexico had this type of information, they would have the home addresses for family members of the Border Patrol. The Russians could use the information to drain people's bank accounts by creating new access codes to acquire private information. The MSS—the intelligence, security, and secret police agency of the People's Republic of China—would know if a Chinese American had family members still living in China in order to potentially extort or use that relationship to apply political pressure.

My information, and that of millions of others, was a gold mine for bad guys across the globe.

"Are you kidding me?" was my response to the letter. "Katherine Archuleta is going to have a bad day tomorrow."

As a first-time congressman, I was a member of the Oversight and Government Reform Committee (OGR) and chairman of OGR's brand-new Subcommittee for Information Technology. OGR was holding a hearing on the theft the day after I received my letter, and the director of OPM, Katherine Archuleta, would be testifying.

I had run my campaign on the promise of being the gold standard in constituent services and a leader on national security. On the campaign trail, I barely spoke about cybersecurity. IT procurement definitely never came up. Before being given the privilege of chairing a subcommittee as a freshman congressman, I had intended to focus on border security and counterterrorism issues. Not IT stuff.

I did have experience in cybersecurity—I had helped build FusionX into a preeminent cybersecurity firm; that's why Jason Chaffetz (R-Utah) wanted me to serve on his committee. While I was at Crumpton Group, our clients were asking for help in defending their digital infrastructure. Being good intelligence officers, we said we knew a guy. That guy was Matt Devost, a crack cybersecurity expert. Because I was the only Crumpton consultant with a computer science degree, I was tasked to work with Matt to help build FusionX. I was the sales guy and account manager, but to pitch our business better, I learned a little something about what our hackers were doing.

The OPM hearing blew me away. One of the most damaging cyber heists in U.S. government history, and the U.S. government just *let them in*. What makes it worse is that OPM had been told for years it needed to improve its digital infrastructure to prevent such an attack.

I quizzed OPM officials about whether they employed basic elements of good digital hygiene like two-factor authentication, how they'd found the breach, and even whether they had a team drinking Red Bull working around the clock to fix this.

Their answers were vague at best, and they declined to apologize or even acknowledge their agency's refusal to implement security best practices that had been recommended for years by the agency's own inspector general.

I asked Archuleta whether the hacker had used a zero-day vulnerability to get into the OPM network. A zero-day vulnerability is a software security flaw for which the vendor of that software doesn't have a fix. It was a simple question, but her reply was a bureaucratic side step.

"I think that would be better answered in a classified setting," she said.

Really? Millions of people had their most personal information stolen, and she won't tell us whether there's a hole in their software. I asked the question even though I already knew the answer. The attackers didn't exploit a zero-day vulnerability. They took advantage of a weakness in the software that *we already knew was a problem.* This could have been easily prevented if basic security measures had been taken. The fact that most of the country knew about an obscure government agency like OPM was an indication of how outraged the American public was that it was so easy for important information to be stolen—and that the theft was enabled by laziness and sloppiness.

The perpetrators were eventually identified: the government of China.

The OPM hack was not about the Chinese government making money. It was about scoring a treasure trove of data to improve their intelligence operations against the United States.

The war is underway. The reality is that the American Revolutionary War was fought by soldiers on the ground. World War II was fought by planes in the sky. And this New Cold War is being waged on the cyber battlefield.

But if a soldier is in battle and has an inferior firearm or doesn't know how to use that firearm, or that firearm doesn't work the way they think it will, then that soldier is unable to fight effectively. *Combat effectiveness* requires *technical fitness*—quality equipment and an ability to use the equipment the way it is intended to work. This is true whether the battlefield is in the air, on land, or inside cyberspace. We must achieve technical fitness for a cyber war we are already fighting, where the winner will control the world.

China isn't the only country with its eyes fixed on the opportunities cyber warfare presents.

In 2021, three North Korean computer programmers were indicted in the U.S. for attempting to extort and steal more than $1.3 billion as part of a global cyber scheme that included the 2014 hack of Sony Pictures Entertainment. In that famous data breach, North Korean hackers dug through Sony's network and released embarrassing emails between executives, executive salaries, and personal information about employees and their families. They demanded that Sony withdraw its movie *The Interview*, a comedy about hapless journalists recruited by the CIA to assassinate North Korean Leader Kim Jong-Un.

Russia has also developed considerable skill in cyber warfare and has been the most brazen in its execution. Without firing a gunshot, launching a missile, or deploying troops, it brought the country of Estonia to its knees. And in 2020, Russian hackers penetrated the Pentagon, intelligence agencies, nuclear labs, and Fortune 500 companies in the SolarWinds operation—one of the worse cyber espionage assaults ever experienced by the U.S. Hackers inserted malicious code into software updates that gave them remote access into computers. As of mid-2021, estimates suggest there would be insured losses of up to $90 million. Even more scary, this hack showed a cyberattack can impact more than just digital infrastructure. It showed it could navigate to operational technology—power distribution units, air handler units, and other control system devices, which can affect the physical world.

What this makes clear is that U.S. government, the private sector, and individuals are still ill-prepared for cyber warfare.

I experienced this lack of preparation firsthand in Congress, as well as at

FusionX, where Matt Devost and his hackers worked to penetrate corporate data security systems to find their vulnerabilities before cybercriminals got there first.

In a meeting at a major financial services firm that was spending millions of dollars defending its digital infrastructure, I watched as Matt spent six hours firing questions at the senior leaders of the firm. It was my first time joining Matt on a security assessment, and I only understood about 40 percent of what was being discussed.

A security assessment is a discussion with the senior technical leaders of a company to determine how they protect their digital systems. This occurred on the first day. Then, on the second day, we would perform a "technical vulnerability assessment" of their network security—pop the hood and look inside. On the way back to the hotel after the first day, Matt commented to me that if this company was doing half of what it said it was doing, then tomorrow would be a very difficult day for us because it would be hard for us to break in.

A technical vulnerability assessment is different than a blind penetration test (which is a simulated cyberattack to find vulnerabilities without the knowledge of company data-security people). In a technical vulnerability assessment, the assessment is performed on the client's premises and the defenders know what's going on. The FusionX hackers would be given the most basic access to see if they could elevate their digital privileges to get deeper into the organization's system. Think of it like this: You connect to the Wi-Fi at an airport during a layover between flights, and with that basic Wi-Fi access, you end up connecting to the air traffic control tower and can direct the planes in the air. In essence, that was what we were testing for.

We had our best guy on the case. That morning, I was settling into a cubicle for the day to work on other projects when Matt walked in and said, "We got in."

"You got in?"

"Yep. In fifteen minutes."

I was shocked. "We hacked into the most sensitive parts of the firm's network, in fifteen minutes?"

"Yeah," Matt said. "This always happens. Everyone talks a good game, but when you test whether they put their theories into practice, things usually fall apart."

This was a tangible lesson in the Russian proverb popularized by Ronald Reagan, *doveryai, no proveryai*—trust but verify. I followed this maxim in Congress but found that too many organizations in the private sector and federal government rely on just the first part of this proverb.

The costs of cybercrime are growing exponentially, with estimates that it has doubled since 2015. Cyberattacks are also literally killing people. The first documented death resulting from a cyberattack happened in Dusseldorf, Germany, in September 2020, when a woman arrived at the Dusseldorf University Hospital for life-saving surgery, only to be turned away. Cyber criminals had just defeated the hospital's security by exploiting a known software vulnerability, allowing them to commandeer the hospital's computer systems needed to process the patient and carry out the surgery. Out of options, paramedics rushed the patient to another hospital, but it was too late—the patient died.

During the COVID-19 2020 shutdowns, the number of cyberattacks skyrocketed. According to the World Health Organization, cyberattacks soared fivefold after the pandemic erupted. Health organizations were the prime target.

Criminals love crises.

In 2021, hackers hacked into the industrial control systems of a water treatment plant in Oldsmar, Florida, and tried to poison the community's water supply. A supervisor on duty was able to stop the perpetrators before they could raise the level of lye in the town's water to a dangerous level. As-yet-unknown hackers had gained access to these sensitive systems because of poor password security and outdated software.

The stunning GameStop stock frenzy in early 2021 presents a scary cyber theft scenario with global implications. Fueled by a Reddit army of individual traders buying shares to squeeze hedge funds that bet the price would fall, GameStop's stock price skyrocketed before falling back to earth. Tens of billions of dollars were won and lost over days of trading.

But what if this phenomena wasn't hatched by Reddit users, but instead was fueled by a digital covert action campaign by a government like the Chinese Communist Party to achieve a financial objective to the detriment of the American public? This is a "black swan" event that woul.. have catastrophic consequences, but against which we aren't prepared to defend.

Improving our technical fitness to defend against catastrophic cyber-crimes isn't just the responsibility of governments and businesses. Individuals have a role to play by practicing good "digital hygiene."

We relearned a lot about personal hygiene during the pandemic. To reduce our chances of getting COVID-19—wash hands, wear a face mask, and practice social distancing. For our online lives, there is *digital* hygiene.

The basics of digital hygiene are to have a fourteen-character-plus password, resist clicking on attachments in your email or texts from someone you don't know, and keep your software on your phone or laptop up to date in order to protect your devices against a vulnerability discovered by the company that wrote the software.

Beyond the individual battle to maintain security on computers, phones, video game consoles, and other digital devices, there is the national digital war to protect our *country*.

Just as you can't fight a war with tanks and planes that break down, we can't fight this New Cold War with crumbling and porous digital infrastructure. During my time in Congress and on the House Appropriations Committee, we focused on modernizing our armed services—new planes, better ships, and improved training facilities. Now it's time to have that same mentality for our digital infrastructure.

To achieve the operational tempo necessary to defend cyberspace, we need a culture of modernization within our government. That begins with being deliberate in paying attention to digital hygiene.

Many people have heard of antivirus software and firewalls. Antivirus software is used to prevent, detect, and remove computer viruses or malware—any kind of software designed to do something bad to your system. A firewall is a device you put on a network that monitors everything coming and going on your network and decides whether to allow specific traffic based on a pre-determined set of security rules. Antivirus software and firewalls have been tools in cybersecurity for more than twenty-five years, but there are always new tools being developed to defend devices and computer networks. Ensuring that government agencies, businesses, and individuals are keeping up with the times requires a culture that prioritizes modernization.

Changing the behavior of the federal government is a momentous job, and Congress has a critical role in making this a reality. One way Congress can do this is through its oversight role and through legislation like FITARA. After three terms in Congress, I now understand how important the oversight function of Congress is. But in the first few months on the job, grappling with learning the ropes of being a chairman of a subcommittee, I thought doing oversight was more of a pain in the ass and a distraction than what it really was—probably the most important thing that I could have done to improve digital hygiene throughout the federal government.

"Tell me again, what the hell is FITARA?" was my question to Troy Stock, the staff director for the IT subcommittee that I chaired.

"It's the bill that Chairman Chaffetz's predecessor, Darrell Issa from California, and Congressman Gerry Connolly from Virginia passed at the very end of last Congress," was Troy's response. "FITARA stands for the Federal IT Acquisition Reform Act."

"And why do I care?"

"You care because FITARA was the first major overhaul of federal IT in over two decades. Its implementation is in our jurisdiction. It's been one year since it passed. We should have a hearing on how it's working."

Troy suggested I meet with Dave Powner, director of IT issues for the Government Accountability Office (GAO), to discuss a scorecard the agency had come up with to systematically measure and grade every federal agency's performance under the law in modernizing their IT infrastructure.

The GAO is an independent, nonpartisan agency, often called the "congressional watchdog." It examines how taxpayer dollars are spent and provides Congress and federal agencies with objective, reliable information to help the government save money and work more efficiently. I had already come to respect it as an agency because it has been identifying problems within the federal government for a long time, and every GAO staff member I had met was smart, thoughtful, and direct.

While I was suspicious about whether using a scorecard to measure the performance of the federal government's IT systems was anything more than a monumental waste of time, I had used scorecards to improve the performance of many organizations in the past.

When I was a high school junior, I had read the book *The 7 Habits of Highly Effective People* by Stephen Covey, the founder of the leadership development company Franklin Covey. Ever since, I have incorporated these principles into my daily living, and because I was a fan of Franklin Covey's products, I read *The 4 Disciplines of Execution* by Chris McChesney, Sean Covey, and Jim Huling during my time in the CIA.

One of the disciplines of execution is to keep a compelling scoreboard. If you have a clear goal and know what the key measures of success are, then you can track the specific behaviors that lead to goal accomplishment, thus making you more successful. Additionally, people play harder when they know someone is keeping score. I had used these pragmatic principles, including the scoreboard, to increase intelligence production and asset recruitment for my unit in Afghanistan.

Powner and his colleagues at GAO had developed a method of assigning a letter grade to how well a government agency was implementing four areas outlined in the FITARA legislation. The easiest thing that was graded was how well an agency was closing down data centers and transitioning digital operations into the cloud. It also graded whether new digital initiatives were delivering results on a regular basis and assessed performance metrics designed to measure whether new IT investments where being implemented within budget and on schedule. The other thing graded was how well an agency was protecting its IT assets and information.

Of the twenty-four large departments and agencies we reviewed, only two had earned Bs and just five got Cs. The rest flunked—they got Ds and Fs, meaning the federal government was failing to do very basic things to improve digital hygiene.

No wonder it was so easy to hack into OPM.

When Robin Kelly (D-Illinois), my Information Technology Subcommittee ranking member, and I called several agency chief information officers to testify about why their grades were so bad, we learned that these agencies failed to have a culture of modernization.

As we saw some slow improvements, we recognized that these agencies were paying attention to what we were keeping track of, so we added categories that would improve digital hygiene and build a culture of modernization. It took five years, but finally all twenty-four federal agencies passed. We demonstrated that aggressive and continued oversight could drive changes that would improve digital hygiene. We also showed that we needed all hands on deck to fix our technical fitness crisis.

The ship is sinking, and to stay afloat we've got to do more than use a small bucket for bailing water.

Winning this struggle is not the responsibility of just one person or organization. It's everyone's, especially at a time when technological change is accelerating at unprecedented speeds.

In 2018, I was getting an award from FCW (Federal Computer Week), a media company that covers technology within the federal government. At the awards dinner, FCW was presenting a special honor to NASA's *Voyager* mission teams for showing what's possible when innovation and dedication are required to keep systems running for the long haul. Dr. Jeffrey Hayes, a scientist at NASA responsible for the support of several missions then in operation, accepted the award on behalf of the *Voyager* team. In his acceptance speech, Dr. Hayes told the story of the *Voyager* program.

Forty-one years before the awards dinner, the day after I was born in 1977, NASA launched *Voyager 2* into space. It was the first man-made object to leave our solar system, and the engineers who designed *Voyager 2* believed it would send data back to Earth for maybe three to five years. Incredibly, *Voyager 2* is still reporting back to us.

During his remarks, Dr. Hayes said, "Even when the radioisotope generators on the spacecraft are finally depleted, both of them will continue to move out into the galaxy—ambassadors of the human race as we take our first tentative steps into deep space."

What's crazy about *Voyager 2* is that we learned so much about our solar system from it—and it only had seventy kilobytes of onboard memory. That's about enough space for a seven-page Microsoft Word text document. A photo taken on your smartphone wouldn't fit on the Voyager spacecraft computer system.

From the time that we launched this space probe, we have commercialized the internet, pretty much everyone has a handheld smartphone, and many schools even have 3D printers. These technological advancements have taken human innovation to places we couldn't have imagined. But they have also increased the surface area available for hackers to attack.

To be prepared for cyber war we need all our cyber systems—government, business, academic, and personal—technically fit. We need a culture of modernization focused on continually improving our digital infrastructure, an infrastructure we can trust because we have verified it does what it's supposed to do when we need it to do it. And combat effectiveness means having the right tools. If we are technically fit, not only will we be prepared for all the unexpected outcomes of a cyber war, but we will put ourselves in a position to stay the global leader in advanced technology.

CHAPTER 22

WIN THE NEW COLD WAR OVER ADVANCED TECHNOLOGY

After six years of representing the largest section of international border in Congress, I'd heard about some strange things being smuggled into the U.S., but Chinese astrophysicists was a new one. In the midst of the pandemic, a senior U.S. law enforcement officer told me Chinese astrophysicists had been caught trying to illegally sneak across the southern U.S. border. I was annoyed that I hadn't learned of these episodes earlier. Turns out, it had happened more than once.

These Chinese astrophysicists had snuck into Texas from Mexico and were masquerading as day laborers in the U.S. to get jobs at SpaceX, the famed commercial space company founded by Elon Musk. Their intended posts were at the rocket production facility, test site, and spaceport in the South Texas town of Boca Chica, less than three miles from the U.S.-Mexico border. In May 2020, before I heard about the Chinese astrophysicists, SpaceX sent four astronauts atop its *Crew Dragon* reusable, reentry spacecraft to the International Space Station. The successful *Dragon* spacecraft mission was the first full-fledged taxi flight for NASA by a private company.

"Why were they acting as day laborers?" I asked the law enforcement official.

"They wanted to get jobs like being a janitor so they could have access to all the rooms in the facility."

"So basically, they would be able to sneak around and look in drawers and take pictures of dry-erase boards or important equipment."

The official nodded grimly. "Bingo."

There was another milestone in space the same month as the SpaceX launch. The Chinese government celebrated its first launch and return of a space capsule that could someday be capable of performing a round-trip to the moon. The reentry spacecraft they used looked almost identical to SpaceX's *Crew Dragon* spacecraft.

Many citizens have questioned the cost of our efforts in space since 1962 when President John F. Kennedy shifted our efforts from low to high gear to be the first nation to the moon. Since that decision, space-based capabilities have been integral to American military, commercial, and civilian applications. Without space programs, we wouldn't have GPS, accurate weather predictions, rapid long-distance communications, or data for climate change research. A burgeoning amount of medical research is being conducted in space that might someday cure diseases and save lives.

But the final frontier is now a war zone. China is connecting its space program to its ruthless economic and military initiatives: Its Made in China 2025 initiative includes aerospace as one area where it is developing "national champion" companies. The Defense Intelligence Agency said in a January 2019 report that the Chinese Communist Party (and Russia) view "space as important to modern warfare and view counterspace capabilities as a means to reduce U.S. and allied military effectiveness."

Eighteen months after this report, former secretary of defense Mark Esper explained in a speech that, "In space, Moscow and Beijing have turned a once peaceful arena into a war-fighting domain. They have weaponized space through killer satellites, directed energy weapons, and more, in an effort to exploit our systems and chip away at our military advantage."

Space is just one area of advanced technology in which the United States is battling to stay ahead of its competitors.

We have prospered as a nation because we have had a competitive advantage in most areas of advanced technology. To continue this prosperity, we need the same competitive advantage in the technologies that will rule the future, from space to AI to 5G to quantum computing.

Technological advances have always caused disruption, and it has often-times been scary. But technological evolution is coming, whether we want it or not. It doesn't have to be scary.

We can be on the front end of pioneering this new world, where *we* control the outcome.

Before Robin Kelly and I held the first hearings in Congress on artificial intelligence, I asked constituents, friends, and strangers for the first thing that came to mind when I said "artificial intelligence." If I asked someone older than me, they described something close to HAL 9000, the scary computer from Stanley Kubrick's 1968 sci-fi film titled *2001: A Space Odyssey*. If the person was younger than me, they described something like Ava, the ma-nipulative and willing-to-kill humanoid robot in Alex Garland's 2014 thriller *Ex Machina*. If they were near my age, they said the Terminator, the cyborg assassin first made famous by Arnold Schwarzenegger in 1984.

The power of artificial intelligence is analogous to the power of nuclear fission. The Office of Nuclear Energy explains: "Fission occurs when a neu-tron slams into a larger atom, forcing it to excite and split into two smaller atoms. . . . Additional neutrons are released that can initiate a chain reac-tion. When each atom splits, a tremendous amount of energy is released." When this process of successive chain reactions is controlled, we get nuclear power—clean, reliable, cheap energy that can power the world. When this chain reaction process is uncontrolled, we get nuclear weapons—devices that can destroy the world.

The implications of AI will allow humans to live longer and healthier lives, nations to be safer and more secure, and our natural resources to be used more efficiently. Right now, AI can detect eye disease and prevent people from losing their vision. It is tracking soil deficiencies and predicting weather changes to improve crop yields so we can feed more people using less land, energy, water, and labor. We have only scratched the service of what artificial intelligence can do. But the machine learning that powers algorithms that are the foundation of artificial intelligence could produce something much scarier than the Terminator, because it wouldn't rely on violence but, rather, exploit its understanding of everything you have ever done online and use that information to influence your behavior without you knowing it.

If populations, governments, and leaders were rational actors, then the U.S. and China would be working together to maximize the benefits of AI for humanity and prevent the development of the AI equivalent of nuclear weapons. But unfortunately, the Chinese government has failed to show willingness to cooperate on such an endeavor.

We are currently the global leader in AI. We have an innovative private sector, world-class universities, and remain the top destination for AI talent. But American leadership is no longer guaranteed.

In fact, experts Eric Schmidt and Bob Work, chair and vice chair of the congressionally established National Security Commission on AI, wrote: "In the next decade, the United States is in danger of losing its global leadership in AI and its innovation edge. That edge is a foundation of our economic prosperity, military power, and ultimately the freedoms we enjoy."

So what is AI? AI is computational technology that works and reacts in humanlike ways, and computational technology is anything that makes calculations using numbers or quantities. Some examples of areas where a machine could react in humanlike ways are visual perception, speech recognition, and language translation.

AI is what makes it possible for machines to learn from experience and adjust their behavior like humans. AI is powered by algorithms, which are sets of instructions that perform calculations on some kind of input to produce an output.

You put something into an algorithm, and you get something different out. Algorithms are AI's secret sauce.

Most of us already use AI daily. The mapping applications on your phone use AI. The purchasing recommendations you get while online shopping are brought to you by AI. However, the potential of artificial intelligence goes much further than predicting what type of juicer you should buy or the car model you're best suited for. AI stands to reshape every industry, and every part of our lives. Our health. Our transportation. Our manufacturing. Our entertainment. The way we work. How we learn. How we communicate. There isn't an area of our existence that won't be affected by AI.

Russian President Vladimir Putin said, "Artificial intelligence is the future, not only for Russia, but for all humankind. Whoever becomes the leader in this sphere will become the ruler of the world." This might be the only thing that he and I agree upon.

The first time I went to Las Vegas for any other reason than to dance at a club or train CIA assets in surveillance was to walk the floor of the Consumer Electronics Show (CES). It's the most influential tech event in the world. The hottest brands show up to introduce the latest and greatest developments in consumer technology. I was two weeks into my second term in Congress, and the producer of the show, the Consumer Technology Association, had arranged for me to receive several presentations on AI.

My first stop was at the booth for NVIDIA, an American company that has redefined computer graphics and ignited artificial intelligence with its electronic circuit called a GPU that acts as the brain of computers, robots, and self-driving cars.

"How many pictures of a cat do you need to show an algorithm in order for it to start recognizing other images of cats?" I asked a NVIDIA employee at the booth.

"At least one million."

"One million images of a freaking cat?!" I was incredulous.

"That's just to recognize a cat," he said. "But what if you have a driverless vehicle that needs to recognize a stop sign? How many different ways can a stop sign have the glare of the sun on it? The AI has to recognize all of those instances, which means you need a lot of images of each instance of the sun on that stop sign."

With that brief exchange I began to understand an important reality: Data is the new currency. The more data, the better the AI. But alternatively, if you have more data, you need the right algorithms to do anything with it.

In one of my Intelligence Committee hearings with the National Geospatial-Intelligence Agency (NGA) director Robert Cardillo, I learned the U.S. government has access to a lot of data. The folks at NGA like to say, "Anyone who sails a U.S. ship, flies a U.S. aircraft, makes national policy decisions, fights wars, locates targets, responds to natural disasters, or even navigates with a cellphone—relies on NGA." Mr. Cardillo told us what he has said publicly many times, that eight million imagery analysts would be needed for us to even attempt to manually exploit *just* the commercial satellite imagery we expect to have over the next twenty years. The imagery collected from government resources is even more voluminous. Every day in a place where we have troops, like Iraq or Afghanistan, a single sensor collects the data equivalent of every NFL game for three seasons in high definition. It's impossible to hire the number of analysts necessary for this type of volume. So we need AI.

But we can't ignore how this powerful tool can be misused, especially when it comes to our personal information online. It's already too easy to hack into our online worlds and exploit our most intimate secrets. Artificial intelligence could make this process even easier and more pervasive.

My first view of the many dangers of AI came at a 2015 Oversight and Government Reform (OGR) Committee hearing on the commercial use of drones, unpiloted aircrafts, often referred to as unmanned aerial vehicles (UAVs) or unmanned aircraft systems (UAS).

I went into this hearing hoping to learn how far we were from the day when I would be able to have a drone deliver a cheeseburger to me while I was barreling down the highway in a self-driving car. But, instead, the hearing focused on the threat of drones to Americans' privacy.

At the hearing, Harley Geiger, advocacy director and senior counsel at the Center for Democracy and Technology, a technology policy organization that concerns itself with civil liberties, privacy, and free speech, was one of those who sounded the alarm.

"Unmanned aircraft systems are a promising technology," he told us, "but have potential to erode civil liberties by enabling pervasive surveillance."

He laid out chilling scenarios of a society where police dragnets of drones continually monitor people in crowds, stifling their right to free expression, free association, and free assembly. Or where networks of commercial drones record footage of virtually every American who steps outside their home.

Under U.S. law, Geiger warned us, these scenarios are legal and could happen.

At the hearing, I queried Paul Misener, vice president of global public policy at Amazon.com, about its drones' impact on privacy. Through its subsidiary Amazon Prime Air, Amazon plans to use drones to deliver packages to customers.

"How are you planning to gain the trust of the American people [on privacy concerns]?" I asked Misener.

"We have to engender trust," Misener responded. He assured us that Amazon had earned the trust of its customers for keeping their data private, "and we will continue to do that when it comes to Amazon Prime Air."

Many of these privacy issues were addressed by the Federal Aviation Administration (FAA) in late 2020 when it passed its final rule for the use of drones. It included a provision to require all drones to have a broadcast transponder, a unique ID number that could be obtained by anyone within range of the drone.

With this inclusion, I agree with the ACLU that, "the broadcast Remote ID should be sufficient to achieve both the security goal of allowing facilities to identify and deter illegal or hostile drone flights and the privacy goal of empowering individuals to know what aerial cameras may be recording them." Just like a license plate of a car allows an individual to find out who might be parked or driving around his or her neighborhood, an individual should be able to trust they can find out who is using a drone wherever they are located.

Just like the situation created by commercial use of drones, where AI is enabling positive outcomes in commerce while introducing the potential erosion of privacy, we need to prepare for other situations where AI can provide a benefit and, at the same time, potentially discriminate against individuals or communities.

Algorithms can become harmfully biased because of their algorithmic design or the data they are trained with. Microsoft learned this in 2016 from its interactive Twitter-bot called Tay, which learned from tweets and direct messages. Users conversed with Tay, trying to corrupt the bot, and Tay ultimately responded with inflammatory and offensive tweets.

A study by MIT and Stanford University researchers released in 2018 found that commercial facial-analysis programs from major technology companies—which can be used to match faces in different photos and assess characteristics such as gender, age, and mood—contained both skin-type and gender biases. The system, for example, erred significantly more when it categorized darker-skinned subjects versus lighter-skinned people because AI is only as balanced as the humans who are coding it. And because we're human, we can inject our own biases into the software.

These deficiencies of AI applications like facial recognition raise concerns around the deployment of this tool by American police departments. In 2020, a Black man in Detroit was arrested after being mistakenly identified as a shoplifter by a facial-recognition algorithm. Police apprehended Robert Julian-Borchak Williams after security footage from a store was run through facial-recognition technology. A review of an archive of driver's license photos identified Mr. Williams as a potential match.

The software was wrong. It had mistakenly identified two Black men as the same person, and the Wayne County prosecutor's office subsequently apologized. And the police department was wrong in how they had incorporated this tool into their operations. Detroit police chief James Craig explained, "facial recognition was used, but that's not why the arrest was bad." He added that the mistake was caused by "sloppy work and lack of management oversight."

Williams's case may be the first known episode of someone in the U.S. being wrongfully arrested based on an inaccurate facial-recognition algorithm, but it likely won't be the last. The U.S. needs to set the standard on AI ethics, and these standards should set the example for the world for how the technology should work, as well as how humans should use the technology for making important decisions.

The Bipartisan Policy Center's 2020 report on AI and ethics, which Robin Kelly and I collaborated on, points out that if the U.S. doesn't lead on AI, "it will result in other countries setting global AI ethics standards that might not be aligned with American values."

As the former chairman and ranking member of the Information Technology Subcommittee of the House Committee on Oversight and Government Reform, Robin and I learned three things: The federal government can accelerate innovation; use of modern technology within federal departments and agencies empowers public servants to create value for the taxpayer, and rapid technological change creates societal trade-offs.

Enlisting the help of the Bipartisan Policy Center, we used these three findings to inform and shape a national AI strategy that would allow America to take advantage of technology in a responsible and effective way that reflects our values.

During our discussions on this national strategy, we debated the risks of AI systems picking up and exacerbating human biases, worsening inequities in things like the healthcare system, and harming those who are most vulnerable. The civil rights movement ushered in a wave of new laws to fight discrimination and promote fairness. These laws promoted equal opportunity and countered discrimination in a variety of areas, including voting, housing, lending, and employment. Regulations to protect civil rights and liberties have been necessary for ensuring fairness and equal opportunity in a market-driven economy.

When it comes to bias and discrimination, we have existing laws on the books, and algorithms should follow these established laws. That means, just like an individual or a company can't discriminate or invade anyone's privacy or be used for unreasonable searches and seizures, an algorithm shouldn't either. If an individual or business incorrectly implements an AI tool, leading to bias or discrimination, then that individual or business has violated the law. If the individual or business implements the algorithm correctly but the algorithm is biased or discriminates, then that is a violation of the law. In the eyes of the law, algorithm developers should be viewed as at fault and suffer the appropriate consequence. It's a pragmatic, realistic approach.

New incidences and stories about algorithmic bias and privacy violations will create a push for new regulations and regulatory agencies. However, there is already a rich body of applicable regulatory authorities across each sector of the economy. In promoting ethics and mitigating unintended bias, the regulation of AI should build off existing regulation and be tailored to different use-cases using a risk-based approach—identify the most damaging risk and prioritize addressing that risk for controls, policies, and procedures. Once those highest risks are reduced to acceptable levels, you move on to lower risks.

Instead of stifling innovation through onerous regulations, Washington needs to coordinate efforts across government, academia, and the private sector to advance research, development, and adoption of AI. This is why Robin and I, based on our work with the Bipartisan Policy Center, passed a national strategy for AI through Congress, to better prioritize limited government resources and more rapidly advance American AI technology.

Close cooperation between the U.S. government and the U.S. private sector, as well as with our allies, will be essential to winning this competition. We have an example of how the lack of coordination and cooperation has allowed the Chinese government to get ahead. This cautionary tale is 5G.

At the beginning of the COVID-19 pandemic, cell phone towers were being set ablaze around the world by people spooked by internet conspiracy theories that claimed new 5G wireless network technology causes cancer and created the COVID-19 pandemic.

In reality, this "5th Generation" mobile technology will change the way we live and work in a positive way. Using new radio frequencies, 5G networks offer connections up to one hundred times faster than 4G, opening the door to a fresh wave of innovations—improving self-driving cars, enhancing virtual education as teachers get real-time feedback from students, revolutionizing smart factories and the healthcare industry, boosting immersive virtual reality technologies to breathtaking levels, and transforming mobile technology—that will change our lives even more.

It's going to be great to download onto my smartphone an entire season of my favorite show at the best quality within seconds. This is one of the things that 5G is going to let us do; we will be able to send more data per second—called bandwidth.

But what is really interesting about 5G is something called "latency." When you perform a task on your smartphone or connected device, that action is encoded into data that travels somewhere into the cloud. Then a response comes back to you. The time it takes the data to travel from your device to the cloud and back to your device is called latency. With 5G, this trip is going to take one millisecond. Why does this matter? Because the scientific community has found that our thoughts happen in 300 to 400 milliseconds. This means we are going to have the entire power of the internet in real time at our fingertips. Computers will react quicker than we think.

The convergence of data, high-power computing, and advanced engineering is causing a super-evolution of technology and public policy that is turbocharging competition and speeding up regulatory, legislative, political, and societal pressures.

But ultimately, the story of 5G is a cautionary tale—an example of what happens when China's advances get so far ahead that the world has limited options. China's control over 5G technology is growing at an alarming rate, and we are losing the ability to catch up.

I remember when the head of a cybersecurity agency from a major European ally came to my DC office with a stark warning. We were talking about how the U.S. and the EU could work together more effectively on emerging technology issues, and ended up discussing 5G. He leaned forward and gave me his grim take on the U.S.'s place in the world.

"You guys have lost the 5G race," he told me. "The rest of the world knows that. China has already won."

I wasn't in full disagreement. "Look," I said, "the Chinese are ahead, the U.S. is losing this global race, but if the federal government, U.S. private sector, and our allies in Europe work together, we can ensure the future of 5G looks democratic and not authoritarian."

There is no denying the fact that China already controls 30 percent of the 5G market through its gigantic tech company Huawei, which has deep ties to the Communist government and is growing fast. Huawei's technology is as good as, but cheaper than, other Western competitors. The U.S. and the U.K. have banned using Huawei products in their 5G networks, but other nations are still debating the issue, seeing no better alternative.

The U.S. and our allies will not prevent countries from doing business with Chinese companies like Huawei over security concerns alone—of which there are many. We must provide alternative services and products that are better, more secure, and less costly. We need to out-innovate our opponent.

If we don't, we could lose the 5G race, which would have dire consequences for the U.S. economy because the Chinese government would own the 5G information highway. To illustrate the precariousness of this situation, let me use an analogy of a highway traveled over by cars. The antennas, cell towers, base stations that process signals, and the computers used to run all these things are the 5G infrastructure making up "the roads" in my analogy, and the data traveling along that infrastructure are "the cars." The Chinese government won't own the "cars" (information) on the highway, but they will control the roads. They could put a stoplight in the middle of the highway. Or a police officer could stop a driver and refuse to allow them to travel until he inspects that vehicle. Or maybe there is even a trapdoor on the highway that can open up and swallow cars.

The improvements in latency and bandwidth presented by 5G will enable us to use AI at *the edge*—on the devices at our fingertips. Advances in high-powered computing are going to lead to significant advances in the near-term that will make artificial intelligence, which is right now fairly dumb, become truly intelligent. Another mind-boggling technology that will enable intelligent AI is an equally momentous and irrevocable breakthrough: the advent of computers that draw their computational capability from quantum mechanics.

A quick explanation. Traditional computers process information in binary bits, *the* most basic unit of information in computing (0 or 1). Bits make up bytes, then kilobytes, megabytes, gigabytes, etc. Quantum computers exploit quantum bits or "qubits." What you need to know about qubits is that they can exist in multiple states simultaneously, which allows them to perform incredibly complex calculations at speeds unimaginable today and solve problems that are beyond the grasp of today's most advanced supercomputers.

The potential benefits, from extraordinary advances in cancer research to unlocking the mysteries of the physical universe, are limitless. But that same computing power can be used to unlock different kinds of secrets— from your personal financial or health records to corporate research projects to classified government intelligence.

Simply put, quantum computers will be able to crack encryption that today is all but unbreakable. Quantum computing will make strong passwords and private internet networks useless. It will rock current encryption protocols we rely on every day to protect global financial markets and the interworkings of government.

We are in the early stages of the development of this technology, but nations around the world—including China—are investing heavily in research to achieve "quantum supremacy," the point at which a quantum computer can outperform a classical computer.

We are likely less than a decade away from the day when a nation state could use quantum computers to render many of today's most sophisticated encryption systems useless. But spy agencies around the world are already archiving intercepted communications transmitted with currently unbreakable encryption. They are waiting to turn what's gibberish now into valuable intelligence in the future. Rogue states could also leverage the power of quantum to create havoc among our banking and financial systems around the world.

It took more than five years and nearly half a trillion dollars for companies and governments to prepare for Y2K (a computer programming shortcut expected to cause worldwide chaos as the year changed from 1999 to 2000). In the end, it resulted in a nonevent for most people.

But we are not ready for what experts call "Y2Q," Years to Quantum. The time to prepare is now. Banks, government agencies, insurers, hospitals, utilities, and airlines all need to be thinking now about how to implement security and encryption that will withstand a quantum attack.

Like AI, quantum computing presents an unprecedented opportunity and a serious threat. These advanced technologies of the Fourth Industrial Revolution are going to make the steam engine, assembly line, cars, planes, and the internet—the technologies of the previous industrial revolutions— look like sticks and stones in comparison. The United States, in collaboration with our allies around the world, must seek global leadership in these advancements at all cost.

Whether it was the discovery of fission or the launch of *Sputnik*, the United States has responded to past scientific challenges with resolve and determination. We must do the same with the next-generation technological challenges that are already upon us. We need to restore and improve America's crumbling federal digital infrastructure. Shore up feeble defenses in government and the private sector against cyber breaches. Ensure that America leads in artificial intelligence, quantum computing, and other technologies that will define the course of this century. We must accelerate innovation and achieve global dominance in advanced technology at all costs, while avoiding the mistakes of the past.

Accomplishing these feats will entail a level of effort that will make the Manhattan Project look like a pillow fight. It needs hardheaded pragmatism wrapped in with reach-the-moon idealism. Both are needed to achieve such a lofty goal.

We need two political parties that can engage in a competition of ideas rather than gotcha politics or politics of fear. We need national leaders willing to lead and ensure we are addressing our domestic issues in a way that allows us to put our financial house in order, to have the resources necessary to take on this generation-defining challenge. We need a foreign policy that shows our friends that we have their backs and puts fear in our enemies.

To ensure that the democratic world continues to set the rules of the world in the global economy, America and its allies must work together to continue to be the world's centers of innovation and technological advancement. By moving past outdated twentieth-century thinking and implementing twenty-first-century solutions to this New Cold War, the United States can remain the world's most important economy and continue to create opportunities for Americans at home, as well as provide inspiration for millions around the world.

We can uplift humanity for another 250 years, but it will require a reboot so we can embrace an approach of pragmatic idealism. This is our destiny.

EPILOGUE

WE ARE ALL IN THIS BOAT TOGETHER

"Y'all ever heard of *Washington Crossing the Delaware?*"

I tended to wrap up most of my DC2DQ tour stops around the Texas 23rd the same way. Not with red-meat rhetoric to enrage the crowd before a quick escape, like some politicians. But with a story about my love for a 171-year-old painting, and what it meant to me and our country.

At each stop at local Dairy Queens around my district for the annual DC2DQ, I'd give my prepared remarks, take questions, then, as we were digging into the final remains of our Blizzards and dipped cones, I'd close with a story.

Over the twirling hum of the soft-serve machine and the faint *ding* outside as cars pulled up to the drive-through window, I would tell the crowd about *Washington Crossing the Delaware.*

Most people have seen images of the painting, and almost everybody at my DC2DQs nodded when I mentioned it. It depicts George Washington standing in the bow of a small boat, erect and proud, looking as if he is invincible. He's in full battle dress, and the icy Delaware River rages around him while his crew strains to make progress to shore.

I first encountered the painting in Kevin McCarthy's office when he was House Majority Leader, I'd tell the crowds. A version of the painting, and there are several, was on display in Kevin's conference room at the U.S. Capitol. Whenever I had meetings there, my eyes would turn to it. Amid ridiculous arguments and unnecessary fights in Congress, this painting reminded me about not only who we are as Americans, but who we *could* be.

The painting commemorates a crucial moment in the War of Independence. General Washington is crossing the Delaware River on Christmas Eve in 1776, the night before his first major victory against the British. In the wake of some humiliating defeats, Washington had ordered thousands of his troops to covertly cross the freezing Delaware River under cover of darkness. The next morning, in Trenton, New Jersey, his troops launched a surprise attack on the Hessians—German troops hired by the British—bringing a much-needed morale boost to the ragtag Continental Army.

I'd always surprise my constituents by mentioning that there are a number of historical inaccuracies in the work of art. The Delaware River doesn't actually look the way it's portrayed. The flag is from a later time period, the boat is way too small for the number of people actually inside, and George Washington had never won a battle before this point.

Plus, it's painted by a *German*, Emanuel Leutze, to inspire *Germans* after the 1848 revolutions throughout Europe, which were a wave of rebellions against European monarchies.

That tended to get some raised eyebrows. A German painted a scene of one of America's greatest moments?

Then I'd point out who is in General Washington's boat. People of different backgrounds, races, and ethnicities. There's a couple of farmers in there. A French dude. A German guy. A woman. A Native American and a Black man are also aboard.

"In total," I'd say, "you can see twelve people and a thirteenth hand."

For some reason, that mention of the thirteenth hand always got chuckles.

I would explain how when you first look at the painting, you assume, of course, that people fighting on behalf of inalienable rights were obviously going to win. But when you pause and think about what they were trying to accomplish, and consider the difficulties and obstacles these Revolutionaries faced, you come to realize how improbable their victory actually was.

"The reason I love this painting is not because it is a depiction of an important historical point in our history," I told them. "I love it because when Leutze painted it nearly 175 years ago, it was a message to future generations—that the way a nation can achieve the improbable is to recognize we are all rowing toward an uncertain future in a little boat together."

Leutze's masterpiece shows how we are a *pragmatic* people. George Washington probably would have liked more men, ammunition, and preparation. But he had to achieve his objective based on the situation he was in right then, and with the resources he had at the time.

And just like George Washington and the Continental Army, we as individuals, and our leaders in government, must try to be our best selves within the context of where we are right now with the resources we have in front of us. We must endeavor to achieve what is achievable within the context of doing what's best for the most people possible.

Yet no problem is too hard when we understand that way more unites us than divides us. We are all united in our founding ideal that all people are created equal. Folks from all over the world know that America is still based on this ideal. Our values have made America the greatest nation to have ever been built on this Earth, and our ideals have served as beacons of hope to so many.

Since our founding, we have defied convention and raised expectations. At our core, we're an *idealistic* people, and that term can mean different things to different people, especially to those viewing our nation from the outside. Some consider idealism to be too naive, too unpractical to work in today's world. Yet for those of us who are part of this struggle to keep this century the American Century, idealism is about aspiring to achieve those noble values enshrined in our foundational documents.

While we haven't always lived up to our principles, we must always continue to try. Our actions as a government, our actions as a nation, and our actions as individuals must strive to reflect these self-evident truths that are the foundation of our country.

As I closed out the DC2DQ stops and thanked everyone for coming, I'd think about my past. Some of my childhood experiences, and certainly the obstacles my parents faced in a society that wouldn't accept my dad's race, could have led me to question my country's principles. But my parents' faith in this grand experiment of America never wavered, and their hopes for our family sustained my brother, sister, and me. Overseas, I saw my fellow countrymen make tremendous sacrifices to perform their sacred obligation to our forebearers who paid the ultimate price to protect our country.

And when I served in Congress, my constituents, like those at DC2DQ who were shaking my hand as they filed out—ranchers in dusty cowboy boots, office workers in khakis, and cashiers from the local Walmart—taught me important lessons. Struggle and hope go hand in hand.

Our generation-defining challenges as a nation don't have to daunt us. In our little boat called America, we can work together to rise to these challenges, the same way previous generations for close to 250 years rose to theirs. That is our shared responsibility as a nation.

As I said in the opening and have detailed throughout this book, it's time for an American Reboot. We all know this undertaking won't be easy, and there are plenty of challenges and obstacles ahead. We can't flinch from our destiny. We should embrace it together.

ACKNOWLEDGMENTS

E ver since I can remember I've had a poster hanging on my wall with a quote from American poet Carl Sandburg that says, "Nothing happens unless first a dream." I've also known for some time that teamwork makes the dream work. This dream of writing a book would never have happened without a phenomenal team, starting with my partner in crime, Jacqueline Salmon. Without Jacqui as a co-writer in this endeavor, it wouldn't have happened. She helped organize my thoughts, instigated the process of writing, and held my hand when I was obsessing over little things. Our weekly Zoom calls for a little over a year will be one of the positive things I remember from the pandemic. I can't thank Jacqui enough for making this dream a reality.

I can thank my last chief of staff, John Byers, for many things, but when it comes to this book, he arranged a meeting in the lobby of the Mandarin Oriental hotel in Washington, DC, in June 2019 with a talent agent from William Morris Endeavor—Mark McGrath. This meeting kicked off the whole process. Mark helped me tease out ideas I had for a book and then he introduced me to his colleague, literary agent Eve Attermann. Eve helped me understand the process for writing a good book, gave me the confidence that I could do it, and had the relationships to make it happen. I am grateful for my WME team.

Eight months after that meeting in the Mandarin Oriental, armed with my sixty-page letter to publishers summarizing my dream, Eve and I met with the calm and cool Stuart Roberts from Simon & Schuster, who would become my editor. He stood out because he immediately got what I wanted to accomplish. I have been reading the acknowledgment sections of books ever since starting to write *American Reboot*, and I understand now why every author says something to the effect that their editor was a hard-ass. Because that's what good editors do. Every one of Stuart's questions, comments, and edits made the final product significantly better and pushed me to be a significantly better communicator. In short, Stuart is the man.

To ensure the stories I told weren't tall tales, Jacqui and I interviewed a number of important people in my life: Callie Strock, Austin Agrella, Barry Hammond, Brian Jeffreys, my brother Charles Hurd, my sister Liz Hurd, my dad Bob Hurd, Chris Malen, Frank Hall, Hector Cerna, Jen Fahrenbruch, John Byers, Joni Carswell, Justin Hollis, Lynlie Wallace, Madison Smith, Rachel Holland, Matt Haskins, my homie Mel, Mia Love, Nancy Pack, Rachel Gonzales-Hanson, Reza Mizani, Sarah Moxley, Connor Pfeiffer, Ambassador Sichan Siv, Stacy Arteaga, Steve Frost, Trae Stephens, Tyler Lowe, and Stoney Burke. I thank all of you for your great memories and willingness to provide insights so this product would be as accurate as possible. Any errors are, of course, my own.

I also want to thank all the people who read different drafts and gave me amazing feedback: Lynlie Wallace, Jen Fahrenbruch, Sophia Houdaigui, Kathleen Keen, Bob Hurd, Charles Hurd, Sophia Steele, Bianca Maldonado, Mike Yantis, Nancy Pack, Tyler Lowe, and Justin Hollis. Your enthusiasm and feedback helped me get across the finish line.

A very special thanks . . .

To the triumvirate of Nancy Pack, Justin Hollis, and Stoney Burke: You three hold very special places in my life. Nancy, I separate my life into two phases, BN and AN—Before Nancy and After Nancy. Without your support, guidance, and help I wouldn't be as effective as I am, and my life would be poorer without your jokes, sass, and straight talk. Thank you for keeping me on task to get this project done. Justin, you have been more than the greatest political consigliere of all times, you have been a brother to me. Thank you for taking my calls at all hours to allow me to run a random idea or turn of phrase by you. I can't thank you enough for taking time away from your family to white-glove the final product. Stoney, I should first thank your amazing wife, Josefina, for putting up with all the crap I've put you through over the years, and I can't thank you enough for being my partner in building an organization and a movement worth writing a book about. I really do love you, man.

To all my colleagues from the Central Intelligence Agency, for all the life lessons you gave me. I wish I could put your names here, but the Agency's publication review board wouldn't allow it.

To everyone on Team Hurd, which includes both the political and official office: We always had a long way to go and a short time to get there but y'all always did it. We became a leader on national security and the gold standard in constituent relations because of your dedication and hard work. Remember, once part of Team Hurd, always part of Team Hurd.

To my family. The older I get the more I realize my success is because I have a rare gift—a great and loving family. Y'all always have my back no matter what it is, and I know that will never go away. Liz, Chuck, Mom, and Dad, I thank you for your love, support, and help.

To Lynlie Wallace. My penultimate thanks goes to you because you taught me everything I know about politics back when I was a neophyte. Your encouragement when I didn't want to write made me write. Your thoughtful perspective on my writing made me want to write better. Your interest in reading about events that you had often participated in, or heard me talk about a thousand times, helped me realize I could be successful. I could fill this entire book with thank-yous to you, and it wouldn't be enough. I wouldn't have been able to do this if you hadn't been in my life.

To everyone who has come up to me over the years and thanked me for my work. All of you were the inspiration for this book because you taught me that way more unites us than divides us as a country. To a person, you have been concerned that our beloved country is on the wrong track, and you believed something needed to be done about it. *American Reboot* is written for you.

NOTES

American Reboot draws on a combination of personal experiences and primary and secondary sources, including reports, surveys, academic studies, speeches, internal campaign and congressional office material, media articles, congressional legislation and hearings, and interviews. What follows is a condensed list of citations to original sources.

1. ALIGN OUR ACTIONS WITH OUR VALUES

6   *Seventy percent of the population in Texas 23 is Latino*: Statistics in this paragraph are from U.S. Census Bureau Census Reporter, Congressional District 23, TX, 2019.

7   *". . . devastatingly, we have lost the ability to be persuasive with, or welcoming to, those who do not agree with us on every issue"*: Republican National Committee, "Growth and Opportunity Project" report, March 2013, p. 5.

8   *Trump only received 26 percent of the non-white vote*: "Exit Poll Results and Analysis for the 2020 Presidential Election," *Washington Post*, December 14, 2020. https://www.washingtonpost.com/elections/interactive/2020/exit-polls/presidential-election-exit-polls/.

9   *they were even written into the Republican platform in 1984*: Republican Party, Committee on Resolutions, "America's Future Free and Secure," August 20, 1984.

2. SHOW UP SO YOU CAN LISTEN

18   *renamed the Tornillo Port of Entry outside El Paso as the Marcelino Serna Port of Entry*: H.R. 5252, 114th Congress (2015–2016): To designate the United States Customs and Border Protection Port of Entry located at 1400 Lower

Island Road in Tornillo, Texas, as the "Marcelino Serna Port of Entry." September 29, 2016.

3. DON'T BE AN ASSHOLE, RACIST, MISOGYNIST, OR HOMOPHOBE

27   *the Equality Act, a sweeping bill*: H.R. 5, 117th Congress (2021–2022): Equality Act. March 17, 2021.

4. APPEAL TO THE MIDDLE, NOT THE EDGES

34   *For some insights, we can turn to the pollster Tony Fabrizio*: Tony Fabrizio, a partner at Fabrizio, Lee & Associates, is widely recognized as an expert in public opinion and politics and one of the nation's leading GOP pollsters and strategists. Fabrizio has served as the chief pollster on four presidential campaigns.

35   *Going into the 2020 election cycle, only thirty-four House seats were considered split districts*: "Representation Differs from Presidential Vote," 270toWin, accessed September 10, 2021. https://www.270towin.com/2020-house -election-find/split-districts-president-congress.

35   *After the 2020 election, only sixteen split districts are still standing*: Stephen Wolf, "These 16 House Districts Are the Only Ones That Split Their Tickets for House and President in 2020," Daily Kos, March 2, 2021. https://www .dailykos.com/stories/2021/3/2/2018802/-These-16-House-districts-are -the-only-ones-that-split-their-tickets-for-House-and-president-in-2020.

35   *But go back twenty years: 86 seats were competitive. Twenty years before that, 143 seats were*: "Ticket Splitting Between Presidential and House Candidates, 1900–2016," Statistics on Congress, Brookings, Chap. 2, Table 2–16, p. 35, updated February 2021. https://www.brookings.edu/wp-content /uploads/2019/03/Chpt-2.pdf.

35   *In 2018, an average of 54,000 people voted in contested primaries*: Drew DeSilver, "Turnout in This Year's U.S. House Primaries Rose Sharply, Especially on the Democratic Side," Pew Research Center, October 3, 2018. The 54,000 average number was obtained by adding the number of people who voted in contested Republican and Democratic primaries in 2018 (10.8 million and 14.6 million), as reported in the Pew Research Center report, and dividing it by the total number of Republican (197) and Democratic (274) contested primaries in 2018. https://www.pewresearch.org/fact-tank/2018/10/03 /turnout-in-this-years-u-s-house-primaries-rose-sharply-especially-on-the -democratic-side/.

36   *roughly 265,000 people voted in the general election for their representative*: "Citizen Voting-Age Population and Voting Rates for Congressional Districts: 2018," Table 1, U.S. Census Bureau, Feb. 2020. From the data in Table 1, the number of voters per district, excluding the District of Columbia, were averaged. If no votes were recorded for a congressional representative in the November 6, 2018, election, the congressional district was not included in the calculations. https://www.census.gov/data/tables/time-series/demo/voting-and-registration/congressional-voting-tables.html.

37   *one of the forerunners to my DC2DQ trips*: To fix this problem, I collaborated with the House Committee on Appropriations. We were then able to work with base leadership to help secure federal funding. Ground was broken for the Laughlin Air Force Base Airfield Drainage System Repair Project on November 23, 2020.

38   *So I collaborated with Robin Kelly (D-Illinois) and Gerry Connolly (D-Virginia)*: H.R. 2227, 115th Congress (2017–2017): Modernizing Government Technology Act. May 18, 2017.

6. ENSURE THE AUDIO AND VIDEO MATCH

56   *I had hoped Lynlie was exaggerating her opinion on the response to the speech*: 116th Congress, House Permanent Select Committee on Intelligence Impeachment Inquiry, Fiona Hill and David Holmes. November 21, 2019.

57   *"An impeachable offense should be compelling, overwhelmingly clear, and unambiguous"*: Ibid.

57   *Among the elements that prosecutors need to prove is intent*: "Bribery: Elements of Offense," USLegal.com, accessed September 9, 2021. https://bribery.uslegal.com/elements-of-offense/.

60   *In 2015, I surprised many observers by voting in support of an amendment*: H.R. 240, 114th Congress (2015–2016): Department of Homeland Security Appropriations Act, 2015. March 4, 2015.

61   *The 826,000 individuals who have been accepted into the DACA program*: "How Many DACA Recipients Are There in the United States?," USA Facts, Nov. 10, 2019, updated September 23, 2020. There are varying methods of calculating the number of DACA recipients, but 826,000 represents the number of people accepted into the program between 2012 and 2020. https://usafacts.org/articles/how-many-daca-recipients-are-there-united-states/.

61   *In Congress, I voted for the American Dream and Promise Act of 2019*: H.R. 6,

116th Congress (2019–2020): American Dream and Promise Act of 2019. June 10, 2019.

61   *I also co-wrote the USA Act*: H.R. 4796, 115th Congress (2017–2018): USA Act of 2018. January 26, 2018.

62   *I voted to release the infamous "Nunes memo"*: 115th Congress, House Permanent Select Committee on Intelligence, business meeting, January 29, 2018. https://docs.house.gov/meetings/IG/IG00/20180129/106822/HMTG -115-IG00-Transcript-20180129.pdf.

7. DON'T PANDER, BUILD TRUST

68   *President Trump's handling of the COVID crisis*: Data from Bruce Mehlman, who founded and heads a bipartisan government relations firm, Mehlman Castagnetti Rosen & Thomas.

73   *My very first bill was aimed at an important group of constituents*: H.R. 5896, 115th Congress (2017–2018): Border Patrol Agent Pay Reform Amendments Act of 2018. September 27, 2018.

73   *I joined my buddy Katko*: H.R. 4239, 114th Congress (2015–2016): Tracking Foreign Fighters in Terrorist Safe Havens Act. December 17, 2015.

8. WAY MORE UNITES US THAN DIVIDES US

77   *As Peter Wehner, a Senior Fellow at the Ethics and Public Policy Center, has written*: "Why Trump Supporters Can't Admit Who He Really Is," *The Atlantic*, September 4, 2020. https://www.theatlantic.com/ideas/archive/2020/09 /predicate-fear/616009/.

10. INCREASE ACCESS TO HEALTHCARE WHILE DECREASING ITS COST

90   *the Republicans' American Health Care Act of 2017*: H.R. 1628, 115th Congress (2017–2018): American Health Care Act of 2017. July 28, 2017.

92   *Why does an MRI cost $1,080 in the U.S. and $280 in France?*: Ezra Klein, "Why an MRI Costs $1,080 in America and $280 in France," *The Washington Post*, March 3, 2012. https://www.washingtonpost.com/news /wonk/wp/2013/03/15/why-an-mri-costs-1080-in-america-and-280-in -france/.

93   *The Trump administration tried to address price transparency*: Exec. Order No. 13,951, "An America-First Healthcare Plan," September 24, 2020.

94   *Thanks to Stefanie, the bill was signed into law in 2017*: Texas H.B. 810, 85th Legislature (2017–2018): Relating to the provision of certain investigational

stem cell treatments to patients with certain severe chronic diseases or terminal illnesses and regulating the possession, use, and transfer of adult stem cells; creating a criminal offense. June 12, 2017.

95 *CHCs have grown into a national network*: Health Resources & Services Administration, Bureau of Primary Health Care, Primary Health Care Digest, "Happy National Health Center Week!," August 11, 2020. https://content .govdelivery.com/accounts/USHHSHRSA/bulletins/299b659.

96 *and they save American taxpayers $24 billion a year in healthcare costs*: Leighton Ku, PhD, MPH; Patrick Richard, PhD; Avi Dor, PhD; Ellen Tan, MSc; Peter Shin, PhD, MPH; and Sara Rosenbaum, JD, "Using Primary Care to Bend the Curve: Estimating the Impact of a Health Center Expansion on Health Care Costs," George Gibson/RCHN Community Health Foundation Research Collaborative at the George Washington University Health Services Research Commons, Policy Research Brief No. 14, September 1, 2009. https://hsrc.himmelfarb.gwu.edu/cgi/viewcontent.cgi?article=1024 &context=sphhs_policy_ggrchn.

96 *eight out of ten of CHCs met or exceeded*: Health Resources & Services Administration, Bureau of Primary Health Care, "Health Center Programs: Impact and Growth, accessed September 2, 2021. https://bphc.hrsa.gov/about /healthcenterprogram/index.html.

11. PROVIDE OUR SENIORS QUALITY CARE AND COMPASSION

104 *one out of every six women*: "Dementia Statistics—U.S. and Worldwide Stats," Braintest, accessed September 2, 2021. https://braintest.com/dementia -stats-u-s-worldwide/.

104 *vascular dementia*: Ibid.

104 *Dealing with the destruction my mom's dementia has caused*: H.R. 34, 114th Congress (2015–2016): 21st Century Cures Act. December 13, 2016.

105 *As of September 2021, more than 186,000 residents and staff*: AARP COVID-19 Nursing Home Dashboard, AARP Public Policy Institute, updated August 12, 2021. https://www.aarp.org/ppi/issues/caregiving/info-2020/nursing -home-covid-dashboard.html.

106 *losing an estimated $2.9 billion each year*: Katherine Skiba, "Older Americans Lose Billions to Scams, Senate Report Says," AARP, January 18, 2019. https://www.aarp.org/money/scams-fraud/info-2019/senate-aging -committee-hearing.html.

107 *median loss from a successful phone scam in 2020*: "Phone scams," AARP

Fraud Resource Center, accessed September 2, 2021. https://www.aarp
.org/money/scams-fraud/info-2019/phone.html.

13. BUILD THE WORKFORCE OF TOMORROW, NOT YESTERDAY

115   *be more than 25 billion connected devices in the world*: Arne Holste, "Number of
Internet of Things (IoT) connected devices worldwide from 2019 to 2030,"
Statista, August 25, 2021. https://www.statista.com/statistics/1183457
/iot-connected-devices-worldwide/.

119   *five thousand students at twenty schools in Texas 23*: Files of Rep. Will Hurd.

120   *Educational technology integrator Sheryl Sokoler has said*: Sheryl Soloker,
"Why we should teach coding in elementary school," *eSchool News*,
March 9, 2018. https://www.eschoolnews.com/2018/03/09/teach-coding
-elementary-school/?630728.

122   *One of the four pillars of the legislation was Workforce Development*: "AI and the
Workforce," Bipartisan Policy Center, July 23, 2020.

14. ENCOURAGE A GLOBAL "BRAIN GAIN" THROUGH IMMIGRATION

125   *Dreamers contribute to our history, culture, and economy*: All statistics in this
paragraph are from the congressional files of Rep. Will Hurd, updated January 3, 2017.

130   *In early 2018, Pete—who had become one of my best friends in Congress*: H.R.
4796, 115th Congress (2017–2018): USA Act of 2018. January 26, 2018.

131   *an estimated two hundred thousand Dreamers*: Nicole Prchal Svajlenka, "A
Demographic Profile of DACA Recipients on the Frontlines of the Coronavirus Response," Center for American Progress, April 6, 2020. https://www
.americanprogress.org/issues/immigration/news/2020/04/06/482708
/demographic-profile-daca-recipients-frontlines-coronavirus-response/.

132   *The USA Act included language from a bipartisan piece of legislation*: H.R.
3479, 115th Congress (2017–2018): Secure Miles with All Resources and
Technology (SMART) Act. August 29, 2017.

15. PREVENT PLANET EARTH FROM TEACHING US A TERRIBLE LESSON

142   *Biologists have determined that about 99 percent of species*: "99 Percent of
the Earth's Species Are Extinct—But That's Not the Worst of It," Ashley
Hamer, Discovery, August 1, 2019. https://www.discovery.com/nature/99
-Percent-Of-The-Earths-Species-Are-Extinct.

144   *Preventing further provocations of planet Earth*: "Summary for policymakers

of IPCC special report on global warming of 1.5C approved by governments," Intergovernmental Panel on Climate Change (IPCC), October 8,
2018. https://www.ipcc.ch/2018/10/08/summary-for-policymakers-of
-ipcc-special-report-on-global-warming-of-1-5c-approved-by-governments/.

16. UNDERSTAND THE REAL SOURCE OF AMERICAN POWER

153   *In its* Freedom in the World Report: Sarah Repucci, Amy Slipowitz, *Free-
       dom in the World 2021,* Freedom House, accessed October 16, 2021. https://
       freedomhouse.org/report/freedom-world/2021/democracy-under-siege.

154   *report on his National Security Strategy to Congress:* Office of the Secretary of
       Defense, Historical Office, *National Security Strategy of the United States.*

156   *I learned they don't want to join us:* 115th Congress, House Permanent Se-
       lect Committee on Intelligence, Full Committee Hearing: China's Threat to
       American Government and Private Sector Research and Innovation Leader-
       ship. July 19, 2018.

156   *A bipartisan commission tasked by Congress to review America's National De-
       fense Strategy:* National Defense Strategy Commission, *Providing for the
       Common Defense,* United States Institute of Peace, November 13, 2018, p. 7.

157   *In 1787, British dramatist Thomas Francklin wrote:* "A Lie Can Travel Half-
       way Around the World While the Truth Is Putting On Its Shoes," Quote
       Investigator, accessed September 2, 2021. https://quoteinvestigator.com
       /2014/07/13/truth/.

17. BE TOUGH WITH TOUGH GUYS

164   *In 2018, the Israeli government provided intelligence:* David M. Halbfinger,
       David E. Sanger, and Ronen Bergman, "Israel Says Secret Files Detail Iran's
       Nuclear Subterfuge," *New York Times,* April 30, 2018. https://www.nytimes
       .com/2018/04/30/world/middleeast/israel-iran-nuclear-netanyahu.html.

169   *I partnered with another former CIA officer:* H.R. 3720, 116th Congress (2019–
       2020): Trafficking and Smuggling Intelligence Act of 2019. July 11, 2019.

18. BE NICE WITH NICE GUYS

172   *In 2019, I voted for a bipartisan resolution:* H. J. Res. 77, 116th Congress,
       (2019–2020): Opposing the Decision to End Certain United States Efforts
       to Prevent Turkish Military Operations Against Syrian Kurdish Forces in
       Northeast Syria. October 17, 2019.

174   *the price tag of our activity in Afghanistan from 9/11 through FY2020 was more*

than $2 trillion: "U.S. Costs to Date for the War in Afghanistan, in $ Billions FY2001–FY2022," Costs of War, Brown University Watson International & Public Affairs, accessed September 10, 2021. https://watson.brown.edu /costsofwar/figures/2021/human-and-budgetary-costs-date-us-war -afghanistan-2001-2022.

174 *a total of 2,461 U.S. military personnel had paid the ultimate price*: Nancy A. Youssef and Gordon Lubold, "Last U.S. Troops Leave Afghanistan After Nearly 20 Years," *Wall Street Journal*, August 20, 2021. https://www.wsj .com/articles/last-u-s-troops-leave-afghanistan-after-nearly-20-years -11630355853.

174 *when 2,977 Americans died*: "Commemoration," 9/11 Memorial & Museum, accessed September 2, 2021. https://www.911memorial.org/connect /commemoration.

178 *As of 2021, 139 countries are participating in the Belt and Road Initiative*: Jennifer Hillman and David Sacks, "Countries in China's Belt and Road Initiative: Who's In and Who's Out," Council on Foreign Relations, March 23, 2021.

181 *and more than a third of its entire population*: Mark Witzke, "How Much of China did Japan Control at its Greatest Extent?," Pacific Atrocities Education, July 24, 2017. https://www.pacificatrocities.org/blog/how-much-of -china-did-japan-control-at-its-greatest-extent.

19. PREPARE FOR THE WARS OF TOMORROW, NOT THE ONES OF THE PAST

186 *Cybersecurity specialist Camille François*: Camille François, *Actors, Behaviors, Content: A Disinformation ABC* (Cambridge, MA: Graphika and Berkman Klein Society for Internet and Society at Harvard University, September 20, 2019), pp. 1–8.

186 *Based on François's research*: Lauren Hamm, *The Few Faces of Disinformation*, EU Disinfo Lab, May 11, 2020. https://www.disinfo.eu/publications /the-few-faces-of-disinformation/.

187 *and trying to suppress their vote*: Report of the Select Committee on Intelligence United States Senate on Russian Active Measures Campaigns and Interference in the 2016 Election, Vol. 2: Russia's Use of Social Media with Additional Views, pg. 6. https://www.intelligence.senate.gov/sites/default /files/documents/Report_Volume2.pdf.

191 *a strategic approach to defending the United States in cyberspace*: The Cyberspace Solarium Commission (CSC) was established in H.R. 5515, 115th

Congress (2017–2018): John S. McCain National Defense Authorization Act for Fiscal Year 2019. August 13, 2018.

191   *In early 2020, this Cyberspace Solarium Commission produced a clear-eyed report*: Cyberspace Solarium Commission, *A Warning from Tomorrow*, March 11, 2020, pp. 23–30.

20. REALIZE WHAT "MADE IN CHINA" REALLY MEANS

202   *building blocks of the information revolution*: Yen Nee Lee, "2 Charts Show How Much the World Depends on Taiwan for Semiconductors," *CNBC*, March 15, 2021. https://www.cnbc.com/2021/03/16/2-charts-show-how-much-the-world-depends-on-taiwan-for-semiconductors.html

202   *American political scientist Graham Allison has explained*: Graham Allison, "What Xi Jinping Wants," *The Atlantic*, May 13, 2017. https://www.theatlantic.com/international/archive/2017/05/what-china-wants/528561/.

21. ACHIEVE TECHNICAL FITNESS FOR CYBER WAR

210   *I asked Archuleta whether the hacker had used a zero-day vulnerability*: 114th House Committee on Oversight and Reform: OPM Data Breach, June 16, 2015, pp. 65–67.

215   *"FITARA stands for the Federal IT Acquisition Reform Act"*: H.R. 1232, 113th Congress (2013–2014): Federal Information Technology Acquisition Reform Act. September 18, 2014.

217   *we learned that these agencies failed to have a culture of modernization*: 115th Congress, House Subcommittee on Informational Technology and Subcommittee on Government Operations joint hearing: The Federal Information Technology Acquisition Reform Act (FITARA) Scorecard 5.0. November 15, 2017.

22. WIN THE NEW COLD WAR OVER ADVANCED TECHNOLOGY

222   *The power of artificial intelligence is analogous to the power of nuclear fission*: "Fission and Fusion: What Is the Difference?," Office of Nuclear Energy, April 1, 2021. https://www.energy.gov/ne/articles/fission-and-fusion-what-difference.

223   *In fact, experts Eric Schmidt and Bob Work*: Eric Schmidt and Bob Work, "The US Is in Danger of Losing Its Global Leadership in AI," *The Hill*, December 5, 2019. https://thehill.com/blogs/congress-blog/technology/473273-the-us-is-in-danger-of-losing-its-global-leadership-in-ai.

225   *Eight million imagery analysts would be needed*: Colin Clark, "Cardillo: 1 Million Times More GEOINT Data in 5 Years," *Breaking Defense*, June 5, 2017. https://breakingdefense.com/2017/06/cardillo-1-million-times-more -geoint-data-in-5-years/.

225   *the commercial use of drones*: 114th Congress, House Committee on Oversight and Government Reform: Drones: The Next Generation of Commerce? June 17, 2015.

228   *The Bipartisan Policy Center's 2020 report on AI and ethics*: "AI and Ethics," Bipartisan Policy Center, August 25, 2020, p. 2.

229   *based on our work with the Bipartisan Policy Center*: H.Res. 1250, 116th Congress (2019–2020): Expressing the Sense of the House of Representatives with Respect to the Principles That Should Guide the National Artificial Intelligence Strategy of the United States. December 8, 2020.

INDEX

ABOUT THE AUTHOR

Will Hurd is a former member of Congress, cybersecurity executive, and officer in the CIA. For two decades he's been involved in the most pressing national security issues challenging the country, whether it was in the back alleys of dangerous places, the boardrooms of top international businesses, or the halls of Congress.

After stopping terrorists, preventing Russian spies from stealing our secrets, and putting nuclear weapons proliferators out of business, Will helped build a cybersecurity company that prepared businesses for the next domain of conflict—cyberspace.

While in Congress, *Texas Monthly* and *POLITICO* magazine called Will "The Future of the GOP," because he put good policy over good politics at a time when America was often consumed with what divided us rather than what united us. He got more legislation signed into law in three terms than most congressmen do in three decades—substantive legislation like a national strategy for artificial intelligence.

Will is currently a managing director at Allen & Company, board member for OpenAI, and trustee of the German Marshall Fund. He has served as a fellow at the University of Chicago Institute of Politics and earned a bachelor's degree in computer science from Texas A&M University.

For more information about Will, go to willbhurd.com.